CRIME AND HUMAN RIGHTS

SOCIOLOGY OF CRIME, LAW AND DEVIANCE

Series Editors: Mathieu Deflem   (Volumes 6–9)
Jeffrey T. Ulmer   (Volumes 1–5)

SOCIOLOGY OF CRIME, LAW AND DEVIANCE   VOLUME 9

CRIME AND HUMAN RIGHTS

EDITED BY

STEPHAN PARMENTIER

K. U. Leuven, Belgium

and

ELMAR G. M. WEITEKAMP

University of Tuebingen, Germany

ELSEVIER
JAI

Amsterdam – Boston – Heidelberg – London – New York – Oxford
Paris – San Diego – San Francisco – Singapore – Sydney – Tokyo
JAI Press is an imprint of Elsevier

JAI Press is an imprint of Elsevier
Linacre House, Jordan Hill, Oxford OX2 8DP, UK
Radarweg 29, PO Box 211, 1000 AE Amsterdam, The Netherlands
525 B Street, Suite 1900, San Diego, CA 92101-4495, USA

First edition 2007

British Library Cataloguing in Publication Data
A catalogue record for this book is available from the British Library

ISBN: 978-0-7623-1306-8
ISSN: 1521-6136 (Series)

For information on all JAI Press publications
visit our website at books.elsevier.com

Transferred to Digital Printing 2007

Working together to grow
libraries in developing countries

www.elsevier.com | www.bookaid.org | www.sabre.org

ELSEVIER   BOOK AID   Sabre Foundation
           International

CONTENTS

v

LIST OF CONTRIBUTORS

Hans-Jörg Albrecht	Max Planck Institute for Foreign and International Criminal Law, Freiburg, Germany
Kai Ambos	Department for Foreign and International Criminal Law, Georg-August-University Göttingen, Göttingen, Germany
Dieter Burssens	Leuven Institute of Criminology at the Katholieke Universiteit Leuven, Leuven, Belgium
Marc Coester	Institute of Criminology, University of Tübingen, Tübingen, Germany
Chris Cunneen	Faculty of Law, University of New South Wales, Sydney, NSW, Australia
Jan Froestad	Department of Administration and Organisation Theory, University of Oslo, Bergen, Norway
Jack R. Greene	College of Criminal Justice, Northeastern University, Boston, MA, USA
Nils Meyer-Abich	Department for Foreign and International Criminal Law, Georg-August-University Göttingen, Göttingen, Germany
James P. Mulvale	Department of Justice Studies, University of Regina, SK, Canada
Stephan Parmentier	Department of Criminal Law & Criminology, Faculty of Law, K.U. Leuven, Leuven, Belgium

Dieter Rössner	Institute of Criminology, University of Marburg, Marburg, Germany
Clifford Shearing	Institute of Criminology, University of Cape Town, South Africa
Ann Skelton	Centre for Child Law, Faculty of Law, University of Pretoria, Gauteng, South Africa
Lode Walgrave	Leuven Institute of Criminology at the Katholieke Universiteit Leuven, Leuven, Belgium
Elmar G. M. Weitekamp	Institute of Criminology, University of Tübingen, Tübingen, Germany

INTRODUCTION: ON THE DOUBLE RELATIONSHIP OF CRIME AND HUMAN RIGHTS

Stephan Parmentier and Elmar G. M. Weitekamp

Since the end of the Second World War, human rights have gained an increasing significance in law, politics and society, both at the national and the international level. According to the American scholar Louis Henkin in his book *The Age of Rights*, human rights have become "the paradigm of our time", and in that process they have displaced previous major paradigms, such as religion and socialism (Henkin, 1990).

The rise of human rights is first and foremost illustrated by the gigantic framework of legal instruments, binding and non-binding, which were and continue to be developed in the realm of international organizations, such as the United Nations (Alston & Megret, 2007; http://www.unhchr.ch), the Council of Europe (http://www.coe.int), the European Union (Alston, 1999; http://www.eu.int), the Organization of American States (Buergenthal & Shelton, 1995; http://www.oas.int), the African Union (http://www.africa-union.org) and others. Related to this is the rapid proliferation of organizations, mostly non-state and civil society based, that aim to promote and to protect human rights and try to foster human rights monitoring and education (http://www.hri.ca). Many of them are quite local and small, and have limited impact, but some of them, like Amnesty International (http://www.amnesty.org) and Human Rights Watch (http://www.hrw.org), are truly transnational and are exercising a strong influence on international

Crime and Human Rights
Sociology of Crime, Law and Deviance, Volume 9, 1–8
Copyright © 2007 by Elsevier Ltd.
ISSN: 1521-6136/doi:10.1016/S1521-6136(07)09011-2

organizations, individual states and public opinion. Finally, the importance of human rights is also demonstrated by the gigantic amount of scholarly work that is generated every year, about the concept of human rights, their philosophical, legal and political underpinnings, their impact in practice, their mobilizing effects on individuals and groups in society, etc. (Steiner & Alston, 2000).

It goes without saying that this rapid proliferation of human rights norms and standards has not come overnight, but has instead been the product of a long development. The French lawyer, Karel Vasak, has argued that human rights have come about in waves or so-called "generations" of rights, thereby distinguishing three such generations: (a) civil and political rights, conceived more in "negative" terms, meaning that the state has to refrain from any intervention; (b) social and economic rights, considered more in "positive" terms as they require an active intervention from the state; and (c) solidarity rights, most often viewed in "collective" terms and requiring the concerted efforts of all social forces, nationally and internationally (Claude & Weston, 2006, p. 8). In doing so, he has linked the three generations to the three principles of the French revolution: freedom (*liberté*), equality (*égalité*) and solidarity (*fraternité*). In recent years, a fourth generation of human rights seems to have gaining ground, according to some covering bio-ethical issues that relate to the beginning and the end of human life (e.g. on the use of embryos, cloning, euthanasia, etc.), according to others relating to the rights of women and of future generations, and the rights of access to information and communication. American scholars Richard Claude and Burns Weston (2006), while following the three-prong approach in their excellent textbook, have suggested different names for these categories, being: (a) participatory rights, also including equality and the rights of refugees and indigenous peoples; (b) security rights, encompassing work, food, health, education and culture; and (c) community or group rights, including self-determination, development, environment and peace.

Whatever categorization is chosen, it is crystal clear that human rights nowadays provide a wide menu of legal norms and standards to promote and to protect human life and human relations. They range from the prohibition of torture and the protection of private life, to the promotion of an adequate standard of living and the right to leisure for every human being, and to the promotion of a healthy and peaceful environment for all. These norms foremost cover all of humanity, but some are also targeted to specific categories such as women and children, migrants and refugees, handicapped and impaired persons, and not to forget human rights defenders as well. This international trend is paralleled by the proliferation of human rights standards and norms at the level of nation states and regions thereof. They have – to a greater or a smaller extent – incorporated the international instruments into their domestic legal orders and which, in some cases, even provide the preliminary testing ground for taking the international norms a step further. In certain parts of the world today, it is impossible to refer to human rights before a national court without referring to the legislation and the case-law developed by an international legislative or judicial authority.

Claude and Weston (2006) have sketched a fairly optimistic account of human rights. In their view, human rights nowadays serve at least four major functions: (a) they constitute a challenge to state sovereignty and non-intervention, as they can be used to criticize human rights violations that take place on the territory of independent countries; (b) they have become an agenda for preferred world policy, supplying a general framework for a comprehensive world order of human dignity; (c) they are used as a standard for assessing the national behaviour, of governments and state institutions for sure but also of non-state actors; and (d) they form a populist worldwide movement that influences international relations, with particular reference to the important educational and lobbying roles of non-governmental organizations in the broad sense.

To many people the development of the human rights framework in law and politics may appear as the linear unfolding of civilization, a steady development of a progressive nature, with a view of freeing mankind from the shackles of domination towards an era of liberation and emancipation. Looking at human rights from a social science point of view, however, cannot but reveal many pitfalls and detours on this road, and may even call into question the existence of a clear road altogether. From the work by Claude and Weston (2006) also stem a number of critiques related to human rights. One is that human rights are far from universal, partly because their origins are Western – dating back to the philosophical ideas of the 17th and 18th centuries in Europe – and moreover because they are not firmly rooted in all societies and cultures of the world. As a result, the daily reality seems to display more violations of human rights than it shows compliance with them. Another critique is more of a political nature and relates to the "double standards" with which human rights are applied by governments and other actors. In many cases, human rights seem quite strong when applied at the domestic level, but they wither away in the foreign policy of states and then become subordinate to their national interests. In the same vein, it is argued that human rights are fine for situations of democracy, stability and peace, but they hardly possess any teeth when it comes to times of crisis or breakdown (such as during civil conflicts and outright wars, terrorism of all sorts, poverty and natural disasters). And more recently, the human rights discourse has been criticized for overemphasizing the claims of individual persons, without due attention to the duties and responsibilities they bear in society, and without reference to other entities that may possess rights and responsibilities, such as communities and even states. Whatever the assessment of their legacy and their day-to-day reality, it is clear that human rights do not constitute an ontological reality in se, but are the results of social constructs, and are thus subject to the same possibilities and limits of other social constructs in the life of man and society.

However, it should be emphasized that all of these debates are not at the heart of the present volume, which in fact is not about human rights as such, but about their relationship with issues of crime and justice. This relationship can be sketched from two main angles. First of all, criminal justice systems around the world have not been immune to the rapid rise of human rights over the past half century but contrarily have been very deeply influenced by them. The first and still classical chapter of human rights protection relates to upholding the rules of due process for suspects and offenders in the main phases of the criminal justice system, when police forces are reporting and investigating crimes, when public prosecutors are charging suspects or are dealing with criminal cases outside of court, when judges hear cases and reach their verdict, and when the sanctions are executed in places of detention or through other means. In the last 20 years, another chapter has been added, one claiming attention for the role of victims in the same stages of the criminal justice system, thereby enlarging the traditional dualistic relationship in criminal justice between the offenders and the state, to a triadic relationship that (albeit partly) includes victims of offences and crimes. Both long-term human rights legacies in domestic systems, the protection of suspects and offenders and the increasing attention to victims, have also exerted considerable influence on the recent establishment of and the proceedings in international tribunals and courts that are dealing with international crimes. Secondly, the impact of human rights is not limited to the functioning of criminal justice systems, but it has gradually extended to the conceptualization of crime and delinquency itself. One way has been to add a human rights component to existing criminal behaviour, and thus to open the existing human rights mechanisms to the victims of such crimes. This is very well illustrated by the case of trafficking in human beings, which instead of being viewed as yet another form of criminal behaviour has become to be seen as a violation of the fundamental rights of victims. The other route has been to take specific human rights violations and to redefine them in terms of criminal behaviour and to incorporate these definitions in domestic legal systems. This is the case of serious violations of human rights law and humanitarian law, such as genocide, crimes against humanity and war crimes, which have been re-conceptualized as international crimes and as such have also been incorporated in the domestic law of many states.

This double relationship between crime and human rights cannot be isolated from a number of new, yet important trends in modern-day societies. Arguably among the most salient ones are the trends towards technological innovation, towards economic globalization, towards multiple layers of political decision-making, towards multiculturalism, and towards ideological diversification (Parmentier & Van Houtte, 2003). Criminologists Susanne Karstedt and Kai Bussmann (2000) have convincingly argued that the drastic social and cultural changes of the past two or three decades pose enormous challenges for criminology, both in its theoretical aspects as well as for its empirical work. Of particular interest in this context are the transitions from authoritarian rule to democratic forms of government, and the implications for crime, criminal justice and criminology that derive from such transitions (Neild, 2006; Vande Lanotte, Sarkin, & Haeck, 2001).

Given the impressive development of the human rights framework and its far-reaching impact on issues of crime and criminal justice, it may be called surprising – if not incomprehensible – that criminology as a discipline has paid very little attention to human rights. The references to human rights in the criminological literature can be counted on the fingers of one hand. Among these, specific reference should be made to the work of American criminologists Herman and Julia Schwendinger who, as early as 1970, tried to import the human rights paradigm in the criminological theories and debates of the time (Herman & Julia Schwendinger, 1970). They shifted the focus from crime as a violation of criminal law, predominantly committed by individuals, to "social injury" as an infringement of fundamental values and human rights, for which state institutions bore a heavy responsibility. According to British criminologist Stan Cohen, the human rights connection – and thus the legacy of the Schwendingers – became lost in criminology because the mainstream theories failed to problematize and conceptualize the relationship between crime and politics. Only critical criminology continued to study "crimes of the state", but it got snowed under by the left realism of the 1990s that reclaimed attention for "the state of crime" (Cohen, 1993).

This volume on Crime and Human Rights is intended to address some of the issues raised before and to fill some of the gaps indicated. By way of a caveat, it should be clear that the book is not designed as another legal book with many details about legal standards and norms, although inevitably it will have some references to the national and international human rights framework. Its first and foremost lenses are those of criminology and sociology, precisely because these disciplines have thus far paid scant attention to the rise and the impact of human rights, both in their normative aspirations and in their practical effects. The book is therefore intended to contribute to a better understanding of the complex yet vibrant relationship between crime and justice on the one hand and human rights on the other hand.

This volume has been structured as follows. In the first part, we look at several types of crimes, old and new, from the angle of human rights and human rights violations. This part starts with an overview of the human rights framework in Europe and the Americas (Ambos & Meyer-Abich). Particular attention is paid to trafficking in human beings as a human rights problem (Albrecht), to the new conception of children's rights as related to problematic behaviour and crime (Burssens & Walgrave), to racism and xenophobia as infringements of the right to non-bias (Coester & Rössner), and to the broad category of political crimes and serious human rights violations (Parmentier & Weitekamp). The second part of the book in turn sketches the influence of the human rights paradigm on criminal justice systems and raises important questions about justice in general. It starts with the impact of human rights on police discretion (Greene), it discusses the differences between a traditional approach to criminal justice and a restorative one (Skelton), it investigates how dispute resolution can give effect to human rights (Froestad & Shearing), and it looks at human rights and justice through the eyes of indigenous peoples in the present (Mulvale) and the past (Cunneen). All of the contributions to this book are original and have specifically been written for this purpose.

The volume is addressed to students and researchers in criminology and criminal justice studies, and to professionals and policy-makers in the criminal justice system, primarily but not exclusively in North America and Europe. By being one of the first of its kind (also see Downes, Rock, Chinkin, & Gearty, 2007), this book aspires to be a source of inspiration for all those wishing to explore the exciting relationship between crime and human rights. Needless to say, all comments and suggestions are very welcome.

Finally, this appears the right place to express our thanks to some persons without whom this volume would not have seen the light of day: Mathieu Deflem, for his generous offer to host this book in the series on the Sociology of Crime, Law and Deviance; Ben Davie and Julie Walker at Elsevier Press, for their professional guidance and their patience in nurturing the manuscript; and of course all the authors of this book, who have sometimes worked on harsh time constraints to produce a high-quality volume.

REFERENCES

Books and Articles

Alston, P. (Ed.). (1999). *The EU and human rights.* Oxford: Oxford University Press.

Alston, P., & Megret, F. (2007). *The United Nations and human rights. A critical appraisal.* Oxford: Oxford University Press.

Buergenthal, T., & Shelton, D. (Eds). (1995). *Protecting human rights in the Americas. Selected problems* (4th ed.). Kehl/Strasbourg: Engel Verlag.

Claude, R. P., & Weston, B. H. (Eds). (2006). *Human rights in the world community. Issues and action* (3rd ed.). Philadelphia: University of Pennsylvania Press.

Cohen, S. (1993). Human rights and crimes of the state: The culture of denial. *Australian and New Zealand Journal of Criminology, 26,* 97–115.

Downes, D., Rock, P., Chinkin, C., & Gearty, C. (Eds). (2007). *Crime, social control and human rights. From moral panics to states of denial, essays in honour of Stanley Cohen.* Cullompton: Willan Publishing.

Henkin, L. (1990). *The age of rights.* New York: Columbia University Press.

Karstedt, S., & Bussmann, K.-D. (2000). Introduction: Social change as a challenge for criminological theory. In: S. Karstedt & K.-D. Bussmann (Eds), *Social dynamics of crime and control. New theories for a world in transition* (pp. 1–10). Oxford: Hart Publishing.

Neild, R. (2006). Human rights and crime. In: R. P. Claude & B. H. Weston (Eds), *Human rights in the world community. Issues and action* (3rd ed., pp. 104–107). Philadelphia: University of Pennsylvania Press.

Parmentier, S., & Van Houtte, J. (2003). *Law, justice and social change in the 21st century. The case of Belgium.* Brussels: King Baudouin Foundation.

Schwendinger, H., & Schwendinger, J. (1970). Defenders of order or guardians of human rights. *Issues in Criminology, 7,* 72–81.

Steiner, H., & Alston, P. (Eds). (2000). *International human rights in context. Law, politics, morals* (2nd ed.). Oxford: Oxford University Press.

Vande Lanotte, J., Sarkin, J., & Haeck, Y. (Eds). (2001). *Resolving the tension between crime and human rights. An evaluation of European and South African issues.* Antwerp: Maklu Publishers.

Websites

African Union: http://www.africa-union.org
Amnesty International: http://www.amnesty.org
Council of Europe: http://www.coe.int
European Union: http://www.eu.int

Human Rights Internet: http://www.hri.ca
Human Rights Watch: http://www.hrw.org
Organization of American States: http://www.oas.int
United Nations High Commissioner for Human Rights: http://www.unhchr.ch
University of Minnesota Human Rights Library: http://www1.umn.edu/humanrts

PART I:
CRIME AND HUMAN RIGHTS

HUMAN RIGHTS IN EUROPE AND THE AMERICAS: REGIONAL PROTECTION SYSTEMS AND THE PROCESS OF REGIONAL INTEGRATION

Kai Ambos and Nils Meyer-Abich

1. INTRODUCTION

Although any culture of this world has made efforts in developing its own, often contradictory categories of favoured and undesirable behaviours and treatments, the idea of elaborating a catalogue of universal rights being inherent to every human being regardless of its cultural and social background has a long history (Camargo, 2002, p. 15ff.). Beside the universal human rights instruments, e.g. multilateral treaties and UN declarations,[1] other instruments and systems have – especially in the last decades – emerged on a regional level.[2] Taking as examples Europe and Latin America, it can be observed that human rights play an important role in at least two senses: on the one hand, comprehensive regional human rights systems have been created in both regions; on the other hand, human rights may have an impact on a process of regional (economic) integration in different ways. Both aspects are important to understand the general

Crime and Human Rights
Sociology of Crime, Law and Deviance, Volume 9, 11–38
Copyright © 2007 by Elsevier Ltd.
All rights of reproduction in any form reserved
ISSN: 1521-6136/doi:10.1016/S1521-6136(07)09001-X

framework applicable for dealing with crime, and for preventing crime altogether.

2. THE SYSTEMS OF HUMAN RIGHTS PROTECTION IN EUROPE AND THE AMERICAS

In the following paragraphs we will give an overview of the two regional systems of human rights protection, thereby suggesting the links with issues of crime and justice.

2.1. The European System of Human Rights Within the Council of Europe

The origins of the Council of Europe may be traced back to the political initiatives shortly after the Second World War with the aim of a closer cooperation between the sovereign states of Europe (Blackburn, 2001, p. 3). It was founded on 5 May 1949 in Strasbourg, France, and with its 46 member states is currently the largest European organisation.[3] Its task is to achieve a greater unity between its members on the basis of the maintenance and further realisation of human rights and fundamental freedoms (Art. 1 (a), (b) Statute of the Council of Europe) (Jacobs & White, 2002, pp. 1–3; Oppermann, 2005, pp. 23–24). The Statute contains a quite unique requirement for membership in its Art. 3, namely that every member state "must accept the principles of the rule of law and of the enjoyment by all persons within its jurisdiction of human rights and fundamental freedoms". Complementing this provision, Art. 8 states that a member state which has seriously violated Art. 3 may be suspended from its rights and requested by the Committee of Ministers to withdraw from the Council of Europe or, if the state does not comply, expelled. The most important Convention of the Council of Europe is the European Convention on Human Rights and Fundamental Freedoms (hereafter ECHR or the Convention).

In 1948, when representatives of European states came together in The Hague with the purpose of establishing an organisation to protect democracy and human rights, there was a discussion as to whether all categories of human rights – civil and political as well as social and economic rights – should be included in one instrument. Although the latter rights were recognised, it was decided to include only the political and civil rights into the ECHR and create another instrument for the social and economic rights (Betten & Grief, 1998, p. 27). The ECHR was signed by the then Council of Europe member states on 4 November 1950 and entered into force on 3 September 1953, becoming the first binding regional human rights treaty (Camargo, 2002; Ehlers, 2005a, 2005b; Jarass, 2005). The European Social Charter (hereafter ESC or the Charter) was signed in Turin in 1961 and entered into force in 1965.

Art. 1 of the Convention requires the contracting parties to secure that everyone within their jurisdiction is able to enjoy the rights and freedoms defined in Section I of the Convention (Art. 2–12), i.e. the right to life; the prohibition of torture and inhuman treatment; the prohibition of slavery and forced labour; the right to liberty and security of the person; the right to a fair trial; the prohibition of retrospective penal legislation; the right to respect for privacy and family life; the freedom of thought, conscience and religion; the freedom of expression; the freedom of assembly and asso-ciation; the right to marry and to found a family. Section II (Art. 19–51) refers to the establishment, composition and functions of the European Court of Human Rights, Section III embodies different final provisions. The membership of the Convention is, albeit not legally, de facto linked to the membership in the Council of Europe (Ambos, 2006a, 2006b). As every member state must accept the fundamental human and individual rights via Art. 3 of the Council's Statute (cf. supra), the membership in the Council implies the adherence to the Convention. The relationship between the Convention and national law depends on the rules provided for in the latter, especially in the (unwritten) Constitutions. As a result the Convention has a different status in the different member states (Betten & Grief, 1998, p. 30). Thus in some countries (e.g. Austria and Switzerland) it is granted a formal or factual constitutional status, meanwhile in other countries it is treated as ordinary law (e.g. Germany) (Ambos, 2003, p. 588ff.; Ambos, 2006a, 2006b, pp. 329–330). In any case the majority of the member states attribute a supra-legal value to the Convention.

The original protection system, emanating from the Convention, consisted of two basic institutions: the European Commission on Human Rights (hereafter the Commission) and the European Court of Human Rights (hereafter the Court or ECourtHR). Both institutions were entrusted to guarantee the respect for the Convention by dealing with applications made by states and individuals alleging violations of the Convention (Jacobs & White, 2002, p. 6ff.). The Commission, being the organ primarily in charge of the establishment of facts and the admissibility of a complaint, operated as an entrance door or filter to the Court or the Committee of Ministers. If a case was declared admissible, the Commission could try to reach a friendly settlement, particularly in the case of an individual complaint or – if such a solution was not obtained – transmit a report to the Committee of Ministers (Harris, O'Boyle, & Warbrick, 1995, p. 587; Frowein, 1996, pp. 23–25; Betten & Grief, 1998, p. 37; Jacobs & White, 2002, pp. 6–7). Within three months the report would be forwarded to the Court if the state concerned had accepted the Court's jurisdiction over individual complaints (Art. 25 (I), 46 (I) ECHR). This requirement of a separate acceptance of the ECHR's jurisdiction led to the unfortunate situation that some member states had done so but others not.

This "old" system worked more or less well as long as the Convention remained a "sleeping beauty, frequently referred to but without much impact" (Frowein, 2004, p. 268). But with a higher caseload and more impact on the domestic level a new system was introduced by the Additional Protocol 11 to the Convention coming into force on 1 November 1998. Accordingly, the Commission and the Court were replaced from that date on by a new permanent Court, which is responsible for both the admissibility of the applications and a possible friendly settlement of cases (Art. 32, 38, 39 ECHR). The Court's organisation and procedure is mainly regulated in Art. 19–51 ECHR. It is composed of 46 judges, one from each member state (Art. 20 ECHR). Although the judgments of the Court cannot annul national judgments but only have a declaratory character, the member state concerned is under a treaty obligation to comply with the judgment. In addition, the Court may, at the request of the Committee of Ministers, give advisory opinions on legal questions concerning the interpretation of the Convention and its protocols (Art. 47 (1) ECHR). The execution of the judgments is supervised by the Committee of Ministers (Art. 46 (2) ECHR), i.e. a political, not a judicial organ.

2.2. The Inter-American System of Human Rights

In 1969, 19 years after the creation of the ECHR, the Organization of American States (hereinafter OAS) established the second regional system for the protection of human rights in San José, Costa Rica, with the American Convention on Human Rights (hereafter ACHR) (Camargo, 2002, p. 561).[4] Already more than 20 years before, in 1948, the American Declaration of the Rights and Duties of Man was adopted by the Ninth International Conference of American States in Bogotá, Colombia. Yet, as this was not a binding instrument and provided for no enforcement mechanism, it was merely of symbolic value (Buergenthal, Norris, & Shelton, 1986; Camargo, 2002, p. 566; Kokott, 1986; López Garelli, 2004, p. 92). As in the case of

Europe, also in the Americas, albeit less forcefully, the horrors of World War II played a decisive role in pushing the demand for a human rights convention for all American states (Sánchez Padilla, 2005, pp. 90–91).

On an institutional level, the inter-American human rights system consists of the Inter-American Commission on Human Rights (hereafter IACom) and the Inter-American Court of Human Rights (hereinafter IACourt); thus, it resembles the "old" system of the ECHR. The IACom was founded in 1959 with the aim "to promote the observance and the protection of human rights and to serve as a consultative organ of the Organization in these matters" (Art. 106 (1) OAS Charter). The Commission is, unlike the Court, not only an organ of the ACHR but also of the OAS Charter with jurisdiction over all OAS member states (Art. 53, 106 OAS Charter; Art. 33, 41 ACHR, Art. 1 IACom Statute).[5] It has, above all, a kind of watchdog or "Public Office" function with regard to the observance of the ACHR in the OAS member states (Sánchez Padilla, 2005, p. 115). It shall inform about human rights abuses in the Americas, enabling other organs, instances and authorities to intervene by political, diplomatic or judicial means. Its decisions are compulsory as far as the measures it may impose are provided for in the ACHR (cf. Art. 41 ACHR).

When the IACom receives a petition (individual/non-governmental complaint, Art. 44 ACHR) or a communication (inter-state complaint, Art. 45 ACHR) it primarily has to examine its admissibility (Art. 46, 47 ACHR). If the petition is considered admissible the Commission follows the procedure provided for in Art. 48 ACHR, i.e. it tries to obtain information about the case from the state concerned and, if necessary, carries out own investigations. If the grounds of the petition or communication still exist (Art. 48 (1) (b)) and if no friendly settlement has been reached (Art. 48 (1) (f), 49 ACHR), the Commission sends a preliminary report with conclusions and recommendations to the respective state (Art. 50 ACHR). If, within a period of three months from the date of the transmittal of the report, the matter has not either been settled or submitted to the Court the Commission "may set forth its opinions and conclusions" and shall, where appropriate, "make pertinent recommendations and prescribe a period within which the state is to take the measures to remedy the situation examined" (Art. 51 ACHR). When the indicated period has expired, the Commission decides "whether the state has taken adequate measures and whether to publish its report" (Art. 51 (3) ACHR). Thus, the Commission enjoys certain discretion as to referring the case to the IACourt or to put pressure on the state by publishing the report. According to Davidson (1997, pp. 118, 183), the corresponding Art. 50–51 ACHR have been modelled after

Art. 31–32 ECHR, "but because there was no equivalent to the Committee of Ministers in the American Convention's framework, the Inter-American Commission was empowered to decide whether to submit a case to the Court or to deal with it itself". If the IACom does not refer the case to the Court, it has the possibility to include the final report "in the Annual Report to the OAS General Assembly, and/or to publish it in any other manner deemed appropriate" (Art. 45 (3) Rules of procedure IACom).

The proposal to create a Court was already made by the Brazilian delegation at the Bogotá meeting in 1948, yet it was only after the establishment of the IACom in 1959 that the original idea was reassumed. The Court is the judicial institution of the inter-American system of human rights but it is not an organ of the OAS, despite all attempts to this effect (Sánchez Padilla, 2005, p. 113). It does not enjoy the same support as the European Court, since only 21 out of the 35 states of the American continent have accepted the contentious (adjudicatory) jurisdiction of the Court and the major powers U.S.A. and Canada did neither ratify the ACHR nor accept the Court's jurisdiction.[6] Also, the IACourt is not a permanently sitting institution as its (new) European counterpart. A case can be submitted to the IACourt only by a member state or by the Commission (Art. 61 (1) ACHR), individual victims have no direct access to the Court. They have to refer first to the Commission, complying with some requirements, especially the exhaustion of local remedies. The Court has the power to award monetary compensation or to impose other remedies, but it cannot execute its judgments; in case of non-compliance it may only inform the General Assembly of the OAS (Art. 65 ACHR). This system is complemented by various other institutions on a sub-regional and national level, e.g. human rights commissions and groups, ombudspersons, etc. (Baranyi, 2005, p. 5).

As the ECHR the ACHR only encompasses the civil and political, not the economic and social rights (Art. 3–25). Yet, the catalogue of rights proclaimed by the ACHR is longer than that of the ECHR, especially by drawing on the American Declaration of the Rights and Duties of Man as well as on the International Covenant on Civil and Political Rights. Concretely speaking, the ACHR covers eight rights not protected by the ECHR: the right to juridical personality (Art. 3); the right to compensation (Art. 10); the right to reply to "inaccurate or offensive statements" in the media (Art. 14); the right to a name (Art. 18); the rights of the child (Art. 19); the right to nationality (Art. 20); the freedom of movement and residence (Art. 22); the right to equal protection (Art. 24). Thus, as to the list of rights, the ACHR rather resembles the International Covenant on Civil and Political Rights than the ECHR. States Parties to the Convention are obliged not only to respect, but also to ensure the free and full exercise of these rights (Art. 1). The additional Protocol to the Convention including Economic, Social and Cultural Rights was adopted only in 1988 in San Salvador and is therefore called the "Protocol of San Salvador".

2.3. Assessment

While the Inter-American system has considerably and steadily improved since its creation, there are still many deficits and the "achievements have been the exception rather than the rule" (Buergenthal & Cassell, 1998, p. 540ff.). The widespread impunity with regard to the human rights violations under the military regimes in Central America and the *Cono Sur* could not be effectively impeded by the human rights system. While the ACHR is, on a normative level, a highly advanced instrument, the reality in almost all states is far away from compliance with these norms; there is a wide gap between the de iure situation of the ACHR and the de facto situation on the ground in the respective member states (Buergenthal et al., 1986, pp. 14–15). Apparently the Commission is under too much influence of the states, especially the ones, like the U.S.A., which are not even a (full) part of the human rights system (Camargo, 2002, p. 565). There is no political organ that could effectively supervise the execution of the judgments of the Court.

Against this background many observers look to Europe and argue for a reform with more power and authority for the inter-American Court and a *locus standi* of the individual modelled after the recent reform of the European human rights system (Camargo, 2002, pp. 564–565; Sánchez Padilla, 2005, pp. 115–116). With this reform the former structural similarities between both systems do no longer exist (Quiroga León, 2003). Such a reform would also be welcomed with a view to the increasing case law of the Court. In particular as far as the rights of victims of serious human rights violations are concerned the Court's case law demonstrates a clear commitment to effective legal remedies of the victims (Art. 8 (1), 25 ACHR) entailing, inter alia, a state's duty to investigate the crimes and sanction the responsible, the victims' or their families' right to know the truth and a whole set of measures of reparation (ranging from economic to pure symbolic measures like the setting up of memorials or public acts of apology).[7] Notwithstanding, the Court's strengthening by a reform of the system similar to the one implemented in Europe does not seem to be feasible in the near future (Camargo, 2002, pp. 542–543).

3. HUMAN RIGHTS AND REGIONAL INTEGRATION

In the second half of the 20th century the processes of regional cooperation and integration have become a basic structural element for the "New World Order" (Schirm, 1997, p. 11). Today the most industrialized and "developing" states are members of at least one Regional Integration Agreement (RIA).[8] Having said this, it must not be overlooked that the concept of regional integration encompasses quite different conventions and models of development. Although the most important motive of integration is mostly to further economic development by taking off trade barriers (Kühn, 2003, p. 111), the processes of integration sometimes also lead to profound political changes, such as the formation of common executive, judicial and legislative institutions. The "new regionalism" must be seen within the context of the end of the Cold War and the process of globalization (Kühn, 2003, p. 124ff.). Contrary to a simple economic integration as a "process of reducing the economic significance of national political boundaries within a geographic area" (Anderson & Blackhurst, 1993, p. 1), the so called "new regionalism" can be described as "a comprehensive multidimensional process including new political and economic objectives beyond trade and investment issues within a multi-polar world of globalized markets" (Preusse, 2004, p. 6; also Sangmeister, 2005, p. 12ff.). In this sense an increasing significance of RIAs does not only refer to free trade and economic issues but also intend to promote human rights and democratic principles with the aim to create an investors' friendly infrastructure and to strengthen historical and cultural ties (Kühn, 2003, p. 109; Leuprecht, 2002, p. 129). Despite the fact that the development or strengthening of economic relations normally entails some positive side-effects with regard to the political or social situation, an integration process driven exclusively or predominantly by economic interests is cause of some concern, at least from the perspective of human rights and conflict prevention. Indeed, a "peace-making" effect of economic cooperation and integration (especially by the mutual exchange of goods) has been long recognised by studies of social and legal anthropology (see Malinowski, 1922; Schott, 1970).

Be that as it may, ultimately conflicts can only be prevented if the integration is accompanied by specific political and social projects with that aim. In theory there are quite a number of reasons for regional trade agreements to be supportive of peace, but free trade can also be a factor for the creation of inequalities and social unrest leading to conflicts within or even between states (Brown, Faisal Haq, Shaheen Rafi, & Moeed, 2005, pp. 12–13; Leuprecht, 2002, p. 73). Trade (liberalisation) may have an enormous impact on conflict dynamics and crime prevention. In this sense tensions between different agendas exist, take for example the antagonistic relationship between development policies and the war on terror (as a full fledged military war) or between (asymmetrical) trade liberalisation and structural conflict prevention (Baranyi, 2005, pp. 10–12; Guedes de Oliveira, 2004, p. 26; Russau, 2004, p. 24ff.). The discussion, therefore, in particular in Latin America, should not be limited to the aspect of "economic transnationalisation" but has to take the overall social effects of economic transformations into account (Zuber, 2005, pp. 31–32). A human rights agenda must not come along as a pure side-effect of trade agreements, rather that trade agreements must be human rights oriented (Pitanguy & Heringer, 2001, p. 15). In this sense the sustainable development of a state or a region, especially with a view to the prevention, management and resolution of violent conflicts, presupposes the corresponding social, democratic and human rights measures.[9] Thus, in the following paragraphs the human rights component of the integration processes of EU/EC, MERCOSUR/SUL and NAFTA will be looked at in more detail.

3.1. European Communities and European Union

While the founding treaties of the European Economic Community (EEC), the European Community for Coal and Steel (ECCS) and the European Atomic Agency (Euratom) contained no explicit reference to human rights, the general process of European integration has always been accompanied by the awareness of common values and the need of a politically unified Europe (Zimmermann, 2002, p. 9; Williams, 2004, pp. 137–138). Take as examples the idea of a close cooperation between France and Germany to avoid military confrontations in the future (Ambos, 2006a, 2006b, p. 305; Fischer, 2001, p. 8) or the transition from dictatorship to democracy in Spain and Portugal within the framework of their integration into Europe (Fischer, 2001, p. 10; Oppermann, 2005, p. 13). In this sense even the original focus on (only) economic integration was linked – as a kind of "spill-over-effect" – to the more ambitious aim of a common political organisation which at least led to the creation of the EEC in 1957 (Fischer,

2001, pp. 8–9; Herdegen, 2005, p. 8; Oppermann, 2005, pp. 9–10). With time it was more and more recognised that the Communities are not only economic but also human rights actors, and the protection of human rights was increasingly recognised as an objective and aim of the Communities (e.g. in the preamble of the Single European Act of 1987) (Jarass, 2005, p. 8; Zimmermann, 2002, p. 9). With the formal creation of the Union (Art. 1 of the Treaty of Maastricht of 7 February 1992) the Communities finally developed from a free trade area to a political Union and its inhabitants developed from "market citizens" (*Marktbürger*) to "Union citizens" (*Unionsbürger*) (Kadelbach, 2005, p. 553).

3.1.1. Protection of Human Rights Within the EU

Despite the absence of a written catalogue of fundamental rights the existence of such rights at the Community level has been recognised by the European Court of Justice (ECJ) at least since 1969, invoking the "principles of the Community Legal Order" that must be safeguarded according to Art. 220 EC (ex Art. 164 EC) that entails the fundamental rights of persons.[10] To develop these principles the Court has employed a method of value judgment based comparison of the legal systems of the member states (*wertende Rechtsvergleichung*) in order to identify common concepts and principles of the national constitutional law, in particular with regard to the fundamental rights considering them as an unwritten source of the community law,[11] and thus be used as a source of law. Already in 1974 the ECJ extends its case law explicitly to human rights treaties binding for the member states arguing that these treaties must be taken into account as a further source of law within the framework of Art. 6 (2) EU (former Art. F (2) EU) as general principles of law besides the constitutional principles of the member states.[12] Along the same lines the ECJ often stressed the special importance of the ECHR,[13] which thereby has become the most important catalogue of fundamental rights of the EU. This case law, which established and developed the concept of fundamental rights as part of the general principles of Community law (Philippi, 2002, pp. 47–48; Winkler, 2000, p. 24ff.), was finally also recognised and reinforced by the written law, first by Art. 4 EU of the Maastricht Treaty in 1993, and subsequently by Art. 6 EU. Indeed, Art. 6 (2) EU explicitly refers to the ECHR whose fundamental rights must be respected (Ehlers, 2005a, 2005b, p. 386; Zimmerman, 2002, p. 9).

Despite this positive normative development the ECHR has no jurisdiction *ratione personae* about EU-acts since only the member states but not the EU as such is a member of the ECHR (Peters, 2003, p. 27). Although the ECJ takes into account the ECHR's case law,[14] the double human rights jurisdiction of both ECJ and ECHR entails the risk that different levels of protection exist at the level of the Council of Europe and that of the EU (Ambos, 2006a, 2006b, p. 331; Winkler, 2000, p. 34ff.). Another problem is that the EU, notwithstanding the reference to the ECHR in Art. 6 (2), lacks an own catalogue of fundamental rights (Ehlers, 2005a, 2005b, p. 384); the Charter of the Fundamental Rights of the Union, recognised as part II of the EU Constitution (see more detailed infra), can only take formally effect if the Constitution enters into force. The absence of a formal catalogue of human rights and a clear-cut judicial control gives all the more reason for concerns the more the Communities and the Union and their organs increase their powers and their influence about the law of the member states (Uerpmann-Wittzack, 2005, pp. 152–153; Winkler, 2000, p. 36; Zimmerman, 2002, p. 46). A recent area where this became especially relevant is the fight against terrorism and the insufficient remedies against the implementation of the UN terror lists in European Law (Ambos, 2006a, 2006b, p. 426ff.).

To solve this dilemma basically two possibilities exist: either the EU as such joins the ECHR (Zimmerman, 2002, p. 46), and thereby accepts the ECHR's jurisdiction, or it creates an own human rights catalogue explicitly extending the protection to EU acts. The former solution encounters some legal difficulty since the ECJ is of the view that the existing competencies in the treaties do not allow such an accession without an amendment (Ambos, 2006a, 2006b, p. 331; Betten & Grief, 1998, p. 111ff.; Bulterman, 2001, p. 85; Uerpmann-Wittzack, 2005, p. 153; Winkler, 2000, p. 46ff.).[15] As to a separate rights catalogue one may refer to the Charter of Fundamental Rights of the EU proclaimed as such on 7 December 2000 (Jarass, 2005, p. 5).[16] The Charter is unique in its inclusion in a single text of all categories of rights by unifying economic, social and cultural, as well as civil and political rights (Boyle & Méndez, 2004; Jarass, 2005, p. 9ff.). Notwithstanding, the Charter essentially codifies only the existing law and is as such not a binding European legal instrument (Santer, 2002, p. 13). In fact the crucial question of the legal status of the Charter was left open by the drafters (Boyle & Méndez, 2004; Jarass, 2005, pp. 13–14; Zimmerman, 2002, p. 7). The incorporation of a slightly modified text of the Charter in Part II of the Draft EU Constitution leaves us with two versions of the Charter, namely the original, self-standing one and the one of the Constitution. Given the uncertain future of the Draft Constitution after its rejection by the people of France and the Netherlands, the only possibility at this moment is to give the original Charter a binding effect (Jarass, 2005, p. 11). Such a solution should not, however, set aside the possibility of an accession of the EU to the ECHR (Uerpmann-Wittzack, 2005, p. 154).[17] In any case, the Charter is of utmost importance for the human rights protection within the EU (Walter, 2005, p. 13); this has also been recognised by the European Court of First Instance (CFI) arguing that "[a]lthough this document does not have legally binding force, it does show the importance of the rights it sets out in the Community legal order".[18] The Charter was also invoked by the advocates general in some cases (Calliess, 2005, p. 547; Walter, 2005, p. 14).

3.1.2. Scope and Influence of the EU Fundamental Rights

One can distinguish between an internal human rights dimension concerning the (at first potential, then full) member states and an external human rights dimension regarding the foreign relations of the EU. In fact, the latter was introduced in the early 1990s and the former in 1998 (Bulterman, 2001, p. 76).

Internal Dimension: Accession and Membership. The linkage between membership and human rights is a relatively new feature of EU law and started only in the 1990s. The first crucial summit meeting was the Copenhagen European Council of 1993, where the so called Copenhagen criteria as political conditions for accession to the EU were established (Brasche, 2003, p. 158; Nowak, 1999, pp. 691–692; De Witte & Toggenburg, 2004, p. 59).[19] With the Amsterdam Treaty the political conditions have been explicitly spelled out in Art. 49 EU, whereupon "any state which respects the principles set out in Art. 6 (1) TEU may apply to become a member of the Union".

As to the member states Art. 6 (2) creates obligations in two directions: on the one hand, it must be observed in the execution of directly applicable community law by national authorities; it must also be observed, on the other hand, in case of national restrictions of the EU rights by the member states (Walter, 2005, p. 14).[20] Art. 7 TEU (ex-Article F (1) as amended by the Treaty of Amsterdam) and Art. 309 (ex. Art. 236 TEC) establish a (two-step) procedure to sanction a violation of a fundamental principle as defined in Art. 6 (1) TEU. The sanction is supposed to maintain and re-establish the so called "political conditionality" (Nowak, 1999, p. 690). Art. 7 also provides for the procedure to be followed both for the suspension of rights and for the determination of the existence of such a breach (Bulterman, 2001, pp. 78–79).

External Dimension: Human Rights Clauses. The above-mentioned "conditionality" also possesses an external effect as to non-member states and determines the EU's relationship with these states (Weber, 1995, p. 196). In the human rights field the political conditionality finds its best expression in the human rights clauses of agreements with non-EU states or interstate organisations. The aim of these clauses is to link economic or commercial cooperation to human rights or, in other words, use the economic lever to bring potentially violator states into line with general human rights standards (Brandtner & Rosas, 1999, p. 699ff.; Hoffmeister, 1998, p. 7ff.; Kühn, 2003, p. 100ff.). Thus, the EU pursues the so called stick and carrot approach according to which human rights violations shall be sanctioned by negative – "stick" – measures and compliance shall be awarded by positive – "carrot" – measures (Brandtner & Rosas, 1999, p. 700; Kühn, 2003, p. 97ff.; Simma, Aschenbrenner, & Schulte, 1999, p. 578ff.). In this context of conditionality, reference should also be made to the stabilisation and association agreement between the EU and Serbia on the detention and surrender of Radko Mladic to the UN Tribunal for the Former Yugoslavia (ICTY) (Kohl, 2006, p. 2).

The first of such human rights clauses was introduced in 1989 with Article 5 of the Lomé IV agreement after massive human rights violations by member states of Lomé I at the end of the 1970s (Riedel & Will, 1999, p. 726; Hoffmeister, 1998, pp. 86–87). Yet, this provision was not more than a programmatic principle without concrete guarantees and thus it could not be invoked as a suspension clause (Kühn, 2003, pp. 100–101).[21] Nevertheless this "preambular type" might have become relevant "in case one of the contracting parties invokes the *clausula rebus sic stantibus* in order to suspend its treaty relations with the violator state" (Bulterman, 2001, pp. 155–156).

In 1990 the so called Basic Clause was introduced into the framework treaty with Argentina,[22] providing for a "democratic basis for co-operation" (Riedel & Will, 1999, p. 728). Although this clause did either include an express suspension clause, it was considered a stepping stone for the general introduction of human rights clauses (Riedel & Will, 1999, p. 728). In 1991 the dispute about the suspension of the co-operation agreement with Yugoslavia demonstrated the need for a an express human rights conditionality clause and this led to the so called Essential Element Clause which was then included in the agreements between the Communities and its partners in the Conference on Security and Co-operation in Europe (CSCE),[23] as well as in the new agreements with the Baltic states,[24] Albania, and other states, as well as with the OSCE (Riedel & Will, 1999, p.728; also

Russau, 2004, p. 21). This clause states that "the respect for democratic principles, as set out in the Helsinki Final Act 1975 and in the Charter of Paris for a New Europe 1990, forms an essential and integral part" of the respective agreements (Riedel & Will, 1999, p. 728). Thus, it can – spelling out the conditions of Art. 60 (3) (b) of the Vienna Convention of the Law of Treaties – be invoked to partially or completely suspend such agreements in case of grave human rights violations (Riedel & Will, 1999, p. 729).[25] The *Essential Element Clause* was also included into the revised Article 5 of Lomé IV in 1995 and has since served as a model for future treaties of the Communities (Riedel & Will, 1999, pp. 731–732).[26] Sometimes this clause was complemented by so called non-compliance clauses providing for alternative mechanisms to react to violations, especially in the form of consultation and mediation (Brandtner & Rosas, 1998, p. 474; Riedel & Will, 1999, pp. 729–730). Beyond these clauses there is no human rights policy of the EU (Alston & Weiler, 1999, p. 4ff.; Walter, 2005, p. 14).

3.2. The Americas

Latin America has a long history of regional integration based in its origins – similar to the European process – on mainly economic interests and motivations. Yet, as early as 1820, the idea of a Confederation of Iberoamerican Nations was promoted and founded on the respect for the rights of man.[27] Nowadays, different processes of regional integration exist in Latin America which, on the one hand, are partly overlapping, and, on the other, give the human rights aspect a different weight. Already in 1960 the Latin American Free Trade Association (LAFTA) was founded with the aim to create a free trade area, but it collapsed in 1980 and was replaced by the Latin American Integration Association (LAIA).[28] Also in 1960 the Central American Common Market (CACM) was created, which was revived in 1993, and extended in 2003 by signing the Central American Free Trade Area with the U.S.A. (Bodemer, 2006, pp. 149–197; Kaltenbach, 2005, p. 128ff.). In addition numerous bilateral free trade agreements have been signed in the last 15 years, thus creating the often quoted "spaghetti bowl regionalism" (Bodemer, 2006, p. 157; Kaltenbach, 2005, p. 127; Preusse, 2004, pp. 186–187).

Of particular interest are the organisations Mercosur (*Mercado Común del Sur* – Common Market of the South) and the North American Free Trade Agreement (NAFTA) since, apart from their geographical extension and economic importance, they show in an exemplary way the different forms of how the process of integration has developed. Next to these two organisations, there is also the Andean Community of Nations (*Comunidad Andina de Naciones,* CAN), established in 1969 by the Cartagena Agreement with the aim of creating a free trade area (Marwege, 1995, p. 22ff.; Taccone & Noguiera, 2002, p. 2). The CAN is the oldest subregional system of integration in Latin America and had the objective to promote the balanced and harmonized development of its Member Countries and to facilitate the subregional integration process, the respect for human rights being one of its collective objectives (Taccone & Noguiera, 2002, p. 3, 81).[29]

3.2.1. NAFTA

The North American Free Trade Agreement (NAFTA) between Mexico, the United States and Canada became operative on 1 January 1994 and created the largest economic area of the world. Compared to the EU the historical and political motives for the creation of NAFTA are very different. The idea of a European integration can be traced back to the Middle Ages and – given the experience of two world wars – the idea to create an area of peace and economic development played a dominant role (Kaiser, 1998, pp. 39–40). In the case of NAFTA, apart from the general objective of an increased global competitiveness of the North American markets, the U.S.A. as the major economic power pursued some particular interests with regard to the control or domination of the Latin American markets (Hoffmann, 1995, p. 189; Schirm, 1997, p. 49), in particular a consolidation of its relationship to the Latin American states by extending the influence of NAFTA into South America (Kaiser, 1998, pp. 37, 39). According to some, "the major push behind NAFTA is globalization" (Kaiser, 1998, p. 36). In addition to pure security interests, in particular as to the US-Mexican border, the U.S.A. hoped that NAFTA would slow down migration from Mexico, while Mexico hoped to stabilise its reform process through a better access to the world market (Preusse, 2004, pp. 74–75). Although, against this background, it cannot be denied that NAFTA is also a political project, at least in the sense of the "new regionalism" in the Americas, it is equally clear that economic integration takes centre stage and political integration is not an aim in itself. NAFTA's primary purpose was "to dismantle trade and investment barriers" (Pastor, 2002, p. 87), and potential positive effects as to the strengthening of democracy and civil liberties could only be side-effects of the process of neoliberal, economic integration. For some NAFTA is not a trilateral partnership, but a "double-bilateral agreement" that "reads like a business contract" (Pastor, 2002, pp. 87–88). As a consequence human rights are only relevant as far as they concern economic production and development, e.g., as social or labour rights (Hoffmann, 1995, p. 188; Zapata, 2001, p. 38).

3.2.2. Mercosur

The origins of the Southern Common Market (Mercado Comun del Sur – Mercosur) can be traced back to the diplomatic rapprochement between Brazil and Argentina – in economic terms certainly the most important countries in Latin America at that time – after the end of the military dictatorships of the 1970s. The Brazilean-Argentinean connection led first to the Programme for Integration and Economic Co-operation (PICE) in 1986, extending to cooperation in the areas of technology and energy (Coffey, 1998, p. 6). Already two years later these two countries signed an agreement concerning the creation of a common market until 1995, which became the stepping stone for the creation of Mercosur (Coffey, 1998, p. 6). The Mercosur was then formally created with the Treaty of Asunción (Paraguay) on 26 March 1991 with the aim to promote the development of the socio-economic situation in the member states (Argentina, Brazil, Paraguay and Uruguay) by creating a single market between them based on the free movements of goods, services and means of production (Pacheco Pacífico, 2005, p. 125).[30] Venezuela obtained, thanks to its large oil revenues, full membership in 2005 and thus extended the Mercosur – contrary to its name! – to the North of South America. Apart from Chile also the CAN-member states (Bolivia, Colombia, Ecuador and Peru) are considered associated members of Mercosur.

In the light of these developments one can conclude that there are two major factors favouring the creation of Mercosur: the return to democracy in the *Cono Sur* and the implementation of economic and monetary policies. Interestingly enough, the initiative for the creation of a common market did not come from the business sectors, but from the governments (Coffey, 1998, p. 7). Insofar it is fair to say that the Treaty of Asunción had also a political character, even though it did not contain any social or human rights clauses (Ammon, 1998, p. 159ff.; Hofmeister, 2005, p. 58; Leuprecht, 2002, p. 133). In any case the creation of Mercosur – similar to that of the European Communities – was politically inspired and thus it is not surprising that after some delay the original aim of economic integration slowly opens up to a broader process including political and social issues. In fact, one can say that the accession of Venezuela as such is an expression of a certain political tendency of replacing pure neoliberal policies traditionally promoted by the U.S.A. by a social project of comprehensive development favouring all sectors of society.

As to human rights in particular, its role is stressed in different protocols and declarations (Pitanguy & Heringer, 2001, p. 75). Of special importance is the Additional Protocol to the treaty of Asunción, signed the 19 June 2005,[31] which forms an integral part of this treaty (Art. 7 Protocol) and as such calls for the observance of human rights as "condiciones esenciales para la vigencia y evolución del proceso de integración" ("essential conditions to strengthen and develop the process of integration") (Art. 1); it further provides for different possibilities of reaction in case of grave and systematic violations of human rights by a member state or an associated state (see Art. 8 of the Protocol). According to Art. 3 of the Protocol, in such cases the first step are consultations with the respective state; if these fail the other member states shall consider other measures and eventually sanctions which may even result in the suspension of the membership of the respective state (Art. 4). In addition, at the 10th Meeting of the Common Market Council (CMC) – the superior organ of the Mercosur consisting of the respective Foreign Relations and Economy Ministers – on 25 June 1996 a democracy clause was introduced with the Presidential Declaration on Democratic Commitment in the Mercosur as well as with the Protocol of Adhesion of Chile and Bolivia (Bodemer, 2006, p. 158). Accordingly, the democratic order is the essential condition ("condición esencial") for the existence of the Mercosur community and the non-compliance with this condition constitutes an insurmountable obstacle for the process of integration. Member states have different options for sanctions, up until the suspension of the membership, and there is also a possibility to incorporate democracy clauses in other agreements of Mercosur (cf. the human rights clauses of the EU, as mentioned supra). This principle was confirmed by the "Protocolo de Ushuaia sobre Compromiso Democrático" in 1998 and incorporated into the treaty of Asunción (Hofmeister, 2005, p. 58).

More recently, during the 25 Mercosur Summit in Asunción in 2003, the creation of a centre for the promotion of the rule of law (Centro MERCOSUR de Promoción del Estado de Derecho) was decided in order to further research and capacity building in the area of human rights (Hofmeister, 2005, p. 71; Woischnik, 2004, p. 96). Currently the member states discuss about the adoption of a Human Rights Charter: The Ad hoc Commission on Human Rights established in 2000 (Bizzozero, 2004, pp. 52–53), was followed in 2004 by the "Reunión de Altas Autoridades sobre Derechos Humanos del Mercosur", which inter alia is in charge of discussing the necessity of such a Charter and eventually drafting it; this group, however, produced not yet any concrete results.

3.2.3. Other Projects, in Particular the South American Community of Nations (SACN)

Apart from Nafta and Mercosur there are other processes of integration which, albeit not of the same importance, deserve at least to be mentioned. A *Free Trade Area for the Americas* (FTAA) (Bodemer, 2006, p. 178; Preusse, 2004, p. 186), as promoted by the U.S.A., seems to have no chance to succeed given the resistance of the most important South American states (above all Argentina, Brazil and Venezuela). The counterproposal of a *Bolivarian Alternative for the Americas* (*Alternativa Bolivariana para las Americas*, ALBA) (Arreaza, 2004; Bodemer, 2006, p. 159), promoted by the Venezuelan president Hugo Chávez and explicitly based on ideas of the liberator Simon Bolívar, equally finds no sufficient support (and was in fact delegitimized by Venezuela's joining of the Mercosur, cf. supra).

More recently, during the third South American Summit (7–9 December 2004 in Cuzco), a *South American Community of Nations* (SACN) was announced pursuing the aim of creating a continental free trade zone including Mercosur and the Andean Community. While not reaching a more substantive agreement, the twelve Heads of State present (Argentina, Bolivia, Brazil, Chile, Colombia, Ecuador, Guyana, Paraguay, Peru, Suriname, Uruguay and Venezuela) signed the Declaration of Cuzco by which the SACN is formally established upon a "shared South American identity and common values such as: democracy, solidarity, human rights, freedom, social justice, respect for territorial integrity, for diversity, non-discrimination and the assertion of autonomy, the sovereign equality of States and the peaceful settlement of disputes".[32] At their Meeting in Brasilia on 30 September 2005 the Heads of States of the SACN declared, inspired by these shared values, that the essence of the SACN is "the political understanding and social and economic integration of the peoples of South America".[33] Although Peru's (former) President Alejandro Toledo already at the Cuzco meeting, maybe influenced by the Inka myth surrounding this marvellous city, referred to ambitious aims such as the creation of a "new nation" with "a single currency, a single passport" and "a parliament with directly elected representatives", the truth is that the SACN will be based mainly on existing institutions and will rather be a coordinating than a truly supranational organisation (Art. 7 and 11) (Bodemer, 2006, pp. 174–175). Even though, the different declarations adopted in Brasilia provide for co-operation on economic, technical, scientific, environmental and cultural issues following the aim of converging the Economic Complementation Agreements of Southern America.[34] Such cooperation has already led before, as seen above, to the creation of complex supranational structures with an important impact on human rights, its protection and conflict prevention.

4. CONCLUSION

Both in Europe and the Americas more or less effective regional systems of human rights protection exist. While the European system of the ECHR was reformed in 1998 with the creation of a new Human Rights Court, thereby giving more powers to the judicial component of the system, the Inter American system still consists of the Commission and the Court.

Parallel to the human rights systems processes of predominantly economic (regional) integration have started in the middle of the 20th century in both Europe and the Americas. While these processes have certain things in common, in particular the dominant aim of promoting economic development by free trade, they must be distinguished from each other in historical and political terms. Whereas the European Communities were clearly a result from the atrocities of the Second World War, and therefore economic cooperation and development were seen as instruments to ensure a long-lasting and stable peace, the processes in the Americas were largely economically motivated, especially the mainly U.S.-driven creation of NAFTA; only for the Mercosur did the region's experience with the military dictatorships play a certain role in its creation. Thus, it is not surprising that on a political or human rights level the EU may rather be compared to Mercosur than to NAFTA. Indeed, while the question of human rights plays practically no role in the latter it gained more and more importance both in the EU and in Mercosur through specific democracy and human rights clauses. This corresponds to the general similarity between the EU and Mercosur at an institutional level although the Mercosur has not yet reached the institutional complexity and supranationality of the EU (Borges Moschen, 2006; Hofmeister, 2005, p. 62; Leuprecht, 2002, p. 135; Paulo Pereira, 2006, p. 193ff.). Also, in a negative sense, one may question the legitimacy of the project of integration in both organisations as to its (insufficient) support in civil society (Bach, 2006, p. 151ff.; Mineiro, 2006, p. 181ff.). Concerning NAFTA one may wish that it takes the EU and Mercosur as a model when it comes to the importance of human rights clauses; indeed, it should progress beyond the status of pure market integration (Hoffmann, 1995, p. 194; Rozental, 2002, p. 75).

The existence of both a human rights system in the strict sense and a system of economic integration which promotes human rights as a kind of side-effect or at a secondary level, creates problems with regard to delimiting the judicial organs of both systems as to the human rights protection in the same geographic area. While this is a particular relevant issue in Europe, given the partially overlapping competence of the ECHR and EU courts, it is not yet an issue in the Americas since the process of integration has not yet reached the level of a judicialization implying supranational powers of the respective organs.

This institutional and judicial level of human rights protection cannot be overestimated, as illustrated by the recent European case law on the UN terror lists, and in particular on the insufficient legal remedies of European citizens to be taken off these lists (Ambos, 2006a, 2006b). Indeed, the fight for human rights goes well beyond the formulation of nicely drafted declarations and conventions (Peralta Gainza, 2005; Sangmeister, 2005, pp. 15–16); it depends on the interplay between the official human rights organs and civil society, especially on the access of the latter to the former (Ambos, 2006a, 2006b).

NOTES

1. In particular the UN Universal Declaration, adopted by General Assembly Resolution 217 A (III) of 10 December 1948 (http://www.un.org/Overview/rights.html), as well as the International Covenant on Economic, Social and Cultural Rights (http://www.unhchr.ch/html/menu3/b/a_cescr.htm), and the International Covenant on Civil and Political Rights (http://www.unhchr.ch/html/menu3/b/a_ccpr.htm), both adopted by General Assembly Resolution 2200 A (XXI) of 16 December 1966; for an overview of the numerous special Conventions and the ratification status, see http://www.ishr.ch/About%20UN/UN&Regional.htm

2. See, apart from the European and American Conventions, the African Charter on Human and Peoples' Rights (http://www.africa-union.org/official_documents/Treaties_%20Conventions_%20Protocols/Banjul%20Charter.pdf), as well as the Arab Charter on Human Rights (http://www1.umn.edu/humanrts/instree/arabhrchater.html).

3. For the updated status of ratifications, see http://www.coe.int/T/e/com/about_coe/member_states/default.asp. The Council of Europe must be distinguished from the Council of Ministers of the EC (Art. 202 et seq. TEC) and the European Council (regular meeting of the heads of the member states, Art. 4 TEU) (Ambos, 2006, p. 311ff.).

4. The OAS as a Pan-American Organization was created in 1969 by the adoption of the Charter of the OAS, signed on 30 April 1948 and amended by various protocols in the following decades (http://www1.umn.edu/humanrts/iachr/oascharter.html); since 1994 the OAS organizes the Summits of the Americas, promoting inter alia human rights (http://www.summit-americas.org/default.htm).

The full text of the American Convention on Human Rights, which is also known as the "Pact of San José", and became effective in 1978, is found on: http://www.oas.org/juridico/english/Treaties/b-32.htm. For the text of the American Declaration, see http://www.cidh.oas.org/Basicos/basic2.htm

5. For a better understanding of the interplay of the normative fundaments of the IACom: the OAS Charter states in its Art. 106 that there "shall be an Inter-American Commission on Human Rights", whose "structure, competence and procedure" shall be determined by "an Inter-American convention on human rights". Art. 34–51 ACHR accomplish these duties, which are then concretised by the Statute of the IACom (http://www.cidh.org/Basicos/basic15.htm) and its Rules of procedure (http://www.cidh.org/Basicos/basic16.htm) (Buergenthal et al., 1986, p. 15).

6. Annual Report of the IACHR (2005, p. 4; http://www1.umn.edu/humanrts/iachr/Annuals/annual-06.pdf): Argentina, Barbados, Bolivia, Brazil, Chile, Colombia, Costa Rica, Dominican Republic, Ecuador, El Salvador, Guatemala, Haiti, Honduras, Mexico, Nicaragua, Panama, Paraguay, Peru, Surinam, Uruguay, Venezuela. All of these states are members of the OAS (but the Cuban Government has been excluded from participation in 1962), but only 24 have ratified the ACHR (http://www.cidh.org/Basicos/basic4.htm); Trinidad and Tobago ratified in 1991, but declared its withdrawal in 1998 (http://www.cidh.org/Basicos/basic4.htm).

7. See from the more recent case law, in particular Masacre de Ituango vs. Colombia, judgment of 1 July 2006, para. 289 et seq. and Almonacid Arellano et al. vs. Chile, judgment of 26 September 2006 (confirming, inter alia, the prohibition of amnesties and statutes of limitation for crimes against humanity, e.g. para. 152–153). All case law can be accessed at the Court's website: http://www.corteidh.or.cr

8. For a general introduction to Regional Integration Agreements and its development within the last decades from a mainly economic view see: OECD, Regional Integration Agreements, 1 January 2004, pp. 1 et seq. (http://www.oecd.org/dataoecd/39/37/1923431.pdf); see also American Development Bank (IDB), RE-265, Implicit IDB Strategy for Regional Integration: Its Evaluation, 30 May 2002 (http://www.oecd.org/dataoecd/11/46/35261785.pdf) regarding the American processes of integration.

9. Cf. Speech of the EU External Relations Commissioner Patten, held on the Human Rights Forum, Brussels 28 and 29 May 2001 (http://www.ec.europa.eu/comm/external_relations/news/patten/speech01_243.htm); cf. Baranyi, 2004, pp. 5–6, concerning the work of the Inter-American Commission on Human Rights; in a wider perspective. Baranyi, 2004, p. 4ff. examines the role of the Inter-American institutions with regard to conflict prevention by detecting four pillars of conflict prevention practices: (1) the peaceful settlement of inter-state disputes, (2) the protection of human rights, (3) the defence and promotion of democracy, and (4) other aspects of structural prevention, such as activities of IDB and FTAs.

10. ECJ Case C 29/69 Stauder, ECR 1969, 419, mn. 7 (also Winkler, 2000, p. 44).

11. See Opinion of Mr. Advocate General Roemer delivered on 29 October 1969, ECJ Case C 29/69 Stauder, ECR 1969, 419, 428 (also Walter, 2005, p. 10). A part of the doctrine takes the view, however, that the EC/EU is bound by the ECHR by way of the member states which can only delegate their sovereign powers to the EU together with the duties under the ECHR: *nemo plus iuris transferre potest quam ipse habet* (Winkler, 2000, pp. 28–29).

12. ECJ Case C 4-73, ECR 1974, 491, rn. 13 (Jarass, 2005, p. 17; Walter, 2005, p. 10); also ECJ, Case C 94/00, ECR 2002, I-9011 mn. 23, 25; C 112/00, ECR 2003, I-5659 mn. 71; C 20/00, ECR 2003, I-7411 mn. 65.

13. ECJ, ECR 1986, 1651, mn. 18, ECR 1991, I-2925, mn. 41; ECR 1997, I-7493, mn. 12; ECJ, C 97-99/87, ECR 1989, 3165, mn. 10; C 112/00, ECR 2003, I-5659, mn. 71.

14. Cf. ECJ, C-260/89, ECR 1991, I-2925, mn. 41–45 (Walter, 2005, p. 10; Winkler, 2000, p. 33).

15. ECJ, ECR 1996, I-1759, mn. 34-35 – Gutachten 2/94 = *EuGRZ* 1996, 206 where the Court explicitly rejects the general provision of Art. 235 old/308 new EC as a legal basis for such an accession.

16. *Bull. EU* 12-2000, 8, See already in 1977 the General Declaration on Fundamental Rights by the European Parliament, the Council and the Commission (OJ C 103, 27/04/1977, p. 1), as well as the Declarations of Fundamental Rights and Liberties of 1989 (OJ C 120, 16/05/1989, p. 51) by the European Parliament.

17. See also for an accession Art. I–9 of the Draft Constitution; see also Zimmermann (2002, pp. 18–19), who criticizes the reference to the Charter in the case law, e.g. by the Spanish (STC 292/2000 of 30 November 2000, http://www.tribunalconstitucional.es/STC2000/STC2000-292.htm) and German Constitutional Courts (BVerfG, Beschluß vom 22 November 2001, EuGRZ 2002, 669–670) since this entails a normative significance of the Charter which may make the accession superfluous.

18. CFI, Case T 377/00, Phillip Morris, ECR 2003, p. II-1, mn. 122. According to Jarass (2005, p. 14) the ECJ has not yet invoked the Charta.

19. The "membership requires that the candidate country has achieved stability of institutions guaranteeing democracy, the rule of law, human rights [...]", *Bull. EC* 6-1993, I.13.

20. ECJ, ECR 1989, 2609, mn. 19.

21. See also Commission Communication COM (95) 216 of 23 May 1995, http://www.europa.eu.int/comm/external_relations/human_rights/doc/com95_216_en.pdf

22. [1990] OJ L 295/67; this clause was later also used in agreements with the post-dictatorial governments of Chile ([1991] OJ L 79/2), Uruguay ([1992] OJ L 94/2) and Paraguay ([1992] OJ L 323/72) calling for the respect for democratic principles and human rights in Art. 1 of the respective agreements (Hoffmeister, 1998, pp. 86–87).

23. Predecessor of the Organisation for Security and Co-operation in Europe, cf. *Bull. EC* 5-1992, pt. 1.2.13; concerning Yugoslavia see OJ L 325/23 (Kühn, 2003, pp. 102–103; *EuZW* 1998, p. 694).

24. [1992] OJ L 403/2 (Estonia), 11 (Latvia), 20 (Lithuana), [1992] OJ L 343/2 (Albania).

25. Cf. *Bull. EG* 12-1990, Ziff. 2.4.1.

26. It is also called the *standard human rights clause* (Bulterman, 2001, Part B, Chapter V–X; also Annex 2, p. 293ff. for a list of agreements containing a reference to human rights); as an example for the clause see Title I, Art. 1, Principles, Nr. 1 of the "Political Dialogue and Cooperation Agreement" between the EU and Central America signed in Rome in December 2003: "Respect for democratic principles and fundamental human rights, as laid down in the Universal Declaration of Human Rights, as well as for the principle of the rule of law, underpins the internal and international policies of the Parties and constitutes an essential element of this Agreement", http://www.europa.eu.int/comm/external_relations/ca/pol/pdca_12_03_en.pdf; see also the identical part of the agreement

between EU and the Andean Community, http://www.eu.int/comm/external_ relations/andean/doc/pdca_1203_en. pdf and the Interregional Framework Cooperation Agreement between the EU and Mercosur, http://www.eu.int/comm/ external_relations/mercosur/bacground_doc/fca96.htm

27. In his letter to Francisco Peña, dating from the 27 August 1820, "el libertador" Simon Bolívar stated: "El hombre no tiene más patria que aquélla en que se protegen los derechos de los ciudadanos y se respeta el carácter de la humanidad", quoted according to Camargo (2002, p. 565). According to Bolívar the Confederation should be an example for the world in respect of democracy and freedom (Vargas Martínez, 1990, p. 133; Schirm, 1997, pp. 27–28). Bolívar's initiative finally led to a congress held in Panama from 22. June to 15 July 1826 where the delegates of the newly founded Ibero American republics signed a common treaty of alliance and cooperation (Kühn, 2003, p. 109; Medina Núñez, 2002; Sangmeister, 2005, p. 15).

28. Being composed of Argentina, Bolivia, Brazil, Chile, Cuba, Colombia, Ecuador, Mexico, Paraguay, Perú, Uruguay and Venezuela (Coffey, 1998, pp. 2–3). For a survey of the existing trade agreements in the Americas, see Ammon (1998, p. 16), and for historical developments, see Kühn (2003, p. 108ff.).

29. See also the Andean Charter for the Promotion and the Protection of Human Rights of 2002: http://www.ohchr.org/english/law/compilation_democracy/ andeancharter.htm. As to the relationship with the EU it is worthwhile mentioning that the agreement between the EU and CAN contains a democracy and human rights clause (Kühn, 2003, p. 96).

30. http://www.mercosur.int/msweb/principal/contenido.asp

31. MERCOSUR/CMC/DEC Nr. 17/05: Protocolo de Asunción sobre Compromiso con la Promoción y Protección de los Derechos Humanos del Mercosur, http://www.mercosur.org.uy; see also http://www.sre.gob.mx/dgomra/mercosur/ documentos/Pro_dh_05.doc

32. Declaración de Cuzco: http://www.comunidadandina.org/documentos/dec_int/ cusco_sudamerica.htm; for further information see: http://www.comunidadandina. org/ingles/sudamerican.htm

33. Presidential Declaration and Priority Agenda of the First Meeting of Heads of States of the SACN in Brasilia, 30 September 2005, http://www.comunidadandina. org/ingles/documentos/documents/casa_2005_4.htm

34. See in particular the Program of Action and the Declaration of the Convergence of Integration Processes in South America, First Meeting of Heads of State of the South American Community of Nations, Brasilia, 30 September 2005, http://www.comunidadandina.org/INGLES/documentos/documents/casa_2005_3.htm and http://www.comunidadandina.org/INGLES/documentos/documents/casa_2005_1.htm; see the full text of all the declarations at http://www.comunidadandina.org/INGLES/ sudamerican.htm

REFERENCES

Alston, P., & Weiler, J. H. H. (1999). An "ever closer union" in need of a human rights policy: The European Union and human rights. In: P. Alston (Ed.), *The EU and human rights* (pp. 3–66). Oxford: Oxford University Press.

Ambos, K. (2003). Der Europäische Gerichtshof für Menschenrechte und die Verfahrensrechte. Waffengleichheit, partizipatorisches Vorverfahren und Art. 6 EMRK. *Zeitschrift für die gesamte Strafrechtswissenschaft (ZStW), 115*, 583–637.

Ambos, K. (2006a). *Internationales Strafrecht. Strafanwendungsrecht, Völkerstrafrecht, Europäisches Strafrecht.* München: Beck.

Ambos, K. (2006b). Terrorismusbekämpfung seit dem 11. September 2001. In: M. Becker & R. Zimmerling (Eds), *Politik und Recht. Politische Vierteljahresschrift* (Special issue 36, pp. 416–448). (Updated Spanish version to be published in the Cuadernos de Jimenez de Asua, Madrid, editorial Dykinson.)

Ammon, G. (1998). *Voraussetzungen und Folgen regionaler Integration in Amerika, dargestellt am Beispiel von NAFTA und MERCOSUR.* Nürnberg: Friedrich-Alexander Universität.

Anderson, K., & Blackhurst, R. (1993). Introduction and summary. In: K. Anderson & R. Blackhurst (Eds), *Regional integration and the global trading system* (pp. 1–15). London: Harvester Wheatsheaf.

Arreaza, T. (2004). *ALBA: Bolivarian alternative for Latin America and the Caribbean,* January 30 (http://www.venezuelanalysis.com/docs.php?dno = 1010).

Bach, M. (2006). Integração Européia sem sociedade? In: K. Ambos & A. C. Paulo Pereira (Eds), *Mercosul e União Européia* (pp. 151–180). Rio de Janeiro: Lúmen Júris.

Baranyi, S. (2005). *Inter-American institutions and conflict prevention.* In: FPP-05-04 (http://www.focal.ca/pdf/conflict05.pdf).

Betten, L., & Grief, N. (1998). *EU law and human rights.* London: Longman.

Bizzozero, L. (2004). Derechos humanos y dimensión social en los regionalismos del siglo XXI. Construcción y perspectivas desde el espacio regional del MERCOSUR. In Observatório de Políticas Públicas de Derechos Humanos en el Mercosur (Ed.), *Políticas Públicas de Derechos Humanos en el Mercosur. Un compromiso regional* (pp. 25–54). Montevideo: Observatório de Políticas Públicas.

Blackburn, R. (2001). The institutions and processes of the convention. In: R. Blackburn & J. Polakiewicz (Eds), *Fundamental rights in Europe. The European convention on human rights and its member states, 1950-2000* (pp. 3–29). Oxford: Oxford University Press.

Bodemer, K. (2006). Lateinamerika und die Karibik. Gedanken zu ihrer Bedeutung für Deutschland und Europa. *Lateinamerika analysen, 15,* 149–197.

Borges Moschen, V. R. (2006). Aspectos institucionais do Mercosul: 11 anos do Protocolo do Ouro Preto. In: K. Ambos & A. C. Paulo Pereira (Eds), *Mercosul e Mercosul e União Européia* (pp. 1–15). Rio de Janeiro: Lúmen Júris.

Boyle, K., & Méndez, J. (2004). Foreword. In: S. Peers & A. Ward (Eds), *The European charter of fundamental rights.* Oxford: Oxford University Press.

Brandtner, B., & Rosas, A. (1998). Human rights and the external relations of the European community: An analysis of doctrine and practice. *European Journal of International Law, 9,* 468–490.

Brandtner, B., & Rosas, A. (1999). Trade preferences and human rights. In: P. Alston (Ed.), *The EU and Human Rights* (pp. 699–722). Oxford: Oxford University Press.

Brasche, U. (2003). *Europäische Integration. Wirtschaft, Erweiterung und regionale Effekte.* München: Beck.

Brown, O., Faisal Haq, S., Shaheen Rafi, K., & Moeed, Y. (2005). *Regional trade agreements: Promoting conflict or building peace?* Winnipeg: International Institute for Sustainable Development.

Buergenthal, T., & Cassell, D. (1998). The future of the inter-American human rights system. In: J. E. Méndez & F. Cox (Eds), *El Futuro del Sistema Interamericano de Protección de los Derechos Humanos* (pp. 539–571). San José: Inter-American Institute of Human Rights.

Buergenthal, T., Norris, R., & Shelton, D. (1986). *Protecting human rights in the Americas. Selected problems* (2nd ed.). Kehl/Strasbourg: Engel Verlag.

Bulterman, M. (2001). *Human rights in the treaty relations of the European Community. Real virtues or virtual reality?* Antwerp: Intersentia.

Calliess, C. (2005). Die Europäische Grundrechts-Charta. In: D. Ehlers (Ed.), *Europäische Grundrechte und Grundfreiheiten* (2nd ed., pp. 531–552). Berlin: Walter de Gruyter.

Camargo, P. (2002). *Manual de Derechos Humanos* (2nd ed.). Bogotá: Editorial Leyer.

Coffey, P. (1998). The historical background to integration in Latin America. In: P. Coffey (Ed.), *Latin America: Mercosur* (pp. 1–20). Boston: Kluwer.

Davidson, S. (1997). *The inter-American human rights system.* Aldershot: Ashgate.

De Witte, B., & Toggenburg, G. (2004). Human rights and membership of the European Union. In: S. Peers & A. Ward (Eds), *The European Union charter of fundamental rights* (pp. 59–83). Oxford: Hart Publishing.

Ehlers, D. (2005a). Die Europäische Menschenrechtskonvention. Allgemeine Lehren. In: D. Ehlers (Ed.), *Europäische Grundrechte und Grundfreiheiten* (2nd ed., pp. 23–62). Berlin: Walter de Gruyter.

Ehlers, D. (2005b). Die Grundrechte der Europäischen Union. Allgemeine Lehren. In: D. Ehlers (Ed.), *Europäische Grundrechte und Grundfreiheiten* (2nd ed., pp. 383–409). Berlin: Walter de Gruyter.

Fischer, H. G. (2001). *Europarecht* (3rd ed.). München: Beck.

Frowein, J. A. (1996). Art. 28 EMRK. In: J. A. Frowein & W. Peukert (Eds), *EMRK-Kommentar* (Vol. 2). Aufl. Kehl/Straßburg: Engel Verlag.

Frowein, J. A. (2004). European integration through fundamental rights. In: M. Hartwig, G. Nolte, S. Oeter & C. Walter (Eds), *Völkerrecht – Menschenrechte – Verfassungsfragen Deutschlands und Europas. Ausgewählte Schriften, Beiträge zum ausländischen öffentlichen Recht und Völkerrecht, Band* (Vol. 174, pp. 265–289). Heidelberg: Springer Verlag.

Guedes de Oliveira, M. (2004). Limitations on democratic transitions in Latin America and the fate of Mercosur. In: F. Dominguez & M. Guedes de Oliveira (Eds), *Mercosur: Between integration and democracy* (pp. 17–28). Oxford: Peter Lang.

Harris, D., O'Boyle, M., & Warbrick, C. (1995). *Law of the European convention on human rights.* London: Butterworths.

Herdegen, M. (2005). *Europarecht* (7th ed.). München: Beck.

Hoffmann, R. (1995). Can the EC social charter be a model for the NAFTA? In: R. S. Belous & J. Lemco (Eds), *NAFTA as a model of development: The benefits and costs of merging high- and low-wage areas* (pp. 188–194). New York: SUNY Press.

Hoffmeister, F. (1998). *Menschenrechts- und Demokratieklauseln in den vertraglichen Außenbeziehungen der Europäischen Gemeinschaft, Beiträge zum ausländischen öffentlichen Recht und Völkerrecht.* Berlin/Heidelberg: Springer-Verlag.

Hofmeister, W. (2005). Der MERCOSUR: Stand und Perspektiven des Integrationsprozesses in Südamerika. In: N. Gmelch, A. Kopyciok & A. Meyer (Eds), *Frei Handeln in den Amerikas. Entwicklung und Perspektiven gegenwärtiger Integrationsprojekte* (pp. 56–85). München: Martin Meidenbauer Verlagsbuchhandlung.

Jacobs, F., & White, R. (2002). *European convention on human rights* (3rd ed.). Oxford: Oxford University Press.

Jarass, H. D. (2005). *Die EU-Grundrechte*. München: Beck.

Kadelbach, S. (2005). Die Unionsbürgerrechte. In: D. Ehlers (Ed.), *Europäische Grundrechte und Grundfreiheiten* (2nd ed., pp. 553–587). Berlin: Walter de Gruyter.

Kaiser, R. (1998). *Regionale integration in Europa und Nordamerika*. Baden-Baden: Nomos Verlag.

Kaltenbach, U. (2005). Die CAFTA – Entstehung, Inhalte und Interessenlagen. In: N. Gmelch, A. Kopyciok & A. Meyer (Eds), *Frei handeln in den Amerikas. Entwicklungen und Perspektiven gegenwärtiger Integrationsprojekte* (pp. 127–152). München: Martin Meidenbauer Verlagsbuchhandlung.

Kohl (2006). Carla del Ponte, Chefanklägerin des ICTY, *Frankfurter Rundschau*, 23.2.2006, at 2.

Kokott, J. (1986). *Das interamerikanische System zum Schutz der Menschenrechte*, Beiträge zum ausländischen öffentlichen Recht und Völkerrecht, Band 92. Berlin/Heidelberg: Springer Verlag.

Kühn, W. M. (2003). *Die Andengemeinschaft. Juristische Aspekte der internationalen Beziehungen zwischen der Europäischen Union und lateinamerikanischen Integrationssystemen im Zeitalter des Neuen regionalismus*. Aachen: Shaker.

Leuprecht, P. (2002). Report on Canada's enforcement of human rights and democracy obligations (http://www.dfait-maeci.gc.ca/tna-nac/documents/ANNEXE-e.pdf).

López Garelli, M. (2004). El carácter de los mecanismos de protección de derechos humanos en el sistema interameriocano. In: C. González Feldmann (Ed.), *El Paraguay frente al sistema internacional de los derechos humanos* (pp. 91–107). Montevideo: Fundación Konrad Adenauer.

Malinowski, B. (1922). *Argonauts of the Western Pacific*. London: Routledge and Kegan.

Marwege, R. (1995). *Der Andengerichtshof. Das Rechtsschutzsystem des Andenpaktes mit vergleichenden Bezügen zum Recht der Europäischen Gemeinschaft, Hamburger Studien zum Europäischen und Internationalen Recht, Band 4*. Berlin: Duncker und Humblot.

Medina Núñez, I. (2002). América Latina: Raíces Y perspectivas de la integración. In: *Dinámicas y escenarios estratégicos de la integración en América Latina*, Jaime, Alberto Rocha V. y Elia Marum (Coords) (pp. 29–46). Guadalajara: Universidad de Guadalajara/Centro Universitario de Ciencias Económico Administrativas (CUCEA).

Mineiro, A. S. (2006). Mercosul-EU: As perspectivas da integração birregional e a sociedades civil. In: K. Ambos & A. C. Paulo Pereira (Eds), *Mercosul e União Européia* (pp. 181–191). Rio de Janeiro: Lumen Juris.

Nowak, M. (1999). Human rights "conditionality" in relation to entry to, and full participation in, the EU. In: P. Alston (Ed.), *The EU and human rights* (pp. 687–698). Oxford: Oxford University Press.

Oppermann, T. (2005). *Europarecht* (3rd ed.). München: Beck.

Pacheco Pacifico, A. (2005). Human rights in the constitutions of the member states of the common market of south (Mercosur). *Humanitäres Völkerrecht*, *18*, 124–130.

Pastor, R. A. (2002). NAFTA is not enough. Steps toward a North American community. In: P. Hakim & R. E. Litan (Eds), *The future of North American integration* (pp. 87–117). Washington, DC: Open Society Institute.

Paulo Pereira, A. C. (2006). Diferentes aspectos dos sistemas de integração da Uniao Europeia e do Mercosul. In: K. Ambos & A. C. Paulo Pereira (Eds), *Mercosul e União Européia*, (pp. 193–216). Rio de Janeiro: Lumen Júris.

Peralta Gainza, P. (2005). Mercosur: Derechos humanos y participación ciudadana, Entrevista a Deisy Ventura, Democracia Sur (http://www.democraciasur.com/regional/VenturaMercosur DerHumanos.htm).

Peters, A. (2003). *Einführung in die EMRK*. München: Beck.

Philippi, N. (2002). *Die Charta der Grundrechte der Europäischen Union*. Baden-Baden: Nomos Verlag.

Pitanguy, J., & Heringer, R. (2001). Direitos Humanos no Mercosul. *Cadernos Fórum Civil* 4/3, Rio de Janeiro (http://www.handel-entwicklung-menschenrechte.org/fileadmin/christian /Cepia2001-DHMercosur.pdf).

Preusse, H. G. (2004). *The new American regionalism*. Cheltenham/Northampton, MA: Edward Elgar.

Quiroga León, A. (2003). *El debido proceso legal en el Perú y el sistema interamericano de derechos humanoscontribution*. Lima: Jurista Editores.

Riedel, E., & Will, M. (1999). Human rights clauses in external agreements of the EC. In: P. Alston (Ed.), *The EU and human rights* (pp. 723–754). Oxford: Oxford University Press.

Rozental, A. (2002). Integrating North America. A Mexican perspective. In: P. Hakim & R. E. Litan (Eds), *The future of North American integration* (pp. 73–86). Washington, DC: Open Society Institute.

Russau, C. (2004). Enforcement of international trade regimes between the European Union (EU) and the Common Market of the South (MERCOSUR)? *Foreign direct investment as the object of free trade negotiations: Between investor's rights, development and human rights*. Berlin: FDCL (http://www.fdcl-berlin.de/fileadmin/fdcl/Enforcement-FDI-final_web.pdf).

Sánchez Padilla, E. P. (2005). *Protección Internacional de los Derechos Humanos*. Quito: PNUD.

Sangmeister, H. (2005). Der neue Regionalismus und die lokale Logik der Globalisierung. In: N. Gmelch, A. Kopyciok & A. Meyer (Eds), *Frei Handeln in den Amerikas. Entwicklung und Perspektiven gegenwärtiger Integrationsprojekte* (pp. 12–29). München: Martin Meidenbauer Verlagsbuchhandlung.

Santer, J. (2002). Überlegungen zur Bedeutung der Europäischen Charta der Grundrechte. In: W. Heusel (Ed.), *Grundrechtecharta und Verfassungsentwicklung in der EU* (pp. 13–15). Köln: Bundesanzeiger Verlag.

Schirm, S. A. (1997). *Kooperation in den Amerikas. NAFTA, MERCOSUR und die neue Dynamik regionaler Zusammenarbeit, Aktuelle Materialien zur Internationalen Politik, Band 46*. Baden-Baden: Nomos Verlag.

Schott, R. (1970). Die Funktionen des Rechts in primitiven Gesellschaften. In: W. Maihofer & H. Schelsky (Eds.), Die Funktion des Rechts in der modernen Gesellschaft. *Jahrbuch für Rechtssoziologie und Rechtstheorie* 1, 107–174.

Simma, B., Aschenbrenner, J. B., & Schulte, C. (1999). Human rights considerations in the development co-operation activities of the EC. In: P. Alston (Ed.), *The EU and human rights* (pp. 571–626). Oxford: Oxford University Press.

Taccone, J. J., & Noguiera, U. (Eds). (2002). Andean Report, Buenos Aires: IDB (http://www.iadb.org/publications/search.cfm?language = English&keywords = &title = andean + report&author = &topics = &countries = &searchLang = &fromYear = &toYear = &x = 27 &y = 10).

Uerpmann-Wittzack, R. (2005). Doppelter Grundrechtsschutz für die zukünftige Europäische Union, *DÖV*, 152–157.

Vargas Martínez, G. (1990). Bolivarismo y Monroismo Cien Años despues. *Cuadernos Americanos Nueva Época, IV/5/23*, 116–137.

Walter, C. (2005). Geschichte und Entwicklung der europäischen Grundrechte und Grundfreiheiten. In: D. Ehlers (Ed.), *Europäische Grundrechte und Grundfreiheiten* (2nd ed., pp. 1–21). Berlin: Walter de Gruyter.

Weber, S. (1995). European Union conditionality. In: B. Eichengreen, J. Frieden & J. v. Hagen (Eds), *Politics and institutions in an integrated Europe* (pp. 192–217). Heidelberg: Springer-Verlag.

Williams, A. (2004). *EU human rights policy: A study in Irony*. Oxford: Oxford University Press.

Winkler, S. (2000). *Der Beitritt der Europäischen Gemeinschaften zur Europäischen Menschenrechtskonvention, Schriftenreihe Europäisches Recht, Politik und Wirtschaft*. Baden-Baden: Nomos Verlag.

Woischnik, J. (2004). Institutionelle Konsolidierung im MERCOSUR: neuer Präsident, neues Gericht, neues Sekretariat. *KAS-Auslandsinformationen*, 1, 82–96 (http://www.kas.de/db_files/dokumente/auslandsinformationen/7_dokument_dok_pdf_4077_1.pdf).

Zapata, F. (2001). Nation state, free trade, and economic integration in Latin America. In: N. Saavedra-Rivano, A. Hosono & B. Stallings (Eds), *Regional integration and economic development* (pp. 38–51). London: Palgrave Macmillan.

Zimmermann, A. (2002). *Die Charta der Grundrechte der Europäischen Union zwischen Gemeinschaftsrecht, Grundgesetz und EMRK. Entstehung, normative Bedeutung und Wirkung der EU-Grundrechtecharta im gesamteuropäischen Verfassungsraum*. Baden-Baden: Nomos Verlag.

Zuber, F. (2005). Die politische Dimension der Regionalisierung in Lateinamerika im Schatten des Freihandels. In: N. Gmelch, A. Kopyciok & A. Meyer (Eds), *Frei Handeln in den Amerikas. Entwicklung und Perspektiven gegenwärtiger Integrationsprojekte* (pp. 31–54). München: Martin Meidenbauer Verlagsbuchhandlung.

TRAFFICKING IN HUMANS AND HUMAN RIGHTS

Hans-Jörg Albrecht

1. INTRODUCTION

Trafficking in humans has emerged as an eminent social, political and legal problem with the opening of borders in Europe at the end of the 1980s. Since then, it has become an issue of concern in both national and international systems of crime control and law enforcement (Arlacchi, 2000; David, 2000), as is illustrated by the many norms and standards being enacted in the framework of the United Nations, the Council of Europe, the European Union and other organizations.

This chapter intends to give an overview of the major instruments and policies to deal with the problem of trafficking in humans. It is argued that the fight against trafficking cannot be seen in isolation from policies against organized crime and from migration policies. It also becomes clear that trafficking of humans is increasingly viewed in a human rights framework, both for the victims of trafficking and for their offenders.

2. THE EMERGENCE OF ANTI-TRAFFICKING POLICIES WORLDWIDE

The 1989 UN Convention on the Rights of the Child in Article 34 already expressly confirms the right of the child to be protected from sexual

Crime and Human Rights
Sociology of Crime, Law and Deviance, Volume 9, 39–71
Copyright © 2007 by Elsevier Ltd.
All rights of reproduction in any form reserved
ISSN: 1521-6136/doi:10.1016/S1521-6136(07)09002-1

exploitation, including of course trafficking in children. However, it was in the United Nations Convention on Transnational Crime, signed in Palermo (Italy) in December 2000, that a consensus definition of trafficking in human beings has been achieved in a legally binding international instrument for the first time (protocol to prevent, suppress and punish trafficking in persons, especially in women and children, General Assembly Resolution 55/25, annex II). The Vienna branch of the United Nations has made trafficking in humans a central field of research and international crime policy. The launch of the United Nations global programme to combat trafficking in human beings contains three components: research and assessment, a data base on trafficking flows, and a manual on promising practices (Press Release SOC/CP/210, 11 March 1999). In 2004, the Commission on Human Rights has adopted decision 2004/110 (endorsed by the Economic and Social Council with decision 2004/228), by which it decided to appoint a Special Rapporteur on trafficking in persons, especially women and children. The task of this Special Rapporteur is to take actions (subsequent to individual complaints) on violations committed against trafficked persons and on situations displaying a failure to protect human rights of trafficked persons. The Special Rapporteur visits individual countries in order to monitor the situation and to recommend action to prevent and to combat trafficking and to enhance protection of human rights. Annual reports shall be submitted to the Human Rights Commission (see Report of the Special Rapporteur on the human rights aspects of the victims of trafficking in persons, especially women and children, 2006).

Also in Europe several initiatives have been taken. Within the framework of the European Union several Joint Actions and a Framework Decision on Combating Trafficking in Human Beings (OJ L 203, 1.8. 2002, pp. 1–4) have highlighted the salience of trafficking in humans for European crime and human rights policies (Alexander, Meuwese, & Wolthuis, 2000, p. 489). An Action extended the Europol mandate to trafficking in humans (1996) and a Joint Action of 24 February 1997 aimed at combating trafficking in human beings and sexual exploitation of children. While the Joint Action of 1997 focuses on trafficking in women and children for the purpose of sexual exploitation or prostitution and obliges the member states to penalize behaviour that aims at sexually exploiting children and adults, the Framework Decision of 2002 is a response to the obvious failure of the member states to implement the Joint Action of 1997. The Framework Decision 2002 covers both exploitation of labour and sexual exploitation, and was essentially guided by the trafficking protocol of the UN Transnational Crime Convention of 2000 (Rijken, 2005). The Brussels Declaration of 2002 on trafficking came out of the European Conference on Preventing and Combating Trafficking in Human Beings and aims at further developing European and international co-operation, concrete measures, standards, best practices and mechanisms to prevent and combat trafficking in human beings. It forms now the main basis of the European Commission's activities in the area of human trafficking. On 25 March 2003, the European Commission set up a group of experts the main task of which was to prepare a report on proposals to strengthen the fight against trafficking. The Europol mechanisms are also dealing with trafficking in humans. Article 2 of the Europol Convention refers to the prevention and combating of the trade in human beings. Eurojust, set up in 2002, has been assigned the competence for investigations and prosecutions concerning trafficking cases affecting two or more Member States. The attention paid to human trafficking is shown in the EU Charter on Fundamental Rights as presented during the Summit of Nice in December 2000. Here, Article 5 Sec. 3 simply states that trafficking in human beings is prohibited, and Sec. 1 and 2 of the same article prohibit slave trade and forced or slave labour.

Trafficking is also on the agenda of other international organizations active on European territory. The Council of Europe in May 2005 has opened a Convention on Action against Trafficking in Human Beings (ETS 197) for signature which follows the definitions as set out in the Human Trafficking Protocol of the UN Convention Against Transnational Crime of 2000 (Tschigg, 2005). The Organization for Security and Co-Operation in Europe (OSCE) in December 2003 has adopted an Action Plan to Combat Trafficking in Human Beings which calls on participating States to take initiatives to prevent trafficking, to prosecute traffickers, and to protect trafficked persons. The Action Plan offers the assistance of OSCE institutions and their respective field operations. In 2004, the OSCE appointed a special representative who is supported by an anti-trafficking assistance unit and who cooperates closely with the Anti Trafficking Unit in the Office for Democratic Institutions and Human Rights. The OSCE strategy against human trafficking is based on establishing multi-agency anti-trafficking structures (National Referral Mechanisms, including civil society), mechanisms of identification and assistance of trafficked persons and strengthening access to remedies and rights for trafficking victims.

Non-governmental organizations play an important role in the development of anti-trafficking policies, though it is not clear to what end. Human Rights Watch, IOM (International Organization for Migration) and various other NGOs continue to lobby for their respective clientele and implement their particular interests (immigration, victims in general, violence against women, etc.) under the umbrella of trafficking in human beings when arguing that violence against women and children are a root cause of trafficking in humans (see Human Rights Watch). Beside the eminent insight that evil breeds evil, this points to effective networking among interest groups and between interests groups and states as well as supranational organizations. After all trafficking, as any other crime on the surface, can easily be linked to poverty, inequality, environmental problems and ultimately the absence of democracy. This context then requires "comprehensive programmes and approaches" based on "holistic" views on trafficking.

The discourse on trafficking in humans reveals political agendas that are hidden behind a curtain formed by organized and transnational crime and control of organized crime (Yiu Kong Chu, 2000; Fijnaut & Paoli, 2004; Keidel, 1998; Sieber & Bögel, 1993). It is evident that organized crime groups are involved in trafficking, in particular crime groups that are based in countries plagued by poverty or violent conflicts (Yiu Kong Chu, 2000; Dobinson, 1993) and in destabilized regions (and in weak states). The particular emphasis on human trafficking visible in the Stability Pact for South Eastern Europe demonstrates the relationships between the absence of a strong state and a reliable justice administration and the presence of trafficking in humans (Stability Pact for South Eastern Europe, Task Force on Human Trafficking, 2004). Poverty and violent conflicts represent powerful push factors fanning large scale emigration. It is therefore not only the perspective of organized crime and law enforcement that should be considered in relation to trafficking in humans. Migration and immigration are evidently related to human trafficking (Lăzăroiu & Alexandru, 2003; Ulrich, 1995) and therefore constitute a highly sensitive political issue. Violence against women and children and control of prostitution and red light districts in metropolitan areas further correlate with the trafficking problem (Flormann, 1995; see in this respect also the First World Congress Against Commercial Sexual Exploitation held 1996 in Stockholm and followed by a Second World Congress held in 2001). Finally, economic approaches to the analysis and explanation of black markets and the growing shadow economies point to the significance of demand and supply mechanisms (Fijnaut, 1994). Smuggling and trafficking in illicit goods and services and trafficking in humans represent the "underside" of the (global) legitimate trade (Keidel, 1998, p. 8; Nicolic-Ristanovic, 2004, p. 12). These activities are driven by laws (defining the scope and content of trafficking and smuggling and the goods and services that are provided) as well as by demand (which emerges from conventional society and the established sex markets) (Andreas, 1999; Kelly & Regan, 2000, p. 1). Trafficking hence also concerns a sensitive topic as it raises ideological questions in terms of the explanation and responsibility, as well as moral issues as regards for example the acceptability of prostitution (Le Breton & Fiechter, 2001). However, it would not be adequate to understand trafficking in humans alone from the divide between the industrialized world and the one still struggling with mass poverty, civil war and environmental problems. Countries may at the same time be countries of destination, sending and transit countries of trafficked humans (Laczko & Gozdziak, 2005). Moreover the status of countries can change rapidly (International Organization for Migration, 1999). Then, trafficking of humans may for various reasons play a significant role within a single country, e.g., in China where trafficking in women for marriage purposes evidently plays a considerable role, in particular in rural areas (Lee, 2005; Zhao, 2003).

Most significant is certainly the move toward seeing human trafficking not merely as a law enforcement problem and being linked to organized crime, but to understand human trafficking as a serious violation of human rights (OSCE Berlin Declaration, 2002, p. 22). It is emphasized that the problems of slavery and slave labour remain unresolved despite the proclamation in the Universal Declaration of Human Rights (1948) that "no-one shall be held in slavery and servitude". With that, human trafficking is recognized also as an eminent issue in relation to the protection of victims and access to justice (OSCE, 2006). The victim perspective at large over the last decades has led to the creation and implementation of international standards and national legislation that are protective as regards possible averse impacts of criminal proceedings and the threat of retaliation, and supportive as regards compensation of material and immaterial losses caused by the victimizing event (Council of Europe, 2006).

Trafficking victims, however, find themselves in a complicated web of rules, practices and interests shaped by historical developments, moral judgements and highly sensitive political issues such as organized crime (illegal) immigration, youth welfare and protection, labour market problems, violence against women, prostitution, pornography and the sex industry. Perspectives of law enforcement, immigration control, anti-prostitution movements, victim support and assistance may result in conflicts when implemented and may trigger the question of how these conflicting perspectives and interests can be accommodated. The course of the debate on trafficking in humans and the concerns raised point to the assessment that the law enforcement perspective prevails in many situations and that the interests of victims are sidelined (OSCE, 2006). However, a human rights perspective should not be focused solely on the victims of trafficking.

The creation and enforcement of anti-trafficking laws, of course, also has the potential of affecting the human rights of those to whom criminal offence statutes are applied, in other words the suspects and the offenders.

3. THE HISTORY OF PROBLEMATIZING TRAFFICKING IN HUMANS

International attention as regards trafficking in humans certainly was (and still is) preoccupied with prostitution and child pornography as well as with the sexual exploitation of children and women in general (Kelly & Regan, 2000). However, the debates and developments in international instruments and legislation show that the concept of trafficking in humans is increasingly drawn wider than that. Besides trafficking in women and children for the purpose of prostitution and sexual exploitation, there exist several other phenomena which are covered by the concept of trafficking. These include, *inter alia (i.a.)*:

– international adoption and brokerage of international adoption for profit as well as supply and demand for children for the purpose of adoption (Albrecht, 1994, 2005);
– trafficking of immigrants for the purpose of forced labour or labour outside the statutory safeguards provided today by labour safety regulations, youth protection laws, rules on minimum wages and health insurance (Dreixler, 1998);
– trafficking in human body parts (Dreixler, 1998, p. 75; Foster, 1997; see also the Council of Europe's Decision (78) 29 as of 11 May 1978 where in Article 9 it is declared that providing for a human organ for the purpose of transplantation may not serve financial profits). Commercial interests in human body parts refer to a market for body parts that is essentially structured by the huge demand for body parts for the purpose of organ transplantation. As many as 10,000 Germans as well as 30,000 North Americans are waiting each day for transplantation of some vital part, most of them waiting for transplantation of kidneys (which is priced at up to 50,000 U.S.$ per transplantation; see Dreixler, 1998, p. 75).

International and national efforts to develop instruments to combat trafficking in humans can be traced back to the turn of the 19th and 20th century. It was particularly in two areas in industrialized, modern societies that a sort of moral panic pushed for the international prohibition of the then so-called "white slave trade". The process of creating and implementing international agreements and conventions started in 1904 when in Paris an International Agreement for the Suppression of the White Slave Trade was signed. In 1910, the Paris International Convention for the Suppression of the White Slave Trade was agreed upon by various countries pursuing the goal of putting an end to trafficking in women and underage girls for "immoral purposes". The 1910 Convention was followed by several other international instruments, among them the 1921 Geneva International Convention for the Suppression of the Traffic in Women and Children, the 1933 Geneva Convention for the Suppression of the Traffic in Women of Full Age, and finally the 1949 Convention for the Suppression of the Traffic in Persons and of the Exploitation of Prostitution of Others (Albrecht, 1994; Dreixler, 1998). The United Nations then agreed on 18 December 1979 on the Convention on the Eradication of All Forms of Discrimination Against Women with all parties to the convention being obliged through Article 6 to implement all necessary measures to ensure the abolition of trafficking in women and the exploitation of prostitution.

A major force behind the emergence of the international and UN based system of control of human trafficking is found in the strong beliefs prevailing in Europe and in North America that white women were abducted or seduced into prostitution activities abroad, as well as in interest groups pursuing policies of strict abolition of prostitution (Beiträge zur feministischen theorie und praxis, 2001). However, the international instruments resulted mainly in symbolic legislation as there were obviously nowhere significant signs of serious implementation of the international conventions, neither in Europe nor in North America.

As regards international adoption, however, the situation is quite different. Although there had been – parallel to the creation of the White Slave Trade Conventions – also movements to control (commercial) national and international adoption (Albrecht, 1994, 2005), such attempts proved to be unsuccessful during the first half of the 20th century (Arendt, 1913). Then, during the 1950s and 1960s, a huge demand for families which would be ready to adopt children (from third world countries) emerged. In particular, charity organizations operating in Third World countries were desperately trying to find families in order to be able to place children who would not be adopted in their home countries. This situation started to change in the 1960s and 1970s when a reversal of demand and supply structures occurred with more and more demand being voiced for children in industrialized countries. Then, charity organizations obviously noticed that there was a growing demand for children and that their role had changed into providing children for an adoption market emerging in particular in Europe and North America. The response of charity organizations has been to cut down sharply on international adoption activities and they have subsequently been replaced by commercial business (Albrecht, 2005).

The European Convention on Adoption of 1967 outlines duties and obligations of member states. Article 15 obliges states parties to introduce legislation that prevents "illegitimate profits" stemming from international or cross-border adoption. It is obvious that a distinction was made between legitimate and illegitimate profits. Also charity organizations evidently need to raise fees in order to cover costs of organization, staff, etc., involved in international adoption. This is also part of a political economy where regulation or deregulation of markets occurs. Strict regulation lends itself to the emergence of black markets. Finally, there was obviously no consensus reached among the international community as regards the question of whether international adoption should be left to the free market or whether international adoption should be placed under tight regulations. The United Nations Child's Bill of 1989 defines then rights of the child and deals also with trafficking in children in particular in the Sale of Children Protocol (O'Brian, 2002, p. 115). Article 21d of the Child Convention 1989 says that in case of adoption illegitimate gains should be prevented. However, there was evidently no consensus reached on what gains should be regarded to be illegitimate. Finally, the Hague Convention of 1993 has added rules to the market of international adoptions. A consensus on whether private or commercial adoption should be tolerated was not achieved within that framework either.

While the 1960s, 1970s and 1980s have been rather quiet periods as regards international and national activities in creating laws and regulations concerning trafficking in humans, the 1990s again saw a spread of legislative and political activities headed towards penalizing various phenomena associated with transnational and organized crime. The first related to trafficking in humans for the purpose of sexual exploitation (including child prostitution and child pornography) (Caroni, 1996, p. 21), and ultimately to the emergence of international anti-trafficking instruments and practices that encompass penalization, victim support and protection, prevention, creation of institutions and mutual judicial aid. The second issue is essentially related to illegal immigration and the transborder smuggling of immigrants (Minthe, 2002).

4. DEFINING TRAFFICKING: INTERNATIONAL TREATIES, NATIONAL OFFENCE STATUTES AND HUMAN RIGHTS

Anti-trafficking policies rely today on criminal law and criminal policies and with that on criminal offence statutes pre-designed through international and regional instruments, that both define the activities that fall under this prohibition and also provide rights for victims. Some domestic systems have special provisions too.

4.1. The Scope of Anti-Trafficking Legislation

4.1.1. International and Regional Instruments

The Second Protocol annexed to the 2000 Palermo Transnational Crime Convention has provided for a blueprint for creating trafficking offence statutes that shall apply where offences are transnational and involve an organized criminal group. It defines in Article 3 the act of "trafficking" as recruitment, transportation, transfer, harbouring or receipt of persons. Such acts establish trafficking in humans if use has been made of threats, or the use of force, or other forms of coercion, abduction, fraud, deception, abuse of power, or of a position of vulnerability, or the giving or receiving of payments or benefits to achieve the consent of a person having control over another person, all these with the aim to get control over another person. The act then has to be carried out by the motive (or intent) of exploitation. Exploitation, at a minimum, includes the exploitation of the prostitution of others or other forms of sexual exploitation, forced labour or services, slavery or practices similar to slavery, servitude or the removal of organs. Parties to the Second Protocol are obliged (Article 5) to penalize such acts (also acts of attempts, complicity and of masterminding trafficking) and to foresee that the consent of victims may not be used as a justification (or defence) if control over another person has been established by the means mentioned above. In case of children (under the age of 18) trafficking shall be established even if trafficking and the motive of exploitation are not based on coercive or deceptive means.

The European Community, having signed the United Nations Convention against Transnational Organised Crime and the two Protocols against trafficking in persons and the smuggling of migrants, has issued the Council Framework Decision 2002/629/JHA of 19 July 2002 on combating trafficking in human beings (Official Journal L 203 of 01.08.2002). Article 1 of the

Framework Decision on Trafficking defines trafficking in human beings through:

a. an act in terms of any form of recruitment, transportation, transfer or harbouring of a person;
b. special means applied in carrying out that act in terms of threat or use of coercion or deception or abuse of authority or of a position of vulnerability of the victim or payments or benefits given or received to achieve the consent of a person having control over another person;
c. the purpose of labour exploitation or sexual exploitation, including pornography (removal of organs is not included; however, human organs are covered comprehensively in legislation on (medical) transplantation of human organs).

The consent of a victim of trafficking in human beings to exploitation is irrelevant when any of the means under b. have been used. When trafficking involves a child (below 18 years of age) it shall be a punishable trafficking offence even if coercive or deceptive means have not been used.

Criminal penalties provided for by national legislation must be "effective, proportionate and dissuasive". The maximum penalty is set at no less than eight years imprisonment under certain aggravating circumstances (endangering the life of the victim, serious violence, particular vulnerability of the victim, involvement of organized crime). This makes it possible to apply other legislative instruments adopted for the purposes of enhancing police and judicial cooperation (in particular in the field of organized crime), such as a Joint Action on money laundering, the identification, tracing, freezing, seizing and confiscation of the instrumentalities and the proceeds from crime and a Joint Action (1998) which makes it a criminal offence to participate in a criminal organization. The Framework Decision then introduces the concept of criminal and civil liability of legal persons. Legal persons shall be held liable for offences committed for their benefit by any person acting either individually or a part of the organ of the legal person, or who exercises a power of decision. Penalties on legal persons include criminal or non-criminal fines and specific sanctions such as a temporary or definitive ban on commercial activities, judicial dissolution and the exclusion from public benefits.

The European Convention Against Human Trafficking (2005) also closely follows the model provided by the UN Convention Against Transnational Crime (Council of Europe Convention on Action against Trafficking in Human Beings and its Explanatory Report. Warsaw, 16.V.2005, Council of Europe Treaty Series-No. 197; Tschigg, 2005, p. 47).

A model definition of trafficking is available with the U.S. Government's definition of trafficking in persons (http://secretary.state.gov/www/picw/trafficking). This definition says that all acts involved in the transport, harbouring, or sale of persons within national or across international borders through coercion, force, kidnapping, deception or fraud, for purposes of placing persons in situations of forced labour or services, such as forced prostitution, domestic servitude, debt bondage or other slavery-like practices constitute "trafficking in humans". With this definition, both force on the one hand and cunning behaviour on the other hand are made objective elements of a trafficking offence statute. So, the U.S. Victims of Trafficking and Violence Prevention Act of 2000 has created new forms of felony crimes related to sexual trafficking as well as victim assistance provisions that seek to support victims and to facilitate the prosecution of traffickers (The Victims of Trafficking and Violence Protection Act of 2000, P.L. 106-386; Bensinger, 2001).

The Organization for Security and Co-Operation in Europe (OSCE) has published a report devoted to definitions of trafficking. The report concludes that trafficking in human beings involves the movement of people for the purpose of placing them in forced labour or other forms of involuntary servitude. Thus, trafficking in human beings is defined to include trafficking for sexual as well as non-sexual purposes, and all actions along the trafficking chain, from the initial recruitment (or abduction) of the trafficked person to the end purpose or result, the exploitation of the victim's person or labour (Organization for Security and Co-operation in Europe, 1999).

As regards the international instruments outlined above there is certainly a consensus about the leading characteristics of the trafficking definition such as the use of coercion, violence or deception (in case of adult victims) or abuse of authority and power as well as the motive of exploitation (Siron & Van Baeveghem, 1999, p. 14). Moreover, it is also quite clear that other elements are not evaluated unanimously in international criminal law reform. There exists, e.g., no consensens on the question of how consent voiced by the victim should be dealt with (Siron & Van Baeveghem, 1999, p. 15). Smuggling of immigrants is separated from trafficking as the term "smuggling" is used to describe acts that support or facilitate illegal immigration (or crossing borders) and involve a migrant or immigrant who voluntarily seeks opportunities for immigration and, due to immigration restrictions, relies on criminal groups specializing in cross border smuggling. Besides the criteria of voluntary migration, another element sometimes used to separate smuggling from trafficking activities lies in the duration of the period of exploitation that the migrating individual is subjected to after entering the country of destination (Bajrektarevic, 2000), and whether an immigrant after being smuggled is free to move and make choices in employment or whether he or she is placed in "debt-bondage" or other forms of dependencies (Aronowitz, 2001, p. 167). Proposals to include practices of "forced marriage" are also faced with problems as to how to establish whether illegitimate force or coercion has been used. While it is certainly imaginable that simple force in terms of violence or threat of violence is used to force persons into marriage, in most instances, however, forced marriage will result from a web of dependencies and pressures arising out of emotional, financial and other ties (which again may be backed up by social norms providing for credible threats if not complied with). Such forces are part of any social organization but are particularly relevant in segments of society where pre-modern forms of social integration are still enforced and, moreover, are part of the social life of (immigrant) minorities.

It is thus clear that criminal law addressing trafficking activities in principle has two roots. One of these roots is found in criminal legislation penalizing the exploitation of prostitutes, the organization of prostitution and the living from the proceeds of prostitution, while the other is found in the international white slave trade conventions and corresponding national laws that make bringing females outside the national territory for the purpose of prostitution a crime. Modern criminal policy in continental Europe has reduced anti-pimping statutes from a wide and moralizing criminal law-based approach to a rather narrow criminal law approach aimed at protecting individuals from being brought into prostitution, from being supervised, monitored and exploited while working as a prostitute or from being forced to stay in prostitution. The fact that anti-trafficking offences are rather close to the aforementioned criminal offence statutes to a certain extent explains the problems experienced in drafting and implementing such laws.

4.1.2. National Law

In order to analyze more closely statutory definitions of trafficking, a selection of criminal code books shall be reviewed (see also the comparative overview in Niesner & Jones-Pauly, 2001). However, European legislation addressing human trafficking is pre-designed today through the 2000 UN Transnational Crime Convention as well as through the EU Framework Decision on Trafficking of 2002.

Trafficking in humans is, e.g., defined in the new Polish Criminal Code (see also Lammich, 2000) through Article 253 §1 which penalizes trafficking in persons, even when the trafficked person has expressed consent. Insofar the Polish legislator has chosen a rather wide (and open) definition of trafficking. Moreover, the range of behaviour covered by this definition is evidently not restricted to trafficking for the purpose of sexually exploiting women and children but also covers trafficking of persons with the motive of placing somebody in illegal employment or supporting illegal immigration alone. Article 204 threatens with criminal punishment all actions to facilitate or initiate prostitution activities for personal profit and for profiting from prostitution activities. Furthermore, Article 204 increases penalties provided in case young victims are involved and if victims are brought to prostitution activities abroad.

The Polish trafficking offence statute comes rather close to the trafficking statute found in the Swiss Penal Code Book. The Swiss human trafficking law penalizes in Article 182 not only trafficking in women (for the purpose of prostitution) but also trafficking of humans for labour and for the removal of organs (Capus, 2005, p. 30). Besides the trafficking offence statute Swiss criminal law provides for an anti-pimping statute (Article 195) that criminalizes actions bringing another person into prostitution while exploiting the vulnerable situation or pursuing financial advantages (beside that supervising a prostitute or imposing or enforcing conditions of sex work carry also criminal punishment).

In Austria the trafficking statutes have been amended in 2004 (BGBl I 2004/15). §104a criminalizes acts recruiting, harbouring, transporting, etc. persons with the knowledge that these persons will be subject to sexual or labour exploitation or exploitation through the removal of organs if such acts are carried out by illegitimate means. Such illegitimate means concern deception over facts, abuse of power, exploitation of a precarious situation of the victim, or insanity, or a state which makes the victim helpless, or intimidation, or taking or offering advantages for placing the victim under the authority of another person. The penalty range provided concerns imprisonment of up to three years. Under certain statutorily defined aggravating circumstances the maximum penalty is raised to 10 years imprisonment. Anti-pimping legislation in Austria (§216 Austrian Criminal Code) corresponds to that of Switzerland.

In France trafficking of humans covers a broader scope of situations of exploitation (Loi n° 2003-239 du 18 mars 2003). Article 225-4-1 of the French Criminal Code Book provides for up to seven years imprisonment for trafficking. The latter is defined by an exchange of all kinds of advantages for the recruitment, transport, housing of humans in the interest of a third person in order to subject the trafficked person to acts of pimping, violence, sexual crime, exploitation of labour or inhumane housing or to force the trafficked person to commit criminal offences. The punishment is raised to a maximum of 10 years under certain aggravating conditions and to 20 years imprisonment in case trafficking was committed by an organized crime group. Life imprisonment is provided if during the act of trafficking torture or other barbaric acts have been committed (Law n° 2003-239 as of 18 March 2003, Article 32, Journal Officiel 19 March 2003).

The German criminal code, amended in 2004 to implement the European Union Framework Decision 2002, defines "Trafficking in Humans" (§232) as the exertion of influence on another person with knowledge of a coercive situation (indicated through a state of necessity on the side of the victim or the victims' helplessness due to his or her staying in a foreign country), in order to induce the person to engage in prostitution or to remain in prostitution. If the victim is below 21 years of age trafficking is established without a coercive situation being required. The penalties provided range between 6 months and 10 years. Under certain aggravating circumstances the minimum penalty is raised to one year imprisonment. The German trafficking statute covers not only acts that are related to forced prostitution but also selected acts related to the field of brokering marriages. The purpose of trafficking has been extended to exploitation of labour (§233). Labour trafficking is established through bringing a person into servitude or debt bondage by exploiting a situation of necessity or helplessness due to staying in a foreign country. Labour trafficking is also established by employing a person under conditions that are grossly to the disadvantage of the employed person compared with regular employment conditions if a situation of necessity is exploited or a situation of helplessness. If the victim is under the age of 21, necessity or helplessness is not required to establish the offence of labour trafficking. Facilitating trafficking as defined in §§232, 233 through recruiting, harbouring, etc. a victim of trafficking is penalized in §233a.

The U.S. Victims of Trafficking and Violence Protection Act of 2000 defines "severe forms of trafficking in persons" as (a) sex trafficking in which a commercial sex act is induced by force, fraud, or coercion, or in which the person induced to perform such act has not attained 18 years of age; or (b) the recruitment, harbouring, transportation, provision, or obtaining of a person for labour or services, through the use of force, fraud or coercion for the purpose of subjection to involuntary servitude, peonage, debt bondage or slavery.

The essential questions with regards to determining the borderlines of trafficking offence statutes are twofold: first, what interests should be protected by a criminal offence statute focusing on trafficking in humans, and secondly, how these interests differ from those protected by smuggling offence statutes. Smuggling offence statutes do not point at the protection of personal freedom as migrants demand for being smuggled into a country of destination they themselves have chosen on a voluntary basis. There exist certainly various forms of deception sometimes operative in initiating migration into Europe (Vocks & Nijboer, 2000) with immigrants being provided with false information or distorted pictures of Europe. Thus, immigrants are smuggled into receiving countries that on the one hand do not fulfil those criteria which have been set in immigration countries for legal immigration, and on the other hand are not fully aware of conditions they will face when finally having entered the country of destination. Such deception which triggers individuals into migration activities (and moreover into sometimes significant financial investments) occurs certainly with respect to employment opportunities and possible income as well as concerning the conditions of living and the prospects for a life in economic and social safety. However, such acts of deception do not create the type of coercive situation that is evidently aimed at by trafficking statutes, but they come rather close to behaviour that commonly establishes the offence of fraud.

Criminal trafficking laws are essentially guided by two interests:

(1) the protection of human beings from being treated as objects of trade and commerce: this points at the relevance of human dignity and the principle of equality;
(2) the protection of personal freedom, freedom from being pressured into prostitution or labour, from being held in inhumane conditions of labour or prostitution and from being prevented to exit such conditions.

If violence or threats are not present but just the exploitation of poverty and other pressures, which have not been caused by those individuals or groups who take advantage of such pressures, then the question arises what to do with cases where such pressures are exploited. Some statutes – as, e.g., the German criminal provision of trafficking – require the exploitation of the helplessness of a person (which may be caused by the victim staying in a foreign country) as well as the exertion of influence on the person in order to bring the person to prostitution. Influencing somebody into prostitution in itself cannot be a crime (if there is no violence or other relevant threats involved), as prostitution – at least in most European continental countries – is legal. With that, in fact the exploitation of a vulnerable person is made the incriminated act, which in turn means that the interest involved should be seen in protecting individuals against the mere exploitation of their vulnerability (and herewith arising deficits in autonomous decision-making). Their vulnerability stems from being deprived of a supportive environment, which (in the country of origin) they could in principle mobilize against being influenced into prostitution.

The way trafficking statutes are constructed thus points at a crucial relationship between criminal law protecting individual interests and criminal law protecting moral values. Arguably, the more trafficking statutes depart from violence (or threat of violence) as the core of sources of illicit influence on another person, and the closer the statutory elements describe mere (general and not coercive) "influence" in the context of prostitution, the more the statutes are – in terms of legitimacy – dependent on either the alleged immorality of activities that are required from smuggled or trafficked persons or on the repressive environment into which victims are brought. As immorality alone cannot legitimize the creation of criminal law it is then ultimately the repressive and autonomy-reducing environment within which a person finally will work that is decisive for legitimizing criminal repression of the "exertion of influence". What is created therefore in this area in terms of criminal law concerns "endangering offences" or "risk offences", as opposed to "result offences", where the interest lies in protecting the freedom of will of persons that is bent through unacceptable means. However, the danger arising with getting too close to the mere protection of morality does not only concern the moral language used in analyses of human trafficking but in particular the emergence of problems of law enforcement.

With respect to acts criminalized through trafficking statutes, the range of behaviour offered in current legislation goes from the active exertion of influence through violence or threat of violence and force, up to the exploitation of helpless and vulnerable positions of victims and deception. The statutes vary along the purposes of trafficking, which is sometimes closely restricted to sexual and labour exploitation and then also rather wide with covering all possible ends of trafficking. However, the international discussion as well as international instruments, such as the human trafficking protocol of the UN Transnational Crime Convention and instruments of the European Union and the Council of Europe, have initiated a trend towards extending trafficking beyond women (for the purpose of prostitution and other sexual exploitation) to trafficking in labour force, children and human organs. The problem encountered after all in setting up trafficking legislation concerns the risk of deviating from a concept of criminal law based on protecting individuals and society from behaviour that negatively affects concrete interests, and not just from behaviour representing moral wrong. The cause of the problem is evident. The unequal distribution of wealth and social and economic opportunities, poverty, cross border prostitution markets and mobility, create new vulnerabilities for those who are pushed or pulled towards the world regions that seem to be prosperous and seemingly offer prospects of a better life. However, these vulnerabilities are not easily transformed into criminal offence statutes that precisely and convincingly define the core of the wrong of human trafficking.

A particularly sensitive area of debate is opened with the question of whether penalization should be extended to the clients of (trafficked) prostitutes. In the Council of Europe Convention on Trafficking, Article 19 demands for criminalization of the use of services of a victim of trafficking. Article 19 says that each party to the Convention should consider adopting such legislative and other measures as may be necessary to establish as criminal offences under its internal law, the use of services which are the object of exploitation as referred to in Article 4 paragraph a of this Convention, with the knowledge that the person is a victim of trafficking in human beings. This goes, however, far beyond the classic field of prostitution control, as it applies also in principle to customers of restaurants where staff is held under slavery-like conditions. When applied aggressively this offers unique opportunities of widening the net of criminal law and its enforcement. Precursors of this type of criminal legislation are the penalization of drug use as well as the penalization of the possession and purchase of (child) pornography. With this type of criminal law a market model has been introduced that assigns responsibility not only to the suppliers of illicit services, substances, etc., but also to those who express demand. Of course, parallel to such rationales, moral condemnation of the illicit services and substances plays a significant role, too. Moral entrepreneurship becomes clearly visible in the 2006 report of the Special Rapporteur when addressing the situation in The Netherlands (which parallels the situation in other European continental countries). The report emphasizes the Dutch policy of legalized prostitution and raises doubts about the feasibility of the goal to establish a clear separation between the sectors of legal prostitution on the one hand and illegal activities, involving sexual exploitation, on the other (Special Rapporteur on the human rights aspects of the victims of trafficking in persons, 2006, p. 15).

4.2. Protection of Victims of Trafficking in International Instruments

With the creation of criminal trafficking offence statutes that protect the personal freedom of persons, a victim status has been formally recognized that entitles such victims – on the basis of international instruments – to rights and to an access to justice implementing these rights. Victims of trafficking then also fall under the protection of the principle of "non-refoulement" that forbids the expulsion of a refugee into an area where the refugee might be again subjected to persecution.

The United Nations have addressed the needs of victims in various instruments. The Declaration of Basic Principles of Justice for Victims of Crime and Abuse of Power was adopted by the General Assembly resolution 40/34 of 29 November 1985. In 1999 a Guide for Policy Makers and the Handbook on Justice for Victims has been approved. The 1998 Statute of Rome to establish the International Criminal Court (and the Rules of Procedure and Evidence) deals with victims of crime. And so does the Convention on Transnational Organized Crime in 2000 and its Optional Protocol of 2002 on trafficking, including specific sections for victims. ECOSOC has adopted in 2002 Guidelines on Restorative Justice, in 2002 crime prevention guidelines and in 2005 the Guidelines for Child Victims and Witnesses. The General Assembly has issued Basic Principles and Guidelines on the Rights to a Remedy and Reparation for Victims of Gross Violations of International Human Rights Law and Serious Violations of International Humanitarian Law in 2005. The United Nations Draft Convention on Justice and Support for Victims of Crime and Abuse of Power (14 November 2006) summarizes standards with demands for:

- procedural safeguards as regards confidentiality of proceedings and respect for privacy of the trafficking victim;
- the right of information on the course of criminal or administrative proceedings as well as rights of victims;
- comprehensive rights to compensation;
- (short-, medium- and long-term) assistance in coping with adverse effects of victimization; and
- effective protection of victims from the risk of retaliation.

Article 6 of the Protocol on trafficking to the Transnational Crime Convention of 2000, although emphasizing the creation of criminal trafficking law and law enforcement, also deals with the assistance to and the protection of victims of trafficking. The privacy and identity of victims of trafficking in persons should be protected by making legal proceedings relating to trafficking confidential. Measures shall be implemented that provide information on relevant court and administrative proceedings. The physical, psychological and social recovery of victims of trafficking in persons should be considered. Appropriate housing, counselling and information, in particular as regards the legal rights of victims shall be provided taking into account the age, gender and special needs of victims of trafficking.

Compensation issues are addressed as are questions of immigration laws, in particular concerning the permission to remain in the territory of the receiving state. Article 8 then points to the relationship between trafficking and immigration as to regulating repatriation issues, including questions of the verification of nationality and the issuance of travel documents.

The Council of Europe addressed the issue of compensation to crime victims already in the early 1970s, which eventually led to the establishment of the European Convention on the Compensation of Victims of Violent Crimes in 1983 (ETS No. 116). The Convention entered into force in 1988. The Council of Europe then issued Recommendations on Assistance to Victims and the Prevention of Victimisation on 17 September 1987 (Council of Europe, 2006).

The European Union has dealt with victims of crime in a Green Paper (Commission of the European Communities, 2001), in declarations, joint actions and a framework decision. The attention paid to victims of crime became visible in a Council Joint Action (97/154/JHA) which aims at combating trafficking in human beings and sexual exploitation of children; in the Vienna Action Plan of the Council and the Commission of 1998 that deals with ways to most effectively implement the provisions of the Treaty of Amsterdam on the Area of Freedom, Security and Justice (pointing in particular to Articles 19 and 51(c) thereof); in the Commission's communication to the Council, the European Parliament and the Economic and Social Committee with the title "Crime Victims in the EU: Reflections on Standards and Action"; in the Resolution of 12 December 2000 on the initiative concerning the Council Framework Decision on the standing of victims in criminal procedure, as well as in the final Council Framework Decision of 15 March 2001 on the standing of victims in criminal proceedings.

The European Union Framework Decision 2002 on Human Trafficking in Article 7 demands legislation that provides for the protection of and the assistance to victims of trafficking. Member States shall establish that investigations into or prosecutions of offences shall not be dependent on the report or accusation made by a person subjected to the offence. Children who are victims of trafficking should be considered as particularly vulnerable victims. The status of a particularly vulnerable victim triggers further obligations pursuant to the Framework Decision 2001 on the standing of victims in criminal proceedings.

In the 2005 Council of Europe Convention Against Trafficking the victim of trafficking is addressed comprehensively. Article 10 demands for staff trained and qualified in preventing and combating trafficking in human beings, in identifying and helping victims. Particular emphasis is laid on the identification of trafficking victims and on the determination of the age of victims. The presumption of a child shall apply when the age of the victim is uncertain. Trafficking victims shall be included under those rights normally granted to crime victims in general, in particular as regards compensation by the perpetrator and compensation through other mechanisms (victim funds). Legislative measures should provide for assistance to victims in their physical, psychological and social recovery. Such assistance shall include standards of living capable of ensuring subsistence, appropriate and secure accommodation, psychological and material assistance, access to emergency medical treatment and interpretation services, counselling and information as well as protection of victims against retaliation. Assistance to victims is not to be made conditional on the willingness to act as a witness. Article 13 introduces a recovery and reflection period of at least 30 days. The reflection period shall allow the victim to recover and escape the influence of traffickers and/or to take an informed decision on cooperating with the competent authorities. During this period it shall not be possible to enforce an expulsion order. Residence permits shall be issued to trafficking victims if residence is necessary either due to the personal situation or due to proper investigation or criminal proceedings. Residence permits for child victims shall be issued in accordance with the best interests of the child. In the process of repatriation and return of victims their rights, dignity and safety are to be considered. Receiving and repatriating states are under the obligation of organizing the return without delays and preferably on a voluntary basis. Repatriation programmes shall be created and implemented in order to provide for the safe re-integration of trafficking victims. A non-punishment provision (Article 26) seeks to provide for the possibility of not imposing penalties on victims for their involvement in unlawful activities, to the extent that they have been compelled to do so. The Council of Europe Convention then emphasizes gender equality and non-discrimination. This points also to the problem that the prevention of trafficking in some countries comes with protective restrictions placed on assumed potential trafficking victims as regards access to travel documents and free movement across borders.

5. EVIDENCE ON TRAFFICKING IN HUMANS

The creation of instruments to combat and to contain human trafficking, and criminal trafficking statutes in particular, are based on pictures of trafficking in humans and trafficking victims that simultaneously embrace elements of justification.

From the 1970s the emergence of several phenomena related to what today is defined as trafficking in humans can be observed. First, the globalization and internationalization of certain shadow economies have occurred with prostitution still representing the core of such black market activities and child prostitution and sexual exploitation of children in general becoming core issues of international debates (Kelly & Regan, 2000, p. 9). Second, migration and immigration have to be mentioned, with the most important push factors being poverty, civil wars, environmental disasters and increasing opportunities in terms of cheap, fast as well as global transportation and then, communication systems which establish bridges between cultures (possibly the most powerful facilitator of migration and immigration) (Adepoju, 2005). Third, restrictions in legal opportunities to immigrate, in particular in North America and in Europe, have certainly contributed to produce and to expand an illegal market for immigration as the strong demand for immigration (which remains outside the opportunities offered by immigration law and immigration authorities) results in strengthening illicit supply and the position of criminal organizations. Fourth, there is a vast demand for cheap labour, in particular in countries with over-regulated labour markets and in countries with large agricultural sectors. The demand can lead to internal black or slave labour markets (Aronowitz, 2001, p. 181 with information on West Africa and forced child labour practices).

However, the opening of borders and organized crime do not qualify as factors determining smuggling and trafficking in human beings. These factors are usually presented and stressed by "organized crime fighters" (Aronowitz, 2001, pp. 170–171). The opening of borders certainly would have had the contrary effect (in terms of lessening opportunities for organized crime) as it is essentially the closing of borders and the creation of obstacles for legal immigration that establish a grey or black market for immigration. Organized crime and criminal networks on the other hand are evenly dependent on these kinds of markets. Therefore, organized crime groups evidently are not responsible for establishing the legal and political framework of black markets that produce the kind of problems that come along with smuggling and trafficking of human beings. After all, the problem is not only that of organized crime groups laundering profits that are derived from such markets, but it is essentially problematic that the demand and the financial background of such demand are located in conventional society. That is true in relation to, e.g., prostitution, but it also applies to the second labour markets and drug markets, finally also to gambling and all conventional vices. Insofar, a criminological analysis of human trafficking must first of all focus on the markets that provide for those incentives that again cause traffickers to organize recruitment and placement strategies in relation to women for the purpose of prostitution or in relation to migrants for the purpose of undocumented labour. However, precisely this type of research until now is almost non-existent.

It should be said that research on human trafficking has mushroomed during the 1990s (Herz, 2005; Laczko, 2005). Most of the research on trafficking though is carried out by interested groups lobbying for victims of trafficking (Laczko & Gozdziak, 2005) and constructing a picture of a trafficking victim who is forced to take risks in face of depressing living conditions (Lăzăroiu & Alexandru, 2003).

As regards the extent of trafficking in humans, estimates are available for the number of women who are trafficked for the purpose of prostitution. Estimates put the annual number of women at 200,000 to 500,000 women trafficked to Western Europe (Flormann, 1999; International Organisation for Migration, 1996a; Vocks & Nijboer, 2000, p. 379). Estimates of the number of women and children trafficked worldwide came up with numbers as high as 700,000 to 1,000,000 persons assumed to be trafficked each year across international borders (Bensinger, 2001, p. 11; U.S. Department of State, 2002). According to other estimates, between 1 and 2 million women and children are trafficked each year worldwide for forced labour, domestic servitude or sexual exploitation (Akullo, 2005; Fact Sheet, 1998). Estimates put the number of children subject to commercial sexual exploitation at some 650,000 (Alexander et al., 2000, p. 480).

Research on prostitution and trafficking in women in Italy points to a proportion of some 10% of prostitutes of foreign nationality who have been trafficked into Italy (out of a total of 2,000 prostitutes of foreign descent). Italy displays a special pattern of trafficking, with most women coming from Nigeria and Albania (and most traffickers coming from these areas, too) (International Organization for Migration, 1996b). Insofar, Italian research shows that trafficking of women for the purpose of prostitution follows general immigration patterns (as immigrants to Italy in the last 10 years also tend to come from these regions). German police statistics display significant changes in relation to the sending countries. While before the opening of the borders between the West and the East of Europe most trafficked women came from South America, Thailand and other Asian countries, in the 1990s the most important sending countries were the Baltic States and central and eastern European countries. The belt of sending countries is moving eastwards with Poland, Hungary, and the Czech Republic becoming themselves countries of destination of trafficking (Bundesministerium des Inneren, Bundesministerium der Justiz, 2001, p. 105).

In the context of trafficking in women the question has received some attention whether women recruited for the purpose of prostitution had either known before about what they were expected to do or even had been actively involved in prostitution in the sending country (Müller-Schneider, 2000, p. 152). Research shows for The Netherlands that substantial numbers of women trafficked from Eastern and Central Europe knew about the nature of the job they would carry out in the West of Europe (International Organization for Migration, 1995; Vocks & Nijboer, 2000, p. 383). Data from German police statistics on the contrary demonstrate that almost half of the women had been deceived by promises of placing them in well paid conventional jobs (Bundesministerium des Inneren, Bundesministerium der Justiz 2001, p. 106). However, violence and practices of abduction obviously play a minor role in the recruitment process. Some 7% of victims interviewed by the police indicated that they had been subject to violence. Differences in the rates of deceived, abducted or forced victims may find an explanation in the difference in data sources used. Possibly, police data cover a selection of cases which are characterized by a higher extent of feelings of disappointment on the side of the victims and therefore by more incentives to report cases to police. A study on German trafficking cases shows that not only most of the victims have been informed about the type of activities they would be involved in, but that a substantial proportion had a history of working as a prostitute in Germany (Herz, 2005). Italian research points to a share of some 10% of immigrant prostitutes in Italy having been subjected to some kind of force or deception while the majority belongs to the group of ordinary immigrants (International Organization for Migration, 1996b; see also Kelly & Regan, 2000, p. 20 where for the London area 50% of all women working in the sex industry were foreign, out of whom 5% had allegedly been trafficked to the UK). Substantial proportions of immigrant women who ultimately work as prostitutes in the countries of destination entered the country legally, either on the basis of a tourist visa or on the basis of an entertainer visa (the latter obviously plays a major role at least in some countries; see for Italy, International Organization for Migration, 1996b; for Switzerland, Caroni, 1996). According to German police data most victims of trafficking entered the territory of the Federal Republic of Germany illegally with false passports and/or false visa (Bundesministerium des Inneren, Bundesministerium der Justiz, 2001, p. 105). For women trafficked to the UK it seems rare that entries are organized in an entirely illegal way (Kelly & Regan, 2000, p. 25). A Dutch study points to the involvement of small groups of traffickers and the lack of sophisticated organization. Moreover, it is shown in this study that most victims of trafficking know the traffickers before they are recruited and that this may play a certain role in making the victims more vulnerable to threats, e.g., of disclosing prostitution activities to family members or retaliating against family members (Vocks & Nijboer, 2000, p. 384; these findings are corroborated by the study of Herz, 2005).

In general, research findings concerning recruitment techniques point to a recruitment process that most probably will not differ from general recruitment patterns in local sex markets. Violence and threats evidently play a minor role only for recruitment, if at all. Although, in many reports on trafficking it is pointed out that such cases exist, it seems also clear from available research that these are exceptional cases. Deception evidently plays a certain role in the recruitment of prostitutes, however the conditions that justify establishing a trafficking offence are found most often in after placement conditions (Herz, 2005).

Trafficking or smuggling immigrants across borders for other purposes than sexual exploitation have also attracted attention, in particular related to incidents like the death of 58 Chinese nationals who were found January 2001 suffocated in a container in Dover (Aronowitz, 2001). It is estimated that 60 to 90% of illegal immigrants today have been supported by organized groups in travelling to Europe and crossing European borders (Aronowitz, 2001, p. 169). At large, estimates exist that put the number of immigrants illegally smuggled and trafficked at some 4 million per year (Aronowitz, 2001, p. 164). Estimates put the number of illegal persons entering the European Union at some 500,000 per year at the beginning of the new millennium (Schwarz & Schrader, 2004, p. 386). The brokerage of illegal immigrants into various labour markets obviously is concentrating on the construction business, house services and cleaning, sweatshops and agriculture as well as on various types of shadow economies and street markets. Conventional organized crime evidently is involved in trafficking and smuggling immigrants (Yiu Kong Chu, 2000, p. 115; Zhang & Chin, 2002). In Germany, estimates put the number of illegal immigrants in the construction business at approximately 500,000. In the U.S. according to recent estimates, some 4.5 million illegal Mexicans alone live and work, most of them in the agriculturally characterized areas of the southern states (Out of the Shadows, 2001).

As regards the adoption field, figures provided concern first of all the number of persons who are found on the demand side. For North America it is estimated that approximately 2 million couples are ready to adopt a child while the "supply" of children for adoption is estimated to oscillate around 50,000 (Campagna & Poffenberger, 1988, p. 149). In Germany and

Italy, the numbers on the demand side are said to approximate 20,000 and 16,000 couples respectively (Albrecht, 1994; Eisenblätter, 1992).

However, many of these estimates lack a sound basis of research (Kangaspunta, 2003, p. 84). So, estimates about the number of illegals entering the European Union indicated above are calculated simply by assuming that for each illegal trying to enter the European Union and intercepted by border controls two manage to slip in undetected (Schwarz & Schrader, 2004, p. 386). Estimates sometimes are used to attract attention and they serve therefore more as ideological or political instruments in an ongoing political discourse on prostitution, trafficking, illegal immigration, international adoption, child abuse or other "public bads". So, e.g., the International Human Rights Institute of de Paul University College of Law in a leaflet aiming at justifying research into trafficking of women presents data from various world regions on the numbers of women and children trafficked for sexual purposes. These data are "drawn or projected" from a few case studies, based on NGO and media reports as well as on law enforcement reports. The aim of publishing these data becomes clear when reading in the leaflet that the expected outcomes are the following: "Empirical data will make it impossible for governments and international organizations to continue their ignorance and denial of the phenomenon and the terrible toll it takes on the lives of the world's most vulnerable people" (Investigating International Trafficking in Women and Children, 2001). It is then clear that the data are needed to exert political pressure, and not to serve analytical or theoretical ends.

Another significant issue of research in the field of trafficking in humans concerns illegal profits. Trafficking in prostitutes obviously generates huge turnovers and profits. This is due to the considerable turnover that prostitution in European red light districts still generates. Some years ago, the gross turnovers in the red light milieus were calculated to range between 12 and 70 billion DM (6 to 35 billion U.S.$), according to information generated by German criminal investigations (Flormann, 1999). Data available for local red light districts in Germany put the sum paid for a woman trafficked from Poland to Germany for the purpose of prostitution at 1,000 DM (ca. 450 U.S.$) in the second half of the 1990s (Kruse, 1998). As regards international adoption, the costs of adopting a child from abroad lie between 20,000 and 50,000 U.S.$ per child. Immigration – due to increased controls – also produces considerable profits with fees of transportation, e.g., from China to Germany, estimated to range around 20,000 U.S.$ or from Kosovo to Germany said to be around 1,000 U.S.$ (Walter, 1998; Schwarz & Schrader, 2004, p. 391). What emerges from the literature is that the market model and the concepts of political economy should be regarded to present the most promising theoretical approaches to analyze and explain phenomena of trafficking (and smuggling) in humans (Zhang & Chin, 2004).

6. PROBLEMS OF ENFORCEMENT

Although there has not been much research on law enforcement in the field of trafficking in humans, there is some information to conclude that there are serious law enforcement deficits (Dreixler, 1998, p. 213; Jabornigg, 2005, pp. 33–35). As regards trafficking in women, police statistics throughout Europe show that there are not many cases initiated compared to the large estimates of women actually trafficked from Central and Eastern Europe to Western Europe alone (Bundesamt für Polizeiwesen, 1999). A recently published UN document underlines that few court cases are generated by law enforcement internationally (Economic and Social Council, United Nations, 2005). However, even out of the small number of suspects only a tiny faction is ultimately convicted and sentenced (Economic and Social Council, United Nations, 2005). In Germany, the proportion of trafficking offenders adjudicated and sentenced amounts to approximately 10 to 17% of those suspected of being involved in trafficking in women (Herz, 2005). Law enforcement deficits may be explained through particular enforcement problems posed through victimless crime or crime where victims are not likely to complain because of the possible negative consequences for complainants out of such victim and witness status. In this respect, legal consequences such as the expulsion and deportation of immigrant women working as prostitutes have to be mentioned (Caroni, 1996, pp. 111–112). A study on the outcomes of criminal investigation of trafficking cases shows that in Germany in a substantial proportion of cases victims of trafficking are formally charged with entering illegally into the country or with other immigration law violations (Herz, 2005; Herz & Minthe, 2006). Serious conflicts between immigration authorities and law enforcement agencies can be observed on the tolerance policies allowing witnesses and victims to stay legally in the country, not only for the time it takes to successfully prosecute a case (Dreixler, 1998, p. 234). Furthermore, the problem of vulnerable "victim-witnesses" has to be considered. Reports regularly point to the threat of violent retaliation and to the need for witness protection programmes for those victims who are at risk of retaliatory violence (Bundesamt für Polizeiwesen, 1999, p. 32, where it is criticized that witness protection is not foreseen in Swiss legislation and that this lack in witness protection explains why few immigrant prostitutes are cooperating with the police in trafficking cases). In Germany, some 40% of trafficked women involved in criminal trafficking proceedings have been deported in the course of proceedings and just 1.7% of them have been accepted for witness protection programmes (Flormann, 1999). Furthermore, it has been noticed that in some areas significant proportions of victims repatriated under victim support programmes are re-trafficked after leaving such programmes (National Criminal Intelligence Service, 2002, p. 35). However, another explanation of implementation deficits refers to problems with the trafficking offence statute and the application of other offence statutes, instead of trafficking offences in order to evade problems of evidence and resource consuming investigation. The situation in Switzerland as well as that in Germany point to the switch in offence statutes. While in Switzerland police argue that it is easier to apply the offence statute of illegal prostitution than trafficking or exploitation statutes (Bundesamt für Polizeiwesen, 1999, p. 33), in Germany it seems that smuggling statutes are easier to apply than trafficking statutes (Bundeskriminalamt, 2001, p. 4). However, German accounts of implementing trafficking statutes argue also that the number of trafficking cases initiated by police may be influenced by specialization and resources available for organized crime task forces (Bundeskriminalamt, 2001, p. 3, 2004, p. 4).

In explaining the extent and the course of trafficking in humans, the usual suspects are the lack of proper legislation, the lack of co-operation in law enforcement, and deficits in the implementation of anti-trafficking legislation (Aronowitz, 2001, pp. 184–185; Caroni, 1996, p. 109). As regards implementation deficits, it has been pointed out that sex markets and in particular prostitution during the past 50 years did almost completely turn into low priority policing areas and that even a climate of tolerance can be observed, which then creates difficulties to enforce cases of women trafficking (Kelly & Regan, 2000, p. 35; see also Special Rapporteur on the human rights aspects of the victims of trafficking in persons, 2006), What follows are suggestions to strengthen law enforcement measures (Regtmeier, 1990, pp. 81–94), to strengthen criminal penalties (Streiber, 1998, p. 23), and – ultimately – proposals to develop and implement integrated and comprehensive plans to combat smuggling and trafficking, that embrace repression, prevention and victim assistance (Aronowitz, 2001, pp. 185–190), all set up to cut down smuggling and trafficking activities (and finally also migration and immigration). Victim assistance in particular is thought to contribute to more effective law enforcement as testimony provided by witnesses (and victims) of trafficking obviously plays a crucial role in trafficking trials. This is so because of the precarious status of trafficked women – partly due to immigration laws and the possible deportation to the home country (Herz & Minthe, 2006, pp. 340–342) that prevents women to serve as witnesses in criminal trials against their traffickers (Niesner & Jones-Pauly, 2001, p. 266; Interventionsstelle für Betroffene des Frauenhandels, 2004). In fact, it is in particular the risk of criminalization and other negative consequences of disclosing the illegal status or other illegalities associated with entering or staying in the country of destination that prevents possible victim-witnesses to report to the police and to provide for evidence.

Summarizing the evidence related to enforcing trafficking offence statutes, it may be concluded that the concerns raised in various documents with respect to the precarious position of victims of trafficking and the deficits in implementation have some credit. However, research is limited and evidently does not make use of findings available from the study of other illicit markets.

7. CONCLUSION

Trafficking in humans emerged as an eminent social, political and legal problem with the opening of borders in Europe at the end of the 1980s. Since then, it has become an issue of concern in both national and international systems of crime control and law enforcement. Various United Nations and European instruments, including the 2000 UN Convention Against Transnational Crime, the 2005 Council of Europe Convention Against Trafficking in Persons and the European Union Framework Decision on Trafficking of 2002, aim at the repression and the prevention of trafficking in humans. Most significant is certainly the move toward viewing human trafficking not merely as a law enforcement problem and being linked to organized crime, but to understand human trafficking as a serious violation of human rights. With this shift, human trafficking is also recognized as an eminent issue concerning the protection of victims and access to justice. Criminal trafficking laws are essentially guided by interests in protecting human beings from being treated as objects of trade and commerce, thus emphasizing human dignity and the principle of equality. Moreover, anti-trafficking policies aim at protecting personal freedom, in terms of freedom from being pressured into prostitution or labour, from being held in inhumane conditions of labour or prostitution and from being prevented to exit such conditions.

The way trafficking statutes are constructed point to a crucial relationship between criminal law that protects individual interests and criminal law that protects moral values. Trafficking offence statutes evidently pose problems as far as the determination of the degree of improper influence or exploitation is concerned. The risks of creating moral (and anti-prostitution) criminal law increase with the extent to which trafficking statutes focus on mere endangerment and depart from a narrow range of individually conceived interests.

The experiences with international and national controls of trafficking in humans point to a multitude of problems that for a good part are well known from efforts to control organized crime and related issues at large. Some of these problems are linked to the phenomenon of black markets and victimless crime. When women are pressured into prostitution, the social and legal environment to which trafficked women are exposed prevent their active involvement in controlling trafficking and the sex market, and this is what creates a parallel to other transaction crimes. It is here that policy changes should first of all create the conditions for sex workers that make them less vulnerable to all sorts of negative consequences attached to criminal prosecution of their traffickers, as well as of those profiting from prostitution. In this regard, the legalization of prostitution also in the fields of civil law, in particular contract law and labour law, is assessed to represent a salient step towards creating a safer working environment for prostitutes and improving the conditions of law enforcement. As the implementation of criminal law is dependent on victims reporting crimes and testifying in criminal trials, efforts should be made to establish a legal framework that facilitates the cooperation for victimized foreign nationals. In particular immigration law and victim protection schemes seem to be relevant in this respect. Finally, from a viewpoint of preventing trafficking it is certainly important to insist on the relevance of economic inequality that will continue to produce powerful motives of migration and thus contribute to the vulnerability of large groups in disadvantaged regions.

REFERENCES

Adepoju, A. (2005). Review of research and data on human trafficking in sub-Saharan Africa. In: F. Laczko & E. Gozdziak (Eds), *Data and research on human trafficking: A global survey*, (Vol. 43, pp. 76–98). Special Issue of International Migration.

Akullo, M. (2005). Child trafficking: A metropolitain police service perspective. *SIAK Journal. Zeitschrift für Polizeiwissenschaft und Polizeiliche Praxis, 2,* 24–37.

Albrecht, H.-J. (1994). *Kinderhandel-Eine Untersuchung zum (gewerblichen) Handel mit Kindern*. Bonn: Bundesministerium der Justiz.

Albrecht, H.-J. (2005). Grenzgänger: Internationale Adoption und Kinderhandel. In: T. Marauhn (Ed.), *Internationaler Kinderschutz. Politische Rhetorik oder effektives Recht?* (pp. 97–126). Tübingen: Mohr Siebeck.

Alexander, S., Meuwese, S., & Wolthuis, A. (2000). Policies and developments relating to the sexual exploitation of children: The legacy of the stockholm conference. *European Journal of Crime Policy and Research, 8,* 479–501.

Andreas, P. (1999). Smuggling wars: Law enforcement and law evasion in a changing world. In: T. Farer (Ed.), *Transnational crime in the Americas* (pp. 85–98). New York/London: Routledge.

Arendt, H. (1913). *Kinder des Vaterlandes. Neues vom Kinderhandel mit Jahresbericht über meine Recherchen und Fürsorgetätigkeit vom 1.9.1912 bis 31.8.1913*. Stuttgart: Clausnitzer.

Arlacchi, P. (2000). *Ware Mensch. Der Skandal des modernen Sklavenhandels*. München: Piper.

Aronowitz, A. A. (2001). Smuggling and trafficking human beings: The phenomenon, the markets that drive it and the organizations that promote it. *European Journal on Criminal Policy and Research, 9,* 163–195.

Bajrektarevic, A. (2000). *Trafficking in and smuggling of human beings. Linkages to organized crime: International legal measures: Statement digest*. Vienna: International Centre for Migration Policy Development.

Beiträge zur feministischen theorie und praxis 24 (2001), No. 58: Prostitution.

Bensinger, G. J. (2001). Trafficking of women and girls. *Crime & Justice International, 17,* 11–13.

Bundesamt für Polizeiwesen. (1999). *Szene Schweiz. Drogen, Falschgeld, Organisierte Kriminalität, Menschenhandel*. Lagebericht Nr. 2 1998. Bern: Bundesamt für Polizeiwesen.

Bundeskriminalamt. (2001). *Lagebild Menschenhandel 2000*. Wiesbaden: BKA.

Bundeskriminalamt. (2004). *Lagebild Menschenhandel 2003*. Wiesbaden: BKA.

Bundesministerium des Inneren, Bundesministerium der Justiz. (2001). (Eds). *Erster Periodischer Sicherheitsbericht*. Berlin: Bundesministerium der Justiz.

Campagna, D. S., & Poffenberger, D. L. (1988). *The sexual trafficking of children. An investigation of the child sex trade*. Dover: Auburn House.

Capus, N. (2005). Hundert Jahre Gesetzgebung zur Bekämpfung des Menschenhandels. *Schweizerische Zeitschrift für Kriminologie, 3,* 28–32.

Caroni, M. (1996). *Tänzerinnen und Heiratsmigrantinnen. Rechtliche Aspekte des Frauenhandels in der Schweiz*. Luzern: Caritas.

Commission of the European Communities. (2001). *Green Paper. Compensation to crime victims (presented by the Commission)*. Brussels, COM(2001) 536 final.

Council of Europe. (Ed.) (2006). *Victims. Support and assistance*. Strasbourg: Council of Europe.

David, F. (2000). *Human smuggling and trafficking. An overview of the response at the federal level*. Canberra: Institute of Criminology.

Dobinson, I. (1993). Pinning a tail on the dragon: The Chinese and the international heroin trade. *Crime & Delinquency, 39,* 373–384.

Dreixler, M. (1998). *Der Mensch als Ware. Erscheinungsformen modernen Menschenhandels unter strafrechtlicher Sicht*. Frankfurt: Lang.

Economic and Social Council, United Nations. (2005). *Strengthening international cooperation in preventing and combating trafficking in persons and protecting victims of such trafficking*. Report of the Secretary-General. E/CN.15/2005/8.

Eisenblätter, P. (1992). *History and causes of intercountry adoptions in a "receiving" country.* Contribution to the Expert Meeting "Protecting Children's Rights in Intercountry Adoptions and Preventing Trafficking and Sale of Children", Manila, Philippines, April 6–12.

Fact Sheet. (10 March 1998). *Trafficking in women and girls: An international human rights violation.* Released by the Senior Coordinator for International Women's Issues, Department of State.

Fijnaut, C. (1994). *Prostitutie, vrouwenhandel en (vermeende) politiecorruptie in Antwerpen.* Leuven, Amersfoort: Acco.

Fijnaut, C., & Paoli, L. (Eds). (2004). *Organised crime in Europe. Concepts, patterns and control policies in the European Union and beyond.* Dordrecht: Springer.

Flormann, W. (1995). Rotlichtmilieu – Menschenhandel als Teilbereich der Organisierten Kriminalität. *Der kriminalist, 27,* 178–185.

Flormann, W. (1999). Die Lebensader des Rotlichtmilieus-der internationale Frauenhandel. *Der kriminalist, 31,* 50–55.

Foster, T. W. (1997). Trafficking in human organs: An emerging form of white-collar crime. *International Journal of Offender Therapy and Comparative Criminology, 41,* 139–150.

Herz, A. (2005). *Strafverfolgung von Menschenhandel.* Berlin: Duncker & Humblot.

Herz, A., & Minthe, E. (2006). *Straftatbestand Menschenhandel. Verfahrenszahlen und Determinanten der Strafverfolgung.* München: Luchterhand.

International Organization for Migration. (1995). *The growing exploitation of migrant women from central and eastern Europe.* Migrant Information Programme. Budapest: IOM.

International Organisation for Migration. (1996a). *Trafficking of women to countries of the European Union: Characteristics, trends and policy issues.* Vienna: IOM.

International Organization for Migration. (1996b). *Trafficking in women to Italy for sexual exploitation.* Brussels: IOM.

International Organization for Migration. (1999). *Paths of exploitation. Studies on trafficking of women and children between Cambodia, Thailand and Vietnam.* Geneva: IOM, Center for Advanced Studies.

Interventionsstelle für Betroffene des Frauenhandels. (2004). *Empfehlungen zur Verbesserung der Situation für Betroffene des Frauenhandels in Österreich.* Wien: Interventionsstelle.

Investigating International Trafficking in Women and Children for Commercial Sexual Exploitation. (2001). *Phase I: The Americas.* Chicago: The International Human Rights Law Institute DePaul University, College of Law.

Jabornigg, D. V. (2005). Menschenhandel oder Menschenschmuggel? Einige Überlegungen zu den Hindernissen in der praktischen Strafverfolgung. *Schweizerische Zeitschrift für Kriminologie, 3,* 33–35.

Kangaspunta, K. (2003). Mapping the inhuman trade: Preliminary findings of the database on trafficking in human beings. *Forum on Crime and Society, 3,* 81–103.

Keidel, L. (1998). Menschenhandel als Phänomen der Organisierten Kriminalität. *Der kriminalist, 30,* 321–325.

Kelly, L., & Regan, L. (2000). *Stopping traffic: Exploring the extent of, and responses to, trafficking in women for sexual exploitation in the UK.* Police Research Series, Paper 125. Home Office, London.

Kruse, R. (1998). Organisierte Prostitution auf dem Lande. *Der kriminalist, 30,* 351–354.

Laczko, F. (2005). Introduction. In: F. Laczko & E. Gozdziak (Eds), *Data and research on human trafficking: A global survey,* (Vol. 43, pp. 5–16). Special Issue of International Migration.

Laczko, F., & Gozdziak, E. (Eds). (2005). *Data and research on human trafficking: A global survey.* Special Issue of International Migration. IOM: Center for Advanced Studies.

Lammich, S. (2000). Der internationale Frauenhandel in der polnischen Strafrechtspraxis. *Der kriminalist, 32,* 273–274.

Lăzăroiu, S., & Alexandru, M. (2003). *Who is the next victim?* Vulnerability of young Romanian women to trafficking in human beings. Bucharest: IOM.

Le Breton, M., & Fiechter, U. (2001). Frauenhandel im Kontext von Exklusions- und Differenzierungsprozessen. *Beiträge zur feministischen theorie und praxis, 24,* 114–126.

Lee, J. J. H. (2005). Human trafficking in East Asia: Current trends, data collection, and knowledge gaps. In: F. Laczko & E. Gozdziak (Eds), *Data and research on human trafficking: A global survey,* (Vol. 43, pp. 165–202). Special Issue of International Migration.

Minthe, E. (Ed.) (2002). *Illegale Migration und Schleuserkriminalität.* Wiesbaden: Kriminologische Zentralstelle.

Müller-Schneider, T. (2000). *Zuwanderung in westlichen Gesellschaften. Analyse und Steuerungsoptionen.* Opladen: Leske + Budrich.

National Criminal Intelligence Service. (2002). *UK threat assessment 2002. The threat from serious and organised crime.* London: NCIS.

Nicolic-Ristanovic, V. (2004). Illegal markets, human trade and transnational organised crime. In: P. C. van Duyne (Ed.), *Threats and phantoms of organised crime, corruption and terrorism* (pp. 117–137). Nijmegen: Wolf.

Niesner, E., & Jones-Pauly, Ch. (2001). *Trafficking in women in Europe.* Bielefeld: Kleine.

O'Brian, M. (2002). The contribution of the protocol on trafficking in human beings. In: UNICRI (Ed.), *The United Nations convention against transnational organized crime: Requirements for effective implementation* (pp. 113–120). Turin: UNICRI.

Organization for Security and Co-operation in Europe. (1999). Trafficking in human beings. Implications for the OSCE. Review Conference, September 1999. Paris: ODIHR Background Paper.

OSCE Berlin Declaration. (2002). Berlin Declaration of the OSCE Parliamentary assembly and resolutions adopted during the eleventh annual session on July 10. Edinburgh: OSCE.

Out of the Shadows. (2001). *Time,* 26–29. July 30.

Regtmeier, W. (1990). *Menschenhandel-Erfahrungen einer Sonderkommission in einem besonderen Deliktsbereich der Organisierten Kriminalität.* Münster: Polizeiführungsakademie.

Report of the Special Rapporteur on the human rights aspects of the victims of trafficking in persons, especially women and children. (2006). *Integration of the human rights of women and a gender perspective.* Economic and Social Council, United Nations. Distr. General E/CN.4/2006/62.

Rijken, C. (2005). Combating trafficking in human beings in the European Union. *Schweizerische Zeitschrift für Kriminologie, 3,* 36–45.

Schwarz, A., & Schrader, T. (2004). Menschenschmuggel in Bosnien-Herzegowina. *Monatsschrift für Kriminologie und Strafrechtsreform, 87,* 386–392.

Sieber, U., & Bögel, M. (1993). *Logistik der organisierten Kriminalität. Wirtschaftswissenschaftlicher Forschungsansatz und Pilotstudie zur internationalen KFZ-Verschiebung, zur Ausbeutung von Prostitution, zum Menschenhandel und zum illegalen Glücksspiel.* Wiesbaden: Bundeskriminalamt.

Siron, N., & van Baeveghem, P. (1999). *Trafficking in migrants through Poland.* Antwerpen: Maklu.

Stability Pact for South Eastern Europe, Task Force on Human Trafficking. (2004). *South Eastern Europe's struggle against trafficking in persons. Developments 2000–2004*. Vienna: Stability Pact.

Streiber, P. (1998). *Internationaler Frauenhandel. Funktionsweisen, soziale und ökonomische Ursachen und Gegenmaßnahmen*. Berlin: Freie Universität Berlin.

Tschigg, R. (2005). Konvention des Europarats über die Bekämpfung des Menschenhandels: Einige Bemerkungen aus Schweizer Sicht. *Schweizerische Zeitschrift für Kriminologie, 3*, 46–48.

U.S. Department of State. (2002). *Trafficking in persons report – Report 2001*. Washington: Department of State.

Ulrich, Ch. J. (1995). *Alien-smuggling and uncontrolled migration in Northern Europe and the Baltic Region*. HEUNI Papers, 7. HEUNI, Helsinki.

Vocks, J., & Nijboer, J. (2000). The promised land: A study of trafficking in women from Central and Eastern Europe to the Netherlands. *European Journal of Crime Policy and Research, 8*, 379–388.

Walter, B. (1998). Schlepper-Schleuser-Menschenhändler. Der grenzpolizeiliche Alltag an den deutschen Ostgrenzen. *Kriminalistik, 52*, 471–477.

Yiu Kong Chu. (2000). *The triads as business*. London/New York: Routledge.

Zhang, S., & Chin, K. (2004). *Characteristics of Chinese Human Smugglers*. Research in Brief. Washington: NIJ.

Zhang, S., & Chin, K.-L. (2002). Enter the dragon: Inside Chinese human smuggling organizations. *Criminology, 40*, 737–768.

Zhao, G. M. (2003). Trafficking in women for marriage in China: Policy and practice. *Criminal Justice, 3*, 83–102.

YOUTH, CRIME AND HUMAN RIGHTS

Dieter Burssens and Lode Walgrave

1. INTRODUCTION

Within the United Nations system for the promotion and protection of human rights, the Committee on the Rights of the Child is especially responsible for the design and the follow up of human rights for children, children's and youth rights, and for the social response to youth crime. This Committee is charged with the implementation and the observation of the Convention on the Rights of the Child (CRC), which was adopted unanimously in 1989 by the United Nations General Assembly. It took 10 years of difficult debates to create the CRC as a separate tool to address the peculiarities in children with regard to human rights. But once accepted, the CRC enjoyed a huge international support. Currently, in fact, only the USA and Somalia are the two only countries that have not yet ratified the Convention.

In this chapter, we will discuss some basic provisions of the Convention on the Rights of the Child as they relate to delinquency committed by young people, who are to be understood as persons under the age of 18, and to juvenile justice in general. At the same time, we will also formulate some critical comments in relation to these provisions and to children's rights in general.

Crime and Human Rights
Sociology of Crime, Law and Deviance, Volume 9, 73–91
Copyright © 2007 by Elsevier Ltd.
All rights of reproduction in any form reserved
ISSN: 1521-6136/doi:10.1016/S1521-6136(07)09003-3

2. THE CONVENTION ON THE RIGHTS OF THE CHILD AND OTHER UN GUIDELINES AND RULES ON JUVENILE JUSTICE

The emergence of the CRC is to be understood in the light of some macro-sociological developments, especially the shift in the vision on children and juveniles during the 20th century. Originally, at the beginning of the century, children were seen as "not yet human beings", a social category of "future builders", objects of law, charging adults with duties towards them. But the image changed gradually into seeing children as "fully-fledged human beings". The child is no longer considered as an object of law, but rather as a subject of law, being a full bearer of human rights and competent (Verhellen, 1993). The CRC clearly expresses this new vision on children and positions them in a more active role than as an object of protection by adults only. The CRC proclaims a children's right to participation, including a degree of self determination (Art. 12). Children's own opinion is validated, and their own visions, prospects and interests are to be respected. Moreover, the CRC is steered by three fundamental objectives, i.c., (1) non discrimination (Art. 2), (2) the child's best interest as the fundamental reason for all decisions about them (Art. 3), and (3) the right to survive and to develop in a context adapted to children's needs (Art. 6).

The CRC is not a Declaration, as a moral code, but a Convention, including a legally enforceable status. Under certain conditions, the Convention can have a direct impact. All citizens can claim certain dispositions before their national courts and some of these dispositions even have priority over national law. International control over the implementation is executed by the Committee on the Rights of the Child, which examines among others the national reports. All signing countries are obliged to provide a report every four years.

Two articles in the CRC (Art. 37 and 40) deal directly with the social and judicial response to youthful offending. Besides the Convention, other UN statements concern the reaction to youth crime more extensively. In 1985 already, the so-called "Beijing Rules" (Beijing) issued Standard Minimum Rules for the Administration of Juvenile Justice. Later, in 1990, the "Riyadh Guidelines" (Riyadh) or Guidelines for the Prevention of Juvenile Delinquency and the Rules for the Protection of Juveniles Deprived of their Liberty were adopted. Moreover, the Days of General Discussion held by the CRC in 1995 focussed on the Administration of Juvenile Justice.

3. THE UN APPROACH TO CHILDREN'S RIGHTS AND JUVENILE JUSTICE

The above documents are important for youth criminology, but they also provoke a number of comments and questions from the standpoint of juvenile criminology.

3.1. The Age of Criminal Accountability

States have to define a minimum age below which children are considered not to be able to commit a legally punishable act (CRC, Art. 40.3.a). According to the Beijing rules, this age cannot be too low, in view of the emotional and relational problems and of the intellectual maturity of youngsters (Beijing, Art. 4). For children under the minimum age, specific legislation and agencies must be provided to respond to their offending behaviour:

> Efforts shall be made to establish, in each national jurisdiction, a set of laws, rules and provisions specifically applicable to juvenile offenders and institutions and bodies entrusted with the functions of the administration of juvenile justice and designed: (a) to meet the varying needs of juvenile offenders, while protecting their basic rights; (b) to meet the need of society. (Beijing, Art. 2.3)

While defining such age threshold in criminal accountability is far from evident, it does have important consequences. It seems to mark the limits of the recognition of the juveniles' peculiar living conditions. More than adults, children and juveniles are mainly involved in the task of building an autonomous future. They have to go through a period in which they gradually obtain larger responsibilities, but they remain dependent on others. Especially adolescents live a difficult period, with lots of physical, emotional, psychological, relational and social changes, including uncertainties about themselves and their future position within the larger environment. They live in a period of "drift" (Matza, 1964) and like experimenting, including provocations of expectations, rules and norms. In that period, youthful offending is a statistically normal event, typical for the coming of age, as is demonstrated by all youth criminological research (Rutter, Giller, & Hagell, 1998). By the end of the adolescence, delinquency normally decreases. The drifting transition is coming to an end, and social prospects and social bonds with school, work, and/or in a partner relationship are being installed. By limiting the age of penal majority, the international legislator seems to leave space for this special transition period. It seems to be accepted that, as youth offending is very often mainly age linked, it needs a differentiated response, more than adults' crime seems to need. Not strict punishment according to penal law is the standard, but a reaction oriented to rehabilitation, in order to correct or re-orient the socialisation trajectory of a drifting adolescent.

Such option raises several questions which will be dealt with in the next sections. But we can already mention here that it remains unclear on what basis the ages of criminal responsibility are fixed. They vary between the age of 18 (as is the rule in Belgium, for example) and 10 (as in England and Wales, for example). In Scotland, even young children of eight can theoretically been prosecuted for their offences (Muncie & Goldson, 2006; Walgrave & Mehlbye, 1998). Can youth sciences in psychology, sociology and/or criminology provide reliable data to indicate a more common and better documented age of criminal majority? Would that really be possible? Can legal dispositions anyhow adequately express social scientific categories? It seems that defining the age of criminal responsibility is a matter of local politics which have not much to do with children's rights and interests.

3.2. The Main Objective of the CRC: The 'Best Interest of the Child'

The CRC unambiguously promotes the "best interest of the child" as the main objective of all decisions that concern them (CRC, Art. 3). This "best interest" also applies for children submitted to judicial intervention:

> States Parties recognize the right of every child alleged as, accused of, or recognized as having infringed the penal law to be treated in a manner consistent with the promotion of the child's sense of dignity and worth, which reinforces the child's respect for the human rights and fundamental freedoms of others and which takes into account the child's age and the desirability of promoting the child's reintegration and the child's assuming a constructive role in society. (CRC, Art. 40.1)

There cannot be any doubt that pursuing the best interest of the child is a very worthwhile objective. Aiming at the well-being and the reintegration of children is not only recommendable from a socio-ethical point of view, it is also crucial to take away causes of the problematic behaviour. It is, however, not sure that it must be given priority in all circumstances and in all eventualities. An offence can cause serious victimisation and heavy social unrest, and these consequences must be addressed by social responses as well. Safeguarding security and peace in community, repairing the harm and suffering of the victims and avoiding further victimisation are all objectives that are equally important as is addressing the needs of the young offenders. As a matter of fact, these goals are not necessarily opposed. On the contrary, they are often mutually reinforcing. Involving offending juveniles in the reparation of the harm they caused by their behaviour has proved to be very reintegrative and geared towards capacity building for the juveniles themselves (Bazemore & O'Brien, 2002). Taking care of the social integration of deprived juveniles contributes to social security and peace. The Beijing Rules seem to distinguish clearly between several aims. Besides responding to the young offender's needs, also the interests of society must be safeguarded. But the interests of society are limited to public order:

> Juvenile justice shall be conceived as an integral part of the national development process of each country, within a comprehensive framework of social justice for all juveniles, thus, at the same time, contributing to the protection of the young and the maintenance of a peaceful order in society. (Beijing, Art. 1.4)

An important question relates to the effectiveness. Indeed, orienting interventions towards rehabilitation clearly is an instrumental option which aims at achieving a target, and it can be measured whether the targets are reached in practice. Does juvenile justice contribute systematically and considerably to the constructive social reintegration of most of its clients? After the blunt "nothing works" of the seventies, the empirical pessimism about the effectiveness of treatment programmes has become more nuanced. Especially the "What Works?" research tradition has contributed significantly to this development in the past two decades. A series of meta-evaluations suggests that under some conditions (notably, proper staff training and expertise, and proper implementation and assessment), some programmes work (Lipsey & Wilson, 1998; McGuire & Priestley, 1995). It remains difficult, however, to generalize the conclusions. The evaluations mostly explore experiments in exceptionally optimal conditions. The step toward routine practices, in general, seriously reduces the gains of the evaluated programmes. Moreover, the fact that specific treatment programmes work for specific groups does not mean that the rehabilitation-oriented juvenile justice system as a whole is effective. Finally, the "what works" analyses do not address ethical questions about the acceptability of lengthy and intensive restrictions of liberty, that often seem disproportionate to the modest seriousness of the offences committed, and that are of doubtful effectiveness. The latter brings us to the next comment.

3.3. The Best Interest of the Child versus Legal Safeguards

Focusing primarily on the child's best interest in all aspects of juvenile justice is difficult to combine with legal safeguards that are considered essential in traditional penal law (Feld, 1993). If the crime committed is not the main reason of the judicial intervention, but only an occasion for it, it is problematic to ensure due process, and to safeguard the presumption of innocence or proportionality. It is unfeasible to provide a "right of defence", if you are not "attacked" by a public prosecutor, but submitted only to measures "in your best interest". As a consequence, many countries can, for example, keep children and juveniles in detention without the procedural safeguards that are provided for adults (Cappelaere, 2001). In how far can juvenile justice objectives go together with principles like legality, equality, presumption of innocence, due process or proportionality?

The CRC maintains the legality principle, for example, also for judicial interventions against juveniles who are suspected of having committed an offence (CRC, Art. 40.2.a). But countries that have installed a fully protective-rehabilitative juvenile justice system, as Belgium for example, have in fact abolished legality. Juveniles must not have committed an act qualified as an offence, in order to be submitted to judicial intervention. In the name of the "best interest of the child", children and families "at risk" or "in problematic educational situations" can be submitted to long and intensive intrusions upon their privacy and other civil liberties (Put & Walgrave, 2006). According to the equality principle, an equal sanction has to be imposed on those who commit the same offence in the same circumstances. This is not evident in a juvenile justice system giving priority to the needs of the young offenders, as requested in the CRC. The sanction or measure does then not depend on the kind and seriousness of the offence, but on the needs and problems of the juvenile, as it is meant to cure the underlying causes of the problematic behaviour and to prevent further problems in the future. Such option does of course not only serve the interest of the youngster, but also the interests of the collective of well integrated and useful citizens. It may, however, conflict with the equality principle. Juveniles (and adults) committing the same offence in analogous circumstances may be living in very different social situations, with different problems, different prospects and for different reasons. Referring to those background factors to decide on the measures or the sanctions may result in very different sentences for the same crimes. A question is of course whether sticking strictly to the equality principle is always so desirable, even for adults.

The same arguments apply to wonder whether the proportionality principle can be maintained under all conditions. The Beijing Rules pay ample attention to it:

> The juvenile justice system shall emphasize the well-being of the juvenile and shall ensure that any reaction to juvenile offenders shall always be in proportion to the circumstances of both the offenders and the offence. (Beijing, Art. 5)

This article applies proportionality not only to the offence, but also to the peculiar individual needs of the juvenile. But it is difficult to assess this kind of proportionality. What to do if the offence committed is benign but reveals huge underlying social problems? Can juveniles – and their families – then be submitted to very long and intrusive measures, while the nature of the offence may have been trivial? Contrary to the seriousness of an offence, there is not any objective frame to assess the seriousness of individual needs and to derive from them how much and which kind of judicial coercion is needed to answer to these needs. It all depends on social clinical examination and the individual estimation of the judges. There is in fact no solution to this problem, which raises the suspicion that the proportionality article in the Beijing rules is rhetoric without practical consequences.

3.4. Extra-Judicial Handling and Procedural Safeguards

The CRC promotes the extra-judicial settlement of cases (CRC, Art. 40.3.b), but also underlines the obligation to respect legal safeguards (CRC, Art. 40.2) and fundamental human rights. Avoiding judicial intervention as much as possible is also a general principle of the Beijing Rules:

> Sufficient attention shall be given to positive measures that involve the full mobilization of all possible resources, including the family, volunteers and other community groups, as well as schools and other community institutions, for the purpose of promoting the well-being of the juvenile, with a view to reducing the need for intervention under the law, and of effectively, fairly and humanely dealing with the juvenile in conflict. (Beijing, Art. 1.3)

If juveniles are brought in contact with the justice system, diversion is advised. More concretely, efforts are recommended to set up programmes of temporarily supervision, orientation, restitution and indemnification of the victims (Beijing, Art. 11.4) outside the judicial system.

Many offences qualified for judicial intervention can indeed be resolved outside the judicial circuit. Even after serious events, schools, parents, neighbours, victims, associations and others try to find by themselves a way to define what happened and how the consequences can be resolved constructively. Criminological dark number research provides overwhelming evidence that the great majority of juvenile offences never come to the attention of the police, even if the offender is known, and even in cases of serious offences (Junger-Tas, Terlouw, & Klein, 1994; Rutter et al., 1998). Criminological labelling theory and research is in support of practices to avoid too strong responses against youth crime, because it can yield stigmatisation and thus "secondary deviance", i.e. re-offending (Farrington, 1977; Schur, 1973). Strong judicial interventions create a negative social image in the relevant environment (school, family, labour market), which furthers more social exclusion and marginalisation. Moreover it may have a destructive influence on the self-image and may reinforce juveniles into a criminal lifestyle. Explicit referrals to the labelling theory are found in the Riyadh Guidelines on the prevention of youth crime: "[...] labelling a young person as 'deviant', 'delinquent' or 'pre-delinquent' often contributes to the development of a consistent pattern of undesirable behaviour by young persons" (Riyadh, Art. 5, f).

The promotion of extra-judicial handling holds, however, a considerable risk: dealing with a case outside the judicial circuit means also a loss of procedural safeguards. These safeguards remain nevertheless very important as is apparent in the Beijing Rules:

> Basic procedural safeguards such as the presumption of innocence, the right to be notified of the charges, the right to remain silent, the right to counsel, the right to the presence of a parent or guardian, the right to confront and cross-examine witnesses and the right to appeal to a higher authority shall be guaranteed at all stages of proceedings. (Beijing, Art. 7.1)

The paradox is that procedural safeguards are linked to judicial procedures, but that extra-judicial arrangements or diversion are meant to avoid the negative side-effects of such procedures. One of the consequences is net-widening. While diversion is promoted to avoid judicial handling, the practice is that many diversionary tracks do not come instead of court, but are additional tools for extended social control over juveniles, children and their families (Blomberg, 1983). More juveniles than before are kept under control, and the controls last longer than when such diversionary tracks did not exist. This is not to say that widening the net of social control is negative *per se*. It might, for example, be better to involve a juvenile who committed some petty offence in a reparative scheme than doing nothing because the judicial response is considered too strong a reaction. The problem is that extrajudicial handling cannot be promoted without indicating what the alternative is.

3.5. Children and Detention

In some circumstances, placement or detention of juveniles cannot be avoided. First of all, public security may be threatened seriously. The risk of grave re-offending can be a reason to give priority to avoiding severe re-victimisation, further serious harm and turbulent social trouble, rather than to focus on restorative actions or to try and avoid the stigmatising consequences of detention. But, secondly, detaining juvenile offenders may be necessary also to protect them. Some victims and their families would try to settle matters even by revenge. After offences which have caused deep trouble and/or attract media attention, some children or juveniles are to be hided from persons or parts of the public who might out heavy emotional reactions.

Detention of children and juveniles is not only dealt with in the CRC, but it is also treated in more detail in the UN Rules for the Protection of Juveniles Deprived of their Liberty (UNRPJDL). No child may be deprived of its liberty illegally or arbitrarily. The detention may be used as a last resort, and for the shortest possible duration only (CRC, Art. 37.b). The main argument is that children have the right to be educated as much as possible by their parents (CRC, Art. 7). Separation of the child from his parents is only admitted if a number of safeguards are respected (CRC, Art. 9.1). In case of detention because of an offence, as well as for reasons of welfare and protection, children and juveniles have the right of legal or other assistance, and the right to challenge the deprivation of liberty before a court or other impartial and independent body. These rights and the rights of privacy during the proceedings are very often neglected in the media (Days of General Discussion, 1995). The Committee also stresses that the family must continue playing a crucial role during the detention. The family must be encouraged to keep and to intensify the contacts with their detained children (Days of General Discussion, 1995). The UNRPJDL seek to concretize children's rights for those who are deprived of their liberty, which means any form of detention or imprisonment or the placement of a person in a public or private custodial setting, from which this person is not permitted to leave at will, by order of any judicial, administrative or other public authority (UNRPJDL, Art. 11). The rules do comment in detail on the several aspects of detention, such as the physical environment and accommodation, opportunities of education, work, recreation, medical care, contacts with the wider community, and the disciplinary procedures, the right of legal counsel, inspection and complaints. The guidelines of the CRC are implemented in a concrete manner. Great attention is paid to the remaining possibilities to set up as much as possible activities in the best interest of the detained child:

> Juveniles detained in facilities should be guaranteed the benefit of meaningful activities and programmes which would serve to promote and sustain their health and self-respect, to foster their sense of responsibility and encourage those attitudes and skills that will assist them in developing their potential as members of society. (UNRPJDL, Art. 12)

Such protective attitude is not always appreciated by the public at large, which very often does not understand well the position that "juveniles make trouble because they are in trouble", and that they therefore need support and guidance to be (re-)integrated as full citizens in society. The UN Rules are not blind for this possible public opposition:

> The competent authorities should constantly seek to increase the awareness of the public that the care of detained juveniles and preparation for their return to society is a social service of great importance, and to this end active steps should be taken to foster open contacts between the juveniles and the local community. (UNRPJDL, Art. 8)

3.6. Prevention of Youth Crime

Prevention of youth crime is dealt with explicitly in the UN Guidelines for the Prevention of Juvenile Delinquency (Riyadh Guidelines). The option clearly is to ground prevention on welfare policy: "The well-being of young persons from their early childhood should be the focus of any preventive programme" (Riyadh, Art. 4). Crime and delinquency are seen as symptoms of underlying problems, and these causes are to be tackled.

Locating youth crime prevention in a welfare perspective is not an evident option. One can indeed distinguish two possible approaches to prevention. The most popular with governments is the "security approach", which focuses on actions to decrease the amount of crime in the short run, while neglecting to deal with the underlying social and other causes. Such model of prevention aims at reducing the symptoms, and is limited to situational prevention, punitive deterrence and incapacitation. The reduced effectiveness of such strategy to decrease youth crime is demonstrated by criminological research (Lundman, 2001; Tonry & Farrington, 1995). "Welfare-based prevention", on the contrary, focuses on treatment or social action to reach its objectives. For methodological reasons, its effectiveness is difficult to measure. The presuppositions are more complicated than in the security oriented prevention strategies, and the reduction of criminality is only an indirect aim and one for the longer term. But welfare-based prevention is, according to the Riyadh Guidelines, considered more in line with the best interests of the child: "[...] a child-centred orientation should be pursued. Young persons should have an active role and partnership within society and should not be considered as mere objects of socialization or control" (Riyadh, Art. 3). It is believed that such strategy will be more successful over the longer term. Art. 2 of the Riyadh Rules says that successful prevention of juvenile delinquency requires efforts on the part of the entire society "to ensure the harmonious development of adolescents, with respect for and promotion of their personality from early childhood", and its Art. 6 stipulates that security oriented prevention, based on formal social control, should only be utilized "as a means of last resort".

4. ISSUES FOR FURTHER DEBATE

The CRC and the other UN commitments to children's rights and juvenile justice witness the moral concern within the international community to safeguard the well-being of children and juveniles, and the wish to protect them against neglect and active abuses by arbitrary and ill-motivated adults and institutions. But the above also makes clear that these concerns are not without problems. Many of the texts are based on suppositions that are poorly supported by empirical data, that suffer from internal contradictions and/or irreconcilable requirements, and that leave crucial concepts too open. This seriously diminishes the practical impact of the high moral involvements.

Despite the claim that the CRC, as a convention, has legal force, it only applies in countries that deliberately accept it, and very often interpret it in a doubtful way to insert it into local politics. The CRC does not have any enforceable international power. Not all rights awarded to children in the CRC are actually respected everywhere, to say the least. Even in the most industrialized, educated and democratic countries, serious problems continue to exist in respecting the rights of the child. No sanctions are imposed. Even states that do not sign the Convention are not outcasted from the international community. In fact, the same phenomenon is true with regard to the Universal Declaration of Human Rights. Although the impact of declarations and conventions as social-political tools is to be recognized on many occasions, the real effects on the day-to-day life of children in different regions, different (sub-)cultures, with their different parents and educators, can be questioned.

Moreover, a number of matters of principle remain being debated.

4.1. Is There a Need for Separate Children's Rights?

The very existence of separate rights for children is not without discussion. The CRC in fact is a tool for human rights that does not address all human beings, but children only. The notion "child" in the CRC refers to every human being below the age of 18 years unless under the law applicable to the child, majority is attained earlier (CRC, Art. 1).

It is debated whether or not children need or have an interest in possessing particular children's rights. The Universal Declaration of Human Rights does not mention age as one of the criteria that may not give rise to discrimination. Would that suggest that discriminating children with regard to human rights could be permissible? Are children and young persons under the age of 18 a social category to be distinguished from adults? Is the distinction sufficiently relevant to create separate children's rights and separate tools for supervising respect for these rights? For some, children have exactly the same rights as adults do (among others McGillivray, 1994), while others argue that children do not have equal rights, but that rights are only gradually granted by proof of capacity (among others Purdy, 1994). Instrumental arguments discuss the actual capacities of children to enforce their rights; issues of a philosophical and moral nature are related to the question whether giving too much freedom to children would not be a form of child neglect. In fact, social scientists disagree on the minimum conditions and the ideal context to favour a "healthy" development of children.

It seems obvious that having rights is not the same as exercising them. Newly born children are totally dependent from others to see their rights respected. One might call them second-hand rights, exercised through the goodwill of adults. The rights of children in fact seem to constitute first of all obligations for adults. But one might hope that the dependence of children gradually diminishes over time. As their intellectual, emotional and relational capacities increase, the capacities to exercise their rights and freedoms also do. But as rights and freedoms increase, so do responsibilities. On the other hand, as we find that the ideas mentioned in the debate do contribute a great deal towards a comprehensive, well-balanced socio-ethical reaction on crime, one might reverse the above mentioned question.

Why are adults excluded from children's rights? For it is beyond doubt that many (if not all) principles mentioned with regard to the criminal justice system can be successfully applied to adult offenders as well.

4.2. Limits to Rights

Rights for children are limited, as are rights in general. In the next paragraph we shall mention some possible instrumental limits and moral philosophical objections. But there are also possible conflicts of rights and interests. Human rights may threat other interests such as public order, health, security and rights of others. Child labour, for example, is in conflict with the CRC, but it may be a crucial economic need in some regions of the world. The freedom of expression may be misused to undermine democratic institutions. Different dispositions in the Declaration or in the Convention may be conflicting in certain situations. Freedom of speech (Art. 13) may be limited for the sake of protection against defamation (Art. 16). The children's right not to be separated from their parents (Art. 9) can be overruled by the right for the protection against abuse and neglect (Art. 19). An unsafe environment is an unfree environment in which the rights to live, to security of the person, to physical integrity or to property are endangered. So in order to pursue a safe environment, the human rights machinery has installed many prevention measures that, however, involve infringements on rights and liberties as well. Is there a hierarchy in rights? Some rights, at least, are considered to be non-derogable, such as the right to live, freedom of conscience and religion, legal recognition of the person, safeguarding against torture and cruel treatment, safeguarding against capture because of debts and safeguarding against being punished twice for the same crime (Meuwese, Blaak, & Kaandorp, 2005).

4.3. Rights and Responsibilities

Rights create freedom, because they open up the possibility to choose. The right to unemployment allowances creates the freedom to accept the allowances or not. The right to divorce opens up the possibility to divorce according to certain procedures, but also to stay married. The right of the child to be heard in a divorce procedure of his parents does not create the obligation for the child to choose between both. As we shall see, the rights of the child have sometimes been perverted in that they have been reinterpreted by states as obligations for children. But this is in fact contrary to the very concept of rights. Rights cannot create obligations, but only new opportunities, new options to be chosen by the rights holder. Of course, choices also create responsibilities (which are not the same as obligations). You must use your freedom of choice in a positive way, for yourself and/or for the others. The criteria for your choice, however, depend on yourself as a person. You may choose to increase your personal benefits and enjoyments in a direct selfish way, or you may take an option that best serves the quality of social life. Here, the ethical dimension in behaving according to rights becomes clear. The more humans have rights and are free, the more they have social ethical responsibilities.

If that is true, one may wonder if rights can be attributed to those who are not capable or willing to exert them in a socially responsible way. The right to freedom, for example, is taken away from some citizens who have committed an offence, suggesting thereby that they did not use this right in a socially responsible way. Can we extend this principle? In how far does that apply to children's rights? Do you grant rights to children that might lead to disastrous options and decisions if the children really exercised their rights? This brings us to the next matter of debate.

4.4. How Far Should Rights for Children Go?

This is probably the most difficult issue. First, children can exercise their rights only if they know that they have them. The UN Committee on the Rights of the Child clearly is opposed to children's justice wherein children have a purely passive role only. They should be informed and activated more than currently is the case in most countries: "... Children were seldom made sufficiently aware of their rights, including the right to assistance from a legal counsel, or of the circumstances surrounding the case or of the measures decided" (General Days of Discussion, 1995). The Committee recommends to undertake campaigns to inform children more about their rights and procedural safeguards.

But still, in how far is this realistic? Can granting too many rights to the children not yield counterproductive outcomes? Children must be capable to judge what is in their interest in the short term and in the longer term. As we just mentioned, they also must be able to exercise their rights in a responsible way. They must know the different possible choices and assess the chances and risks. The younger they are, the lower in general their capacities are to take well informed and balanced decisions. A very young child may have rights, but it will depend on the goodwill of the adults to get these rights in practice. But as children grow older, their capacities increase, and they should be given the possibilities to take their own decisions on issues they can overlook, what is in their interest and what the implications for their social context are. In that regard, the CRC imposes an important task on the parents. Following Art. 5, the parents are supposed "to provide, in a manner consistent with the evolving capacities of the child, appropriate direction and guidance in the exercise by the child of his rights".

Finding the balance between a responsible exercise of rights and being dependent on others to implement them, is a matter of continuous debate between pedagogues, developmental psychologists and lawyers. On the one extreme, the protective approach keeps children away from all risks of taking unfavourable decisions, and submits all crucial options to the discretion of the adults. Such model, however, does not lead to the emancipation of children into being autonomous and socially constructive adults. On the contrary, it must be feared that such children will remain dependent, too conformist, easy to manipulate, and that they will in fact not be able to find their way in the always changing conditions of life. On the other extreme, some believe that children are capable to sense their interest and are intrinsically socially constructive. They must be given the maximum possible space for their own visions and choices. The experiences of successes and mistakes are the best possible ways for learning to find ones way in the social and material environment. But going too far here, may amount to a form of child neglect.

Children must have the opportunity to learn from experience based on their own options and choices. That means that they must be given the possibility to make choices which are risky in the eyes of their parents. The amount of risks allowed must increase gradually, depending on information, maturity and responsibility. But the risk-taking should be monitored by feedback and support, and framed by care and, if needed, by control. How many children who have the right to education would go to school and do their best to get good results, if they were not under pressure by their parents? Is it really a right to education in the strict sense of the word, or is it in fact an obligation for authorities to provide education and for the parents to send their kids to school? It is probably more of the latter. Many rights for children are to be reformulated in the first stage as obligations to authorities and parents. They only gradually become rights of free choices to be exerted by the children and adolescents.

It must be clear by now that having rights is not the same as being able to enforce them. Lack of knowledge, lack of capacities, lack of responsibility originally limit the possibilities of children to enforce their own rights, and leaves it to competent adults to do it in their name. But the gradual development in knowledge, in capacities and in sense of responsibility, should also lead to gradually handing over the actual exercise of rights to the adolescents themselves. And that is not without problems. As the Flemish Commissioner for the Rights of the Child has observed, the stipulations with regard to the protection and the agencies for children are very well respected; on the contrary, more emancipatory regulations appear to cause much more resistance in society and are complied with to a much lesser extent (Vandekerckhove, 2004).

4.5. A Fundamental Debate: What are Rights in General?

A "right" suggests a legitimate due, a just claim which cannot be disputed. The Universal Declaration of Human Rights suggests that all humans enjoy these rights, only by the simple fact that they are humans. The Convention on the Rights of the Child proclaims by authority that all humans under the age of 18 have special rights that are unseparably linked to the status of being a child. It is as if humans and children have rights by nature.

But daily practice shows that they have not. Rights in fact are legitimized interests (or hidden obligations). Roughly and tentatively, we can see the development of interests into "rights" in different stages:

(1) First, and basically, rights are claimed by interest groups. Trade unions claim the right to post strikers' pickets, whereas the employers claim the right to work; terrorists claim the right to defend the integrity of their nation or their religion by violence, whereas governments claim the right for exceptional repressive and restrictive counter actions, etc. By calling their interests "rights", they suggest that what they claim is inherent to their position, that they will not discuss the legitimacy of their claim.

(2) Secondly, some interest groups can succeed in having their interests accepted by others, because the claims are recognized as being legitimate, because the interest group can impose its interests by power, or because different interest groups make compromises to recognize mutually the respective interests. The interests are then recognized and proclaimed as "rights". Recognized rights create obligations for those who do not necessarily share the interests but who adhere to the proclamation. This is the status of the Universal Declaration of Human Rights and of the CRC. All the states signing the Convention accept the

obligation to respect its content, but morally only. If they do not, they may be morally condemned by the other signatories.

(3) Furthermore, some proclamations include possible sanctions if the obligations are not met. But even if sanctions are provided, as in some issues of the UN Security Council, they only apply if they can be enforced. Inequality of power often impedes the imposition of sanctions to the most powerful non-compliant members, who can act as if the sanctions did not exist. The less powerful members, however, risk to be really sanctioned if they would not comply. General declarations including sanctions may thus have counterproductive effects, because they can be misused by stronger members to control the weaker members even more.

(4) And finally, legitimized interests may be shared so broadly that they are recognized by an entire political community or a state. Rights such as the right to physical integrity, to privacy, to property, and other rights, are then transformed in laws by consensus or by majority rule. The obligations and prohibitions linked to the rights then become enforceable in the state, and their transgression can be sanctioned by the state.

5. CONCLUSION

This above gradual development illustrates that rights are not given by nature, but that they are interests, reconstructed as legitimized rights by human interactions and power games. Children's and other humans' interests have been recognized as being legitimate, and have been reconstructed as "rights" by the official international community. The "rights" status of the interests adds to the moral authority of claims to respect them. That does not mean that they are respected always everywhere in all circumstances, or that they can be enforced by an international power. In many situations, the economically, militarily or physically weaker human beings are not given what the international community has proclaimed as their rights and they have no means to enforce them. In the war against terrorism, for example, the enemy is called a "terrorist" and is thus de-humanized by warfare propaganda, which in the mind of the warmongers cancels out the applicability of human rights and fundamental freedoms.

At the same time, the strengths of the Convention on the Rights of the Child cannot be underestimated totally. It does constitute a convention, with provisions that can be legally enforced in national jurisdictions. But it is most of all a social and political tool. In most of the articles, the States Parties are urged to take measures in order to respect children's rights. The philosophy of the CRC may thus ground a comprehensive youth policy. Moreover, the CRC issues an important pedagogical message, namely to recognize the development of children's capacities and their maturity, and to respect the best interest of the child. Moreover, the CRC also holds important guidelines for educators (Meuwese et al., 2005).

REFERENCES

Bazemore, G., & O'Brien, S. (2002). The quest for a restorative model of rehabilitation: Theory for practice and practice for theory. In: L. Walgrave (Ed.), *Restorative justice and the law* (pp. 31–67). Cullompton: Willan Publishing.

Blomberg, T. (1983). Diversion's disparate results and unresolved questions: An integrative evaluation perspective. *Journal of Research in Crime and Delinquency, 20,* 24–38.

Cappelaere, G. (2001). De internationale normen met betrekking tot jeugdbescherming. Minimale garanties en één enkel objectief! *Tijdschrift voor Jeugdrecht en Kinderrechten, 1,* 158–160.

Farrington, D. (1977). The effect of public labelling. *British Journal of Criminology, 17,* 112–125.

Feld, B. (1993). Criminalizing the American juvenile court. In: M. Tonry (Ed.), *Crime and justice: A review of research* (Vol. 17, pp. 197–267). Chicago: University of Chicago Press.

Junger-Tas, J., Terlouw. G. J., & Klein, M. (1994). *Delinquent behavior among young people in the Western World.* Amsterdam/NewYork: Kluger.

Lipsey, M., & Wilson, D. (1998). Effective intervention for serious juvenile offenders. In: R. Loeber & D. Farrington (Eds), *Serious and violent juvenile offenders: Risk factors and successful interventions* (pp. 313–345). Thousand Oaks: Sage Publications.

Lundman, R. (2001). *Prevention and control of juvenile delinquency* (3rd ed.). Oxford: Oxford University Press.

Matza, D. (1964). *Delinquency and drift.* New York: Wiley.

McGillivray, A. (1994). Why children do have equal rights: In reply to Laura Purdy. *The International Journal of Children's Rights, 2,* 243–258.

McGuire, J., & Priestley, P. (1995). Reviewing 'What Works': Past, present and future. In: J. McGuire (Ed.), *What works: Reducing re-offending. Guidelines from research and practice* (pp. 3–34). Chichester, NY: Wiley.

Meuwese, S., Blaak, M., & Kaandorp, M. (Eds). (2005). *Handboek Internationaal Jeugdrecht.* Nijmegen: Ars Aequi Libri.

Muncie, J., & Goldson, B. (2006). States in transition: Convergence and diversity in international youth justice. In: J. Muncie & B. Goldson (Eds), *Comparative youth justice* (pp. 196–218). London: Sage.

Purdy, L. (1994). Why children shouldn't have equal rights. *The International Journal of Children's Rights, 2,* 223–241.

Put, J., & Walgrave, L. (2006). Belgium: From protection towards accountability? In: J. Muncie & B. Goldson (Eds), *Comparative youth justice* (pp. 111–126). London: Sage.

Rutter, M., Giller, H., & Hagell, A. (1998). *Antisocial behavior by young people*. Cambridge: Cambridge University Press.

Schur, E. (1973). *Radical non-intervention*. London: Prentice Hall.

Tonry, M., & Farrington, D. (Eds). (1995). *Building a safer society. Strategic approaches to crime prevention, Crime and Justice. A Review of Research* (Vol. 19, pp. 1–20). Chicago: University of Chicago Press.

Vandekerckhove, A. (2004). Ook minderjarigen hebben rechten. In: R. Boonen (Ed.), *Kinderrechten aanpakken. Congresboek* (pp. 16–25). Antwerpen: Garant.

Verhellen, E. (1993). Children's rights in Europe. *The International Journal of Children's Rights, 1*, 357–376.

Walgrave, L., & Mehlbye, J. (1998). An overview: Comparative comments on juvenile offending and its treatment in Europe. In: J. Mehlbye & L. Walgrave (Eds), *Confronting youth in Europe* (pp. 21–53). Copenhagen: AKF Forlaget.

RACISM AND XENOPHOBIA AND THE PREVENTION OF BIAS CRIMES IN GERMANY: RESULTS FROM A NATIONWIDE TASK GROUP

Marc Coester and Dieter Rössner

1. INTRODUCTION

Racism and Xenophobia are constantly present in the public debate as well as in social science in Germany. For more than 30 years research is focusing on this topic and concentrating mostly on attitudes, ideologies and actions of German right wing youth. Since the new millennium a shift in perception of this phenomenon can be noticed that centres mainly on the prevention measures as well as on the victims of crime against social group members within society. This concept of hate and bias crimes respectively was the initial point of a German-wide task group which has been working between 2001 and 2005 in order to find new solutions and better concepts for the handling, and especially for the prevention of right wing violence, racism, xenophobia and bias crimes. It should be noted that the terms "right wing", "right extremist", "right radical", "xenophobic" or "racist" violence/crime are mostly used synonymously in Germany (Coester & Gossner, 2002). The terms "hate" or "bias crimes" are also used synonymously in the (mostly) English literature (Jacobs & Potter, 1998).

Crime and Human Rights
Sociology of Crime, Law and Deviance, Volume 9, 93–107
Copyright © 2007 by Elsevier Ltd.
All rights of reproduction in any form reserved
ISSN: 1521-6136/doi:10.1016/S1521-6136(07)09004-5

The following chapter presents an overview of the results of this task group and demonstrates the need for early, long-termed and comprehensive interventions as well as the view for fighting bias crimes at the international level.

2. SETTING THE SCENE

Before illustrating some substantial results, two important assumptions should be outlined that show the initial point of the establishment of the task group under review.

The starting point relates to the fundamental significance of this topic for Germany in general. Due to the special historical situation characterized by both the rising numbers of right wing crime and young people joining groups of the German right extremist subculture, politics as well as science and society are dealing constantly with this particular social problem.[1] Already absolute numbers are able to demonstrate the importance of this problem. As can be seen in Fig. 1, the amount of right wing crime in Germany as registered by the police rose immensely between 1969 and 2005 (numbers for the year 1983 not available), especially during the last decade and therefore in coincidence with the process of German reunification that started in 1989 (Federal Ministry of the Interior, 1987–2005). Next to the violent offences (which include assault, homicide, arson, etc.), the other offences listed in Fig. 1 are mainly propaganda offences (§§ 86 et sqq. German Criminal Code).

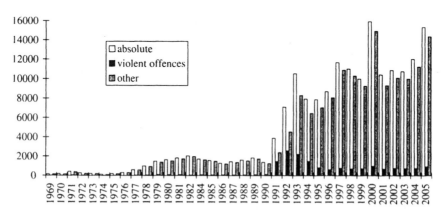

Fig. 1. Right Wing Crime in Germany 1969–2005 (absolute numbers). *Source:* Official data from the Federal Office for the Protection of the Constitution.

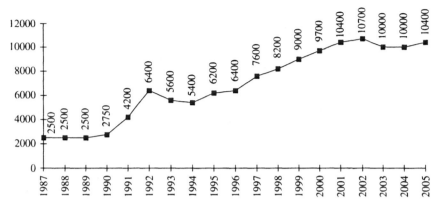

Fig. 2. Members of Violent Right Wing Subgroups in Germany 1987–2005 (absolute numbers). *Source:* Official data from the Federal Office for the Protection of the Constitution.

A similar increase shows the number of members from subgroups that are considered to be disposed towards violence (skinheads for example). Their population has risen from 2,500 to 10,400 between 1987 and 2005 (Fig. 2) (Federal Ministry of the Interior, 1987–2005). Notwithstanding the usual and well-known limitations of official registered crime records, the current research in the field of right wing crime in Germany confirms this trend consistently (Heitmeyer, 2002).

The second assumption for the establishment of the task group – next to the understanding of a constant rise of right wing violence and particularly in respect of the German history – is a new trend in social studies of right wing crime. Until the beginning of the new millennium the empirical and theoretical work focused on the offence and offender. Therefore data, research, practical and preventive implications with regard to victims did not exist. Of course the offender-oriented approach and its theoretical framework were and will remain important for the understanding of xenophobic violence. Relevant insights pertain to the sociological and psychological background of the offenders. Profiles help categorizing different groups. Next to the offender motivation profile of Levin and McDevitt (1993) that includes the thrill-seeking, reactive, mission and retaliatory hate crime, Willems (1995) introduced on an empirical basis four offender types for the German situation: the follower, the criminal, the xenophobic and the ideological-motivated offender. Focusing on preventive measures and the view to the genesis and escalation of socially conflicts create a better knowledge of the offence itself (Coester & Gossner, 2002, for an overview of the statistical, empirical, theoretical and preventive work in the field of right wing crime in Germany). But leaving the victim out of the scope creates a scientific vacuum and a lag behind international research. When in 2001 the statistical coverage of right wing crime among the German police forces was renewed and improved it combined for the first time victim-related data.[2] The analysis of this material as far as possible and other victim-oriented research demonstrates a shift that widens the focus: from right wing or xenophobic to "bias crime" (introduced by the task group, see infra) or 'group-focused enmity'.[3] The victim is no longer a "faceless part" of the crime but portrays the diversity of society and therefore reflects the casual, inhuman and bias motivated selection of the innocent. In a forthcoming dissertation, Coester (forthcoming)[4] shows the importance of distinctive differences between the offender and victim as well as the group context of the victims and the consequences of these insights for research and practice. Fig. 3 illustrates the variety of different characteristics of victim groups (Coester, forthcoming).

The background of this change in the perception of this topic derives from international studies, especially the hate crime research in the United States. The term "hate crime" was coined there in the mid-1980s by the

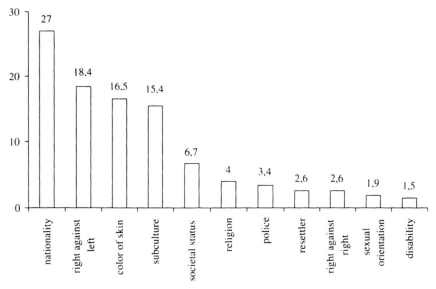

Fig. 3. Political Motivated Violence from the Right in Germany 2001. Attribute of the victim (Victim N = 307) (in %) *Source:* Coester (forthcoming).

introduction of special laws in several states and in particular the Hate Crime Statistics Act of 1990 (Jacobs & Potter, 1998). This act obliged the federal attorney general to collect and publish data about the causes and the prevalence of crimes committed by prejudice based on race, religion, sexual orientation and ethnicity.[5] The U.S. became the first nation worldwide to create and implement a state-wide strategy against hate crimes (Grattet & Jenness, 2001). It consisted of new legislation, but also encompassed the development of new institutions that are dealing with the problem on a scientific and practical basis, e.g. the Hate Crime Research Network, the Department of Justice National Hate Crime Training Initiative or the National Center for Hate Crime Prevention, to name a few. In Germany the research focusing on the right wing or right extremist crime and criminals developed simultaneously to the hate crime debate in America (Neureiter, 1996). Particularly because of the xenophobic excesses in the beginning of the 1990s social sciences and practice concentrated increasingly on this area and blinded out the considerations and results of the hate crime research. Shaw (2002, p. 2) has rightly argued that "Germany (…) primarily emphasize crimes which have a racial motive (…)". While in Germany the focus was on the disintegration theory by Wilhelm Heitmeyer (1994) and the situational theory approach by Willems, Würtz, and Eckert (1994) and Willems (1997) that concentrated on the offender and his socialization, the theories about hate crimes took into consideration the victims in their group specific context and as a selected object of hate (Coester & Gossner, 2002).

3. A TASK GROUP FOR GERMANY

With this in mind the German Federal Ministry of Justice (www.bmj.bund.be) requested in August 2001 the German Forum for Crime Prevention[6] to set up a task group to discuss the concept of the so-called hate crimes for the German situation with a special focus on its prevention. By doing so the international research on this important topic was to be appreciated and implicated with the right wing and xenophobic violence that convulses the German public consistently (Fuchs, 2003; Neidhardt, 2002). The name of the project "Primary prevention of violence against group members-especially: young people" is aiming exactly at this widening view: the hated groups – foreigners, homosexuals, disabled, etc. – are becoming victims just because of their symbolic status and the affiliation to a social group with which the offender does not agree (Conklin, 2001). The impacts of these offences can be described as devastating because they aim at attributes that the victim cannot affect; they send a frightening and fearing message of hate to the entire group of victims; and they suggest an invitation for more violence to the group of offenders (Schneider, 2001).

Following this model the 14 constant members of the German task group studied in regular sessions different theoretical aspects and the prevention of violence against group members. This work process was complemented by speeches of well-known experts in specific areas, a criminological documentation, a social psychological report, a workshop "primary prevention of hate crimes in Germany" on 2 December 2002 in Bonn, as well as the international symposium "National and international strategies for the prevention of hate crimes" on 7 March 2003 in Berlin (Bannenberg, Rössner, & Coester, 2005, 2006; Coester, 2003, 2006; Rössner & Coester, 2003a, 2003b, 2003c, 2005). Besides that the work of the group was externally evaluated.

4. MAIN RESULTS

In the following paragraphs the results of the working process of the task group will be discussed. At first the definition and the connotation with worldwide used terms was the group's main focus. The international term "hate crime" (Bender, 1996; Levin & McDevitt, 2002; Perry, 2001; Schneider, 2001) was not chosen, since it is mistakable because of its focus on the offenders' motivation and leaves the societal dimension of the community damage out of sight. More accurate to capture the implication of the phenomenon is the term "bias crime" (Bufkin, 1996; Lawrence, 1994), which can be found in the actual discussion. This term was chosen by the task group and translated into "Vorurteilskriminalität" or "Vorurteilsverbrechen" to describe this criminological and political topic:

> Bias crimes (*Vorurteilsverbrechen*) are violent crimes against persons or objects, which the offender commits on the background of the own group membership and against a member of a different social group because of their attributes like race, nationality, religion, sexual orientation or other lifestyles. The offender aims to frighten all members of the foreign group and to affect members of the own group for similar offences.

Another aspect of the definition appeared to be important: the name of the project refers to primary prevention and follows the classical arrangement oriented around medicine that categorizes the risk stadium in primary, secondary and tertiary prevention. In this scheme primary is understood to affect known causal factors of bias crime in the sense of a general prevention while secondary prevention is aiming at a specific treatment for certain risk factors and constellations and finally tertiary refers to the re-socialisation of already delinquent persons (Riedel, 2003, p. 13ff.). As obvious as this scheme seems, it only reflects a gross pattern because the development of criminality follows a gradual development process with many passages in one or the other direction (Kube, 1999; Lösel, 1987). Therefore a strict schematic categorisation would not meet the task to find effective strategies to prevent bias crimes. For its purposes, the task group defined it as follows:

> Primary prevention of bias crimes (*Vorurteilsverbrechen*) is aiming to avert the process of socialisation and socio-cultural deficiencies as well as attitude and value patterns in a way that bias crimes can be prevented.

In this perspective of primary prevention it is clear that the exertion of influence on risk groups that are affected by deficiencies are taken into account as well as the control by criminal law with which the value patterns of the general public are stabilised in the end and therefore the fortification of the potential victims. This perspective becomes clear by supplementing the classical arrangement by recent classification systems, for example by Tonry and Farrington (1995). They differentiate between developmental prevention, social structural measures and situational prevention. In this understanding, primary prevention is more or less identical to the first two forms of prevention that focus on the process of socialisation and the arrangement of the habitat. Situational/technical prevention is not covered.

According to the task group, the prevention of bias crime has to consider mainly three basic conditions that promote its development and therefore have to be influenced positively: (a) the disposition of violence, i.e. the mostly high and aggressive affinity of the offender for prejudice, (b) situational factors of the opportunity to commit an offence, and (c) the pressure on members in peer group situations. Aggressive behaviour as well as group-related prejudice is developing in an early stage and steps up in an accumulation process of present risk factors and resulting problems in the direction to social disintegration. In this context primary prevention includes the influence on socialisation processes and social cultural deficiencies as well as on attitudes and value patterns. In doing so it can be assumed that appropriate learning processes work the best in the early basis of socialisation and within a close personal reference. The effectiveness of every intervention gets weaker from the family to the kindergarten and

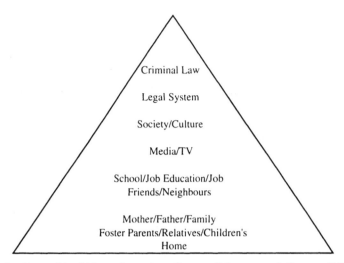

Fig. 4. Pyramid of Norm Learning. *Source:* Rössner and Coester (2003a).

school until the state alternatives of a tertiary encroachment. The loss of effectiveness can be shown by the picture of a pyramid from its wide and bearing basis up to the small and attached peak which is grounded on the fundaments underneath (Fig. 4).

The resources for preventing the general disposition of violence and the affinity to prejudice can be extracted from the knowledge of effectiveness research. Firstly the constant focusing, isolating and sanctioning on and of violent behaviour are to be mentioned. This must happen in every important area of education. Most important is that this process is taking place within a climate that is addressed to the child and the juvenile, and with the goal of social integration and not exclusion (integrative sanctioning). It is required that norms are clearly defined and applied with consistency. When the conspicuousness of children and juveniles has emerged, the cognitive dispute over the violent behaviour is most important, especially by taking the victims' position into account. This is also true for efforts from behaviour therapy. Within the context of institutional education (kindergarten and school) so called multi-level-concepts have been approved worldwide. According to the best proven and evaluated school programme Olweus, parents, teachers and pupils are getting committed to the goal of absence of violence by bringing up problems for discussion, dealing with incidents, supporting victims and treating violent pupils on a regular basis. In often repeated international scientific studies the violent crimes in schools could be lowered significantly (Wilson, Gottfredson, & Najaka, 2001). Also sport plays an important role because like nowhere else the physical energy and power of young men can be directed and adopted into normatively and socially acceptable behaviour. Counterproductive are family and life circumstances in which the child feels declined, and receives a violent and hostile education through punishment, if it receives any attention at all.

On a societal level the message and the demanding character of bias crimes are calling for explicit signals of assistance towards the victims and strict actions against the offenders. Against all sorts of messages that create fear, a powerful anti-message from society must be the reaction to encourage potential victims. Like nowhere else, criminal law in cases of bias crime acts as a shield for human rights. Accordingly, to clarify norms in a visible way through sanctioning serves the victims' rights and also norm conformity, and it is also important compared to offenders that justify their actions by blaming the victims.

Recapitulating the basic considerations of preventing bias crimes the following issues should be noticed. In the view of the German task group, focal issues for the prevention of bias crime were deemed to be:

– Prevention must contain the reduction of risk and the enhancement of the protective factors during childhood and youth. This means the reinforcement of primary or social prevention so that social structural lacunae, attitude patterns and values can be influenced positively.
– Successful programmes address several systems at the same time (family, school, etc.), integrate different services (youth welfare office, school, youth work. etc.), and are installed at an early stage, consistently and in the long run.
– Most effective in national and particularly in international evaluation studies turned out to be the contact programmes as well as approaches in schools. Examples of the first category are contacts in segregated neighbourhoods (Pettigrew & Tropp, 2000), contacts at the work place (Pettigrew & Tropp, 2000), integrated schools (Dollase, 2001), and co-operative group education (Slavin & Cooper, 1999). Examples of the second category include information within the class (Stephan & Stephan, 1984), activities around the 'multicultural school' (Banks, 1988), the already mentioned Olweus programme (Knaack & Hanewinkel, 1999), and the National Centre for Hate Crime Prevention's programme for the prevention of bias crimes (McLaughlin & Brilliant, 1997). Besides these approaches, especially programmes are to be rated positively that focus on the prevention of personal development. Examples comprise parent

education training (Kazdin, 1994), social competence training for children (Wasserman & Miller, 1998), the class-contingent-programme for teachers (Howell & Hawkins, 1998), parents–child interaction training within pre-school education (Zigler, Taussig, & Black, 1992), and cultural awareness training (Wallace, 1998).
- In respect to the message and demanding character of bias offences the legal answer requires a clear signal of support to the victim(s) as well as a strict procedure against the offender(s).

Furthermore the task group compiled recommendations for the prevention of bias crime (for the final report, see: http://www.kriminalpraevention.de). These contain for example:

- Modular structuring and evaluation of internationally established education programmes (mentoring models and multi-systematic family treatment programmes), as well as therapeutic approaches and their adjustment to the German situation.
- The development of intercultural learning in kindergarten/day care centres for children on the basis of successful models from the national and international level. Therefore expert advisors have to be available area wide. Projects are to be monitored scientifically and should be evaluated from the beginning.
- Since internationally positive results are present it is recommended to implement a research agenda for cooperative contact programmes that compile five examples of cooperative group education and its effects on prejudice in elementary and secondary school. A system of scientific monitoring as well as documentation should guarantee the quality and transferability of such programmes.
- The promotion and scientific monitoring of school multi-level concepts for the prevention of violence. This includes sufficient financial support, the development of a German manual, the control of the implementation and a methodically appropriate process, and an effect evaluation.
- Multi-level concepts within the field of sport clubs that are proven successful at the national and international level for the prevention of violence and conflicts. They contain among other things the training of the coaches as conflict mediators, and referee training or co-operation strategies on the local level. These concepts should be promoted and accomplished especially by the sports federations.
- A wide co-operation between the educational institutions among themselves and with independent institutions as well as with the police and justice institutions to bundle resources and to integrate preventive

measures that are only effective in cooperation. This cannot be attained without a change of laws. Because the current situation for the protection of legal data is deplorable, a new § 4a has to be included in the Code of Social Law VIII that – similarly to Denmark – obliges kindergartens, schools, youth welfare offices, agencies of the juvenile welfare service as well as the police and justice authorities to co-operate within the field of primary prevention. This also includes the co-operation in a context with individual cases and not only in the stage of planning actions as before described in § 81 Code of Social Law VIII.

– In principle, assured insights about the manifestation and the causes of bias crimes are missing to a large extent. The effectiveness of prevention programmes is often not controlled systematically. The implementation and the quality assurance of educational approaches should be examined by external process evaluations.

5. CONCLUSION

In summary, it can be stated that what seems most effective is especially primary or social prevention that on the one hand addresses young members of our society and on the other hand is situated in institutions having the largest influence on these persons. This is also true for the prevention of negative attitudes and aggression against members of foreign groups. Secondary prevention is not excluded but the development of early interventions must be promoted, in particular by the state. Clear rules against intolerance and violence and the strict application of sanctions obviously possess a larger degree of effectiveness within the primary scope than criminal law does. At this point financial means are very important for the evaluation of such measures. Without any quality assurance funding is not recommended.

It can be argued that a lasting prevention requires more than a deterring punishment or a short-term offer of social measures if a spectacular bias crime has convulsed society. In every respect primary prevention of bias crime is necessary.

NOTES

1. One example for the constant dispute in this field might be the societal handling of political parties which are located on the far right. Shortly after the Second World

War the *Wirtschaftliche Aufbau Vereinigung* (Economic Development Coalition) reached in 1949 14.4% of the votes and therefore joined the first German *Bundestag* (House of Parliament) after Nazi Germany. In 1952 -eight years after World War Two and only three years after the enactment of the *Grundgesetz* (German Constitutional Law)- the Federal Constitutional Court of Germany banned for the first time a right wing party in Germany: the *Sozialistische Reichspartei* (Socialist Reichs Party). The prohibition Section 21 Paragraph 2 of the constitutional law says: "Parties which, by reason of their aims or the behaviour of their adherents, seek to impair or destroy the free democratic basic order or to endanger the existence of the Federal Republic of Germany shall be unconstitutional". Until today the struggle between right wing parties and the government continues. Just recently up to March 2003 the Federal Government tried to ban the *Nationaldemokratische Partei Deutschlands* (National Democratic Party of Germany). The NPD was formed in 1964 and is today the most right wing or right extremist party in Germany with over 6.000 members, a monthly journal with a run of 10.000 copies as well as a youth party organization *Junge Nationaldemokraten* (Young National Democrats) that recruits mainly young neo-Nazi skinheads and the militant scene.

2. The statistical coverage follows a new definitional system of political motivated crimes. This allows for a differentiated registration of right wing, racist, xenophobia and anti-Semitic crime and violence, since the focus is on the political motivation of the crime and not on the extremism of the offender. On the homepage of the Department of Foreign Affairs more information can be found: www.auswaertiges-amt.de

3. As introduced by a comparative survey (International Comparative Investigation of Group-Focused Enmity) by the Institute for Interdisciplinary Research on Conflict and Violence (Prof. Dr. Wilhelm Heitmeyer). For more information see: http://www.uni-bielefeld.de/ikg/eng/index.htm

4. Dissertation by Marc Coester of the Institute of Criminology at the University of Tübingen. For more information visit the author's webpage: http://www.jura6.ifk.jura.uni-tuebingen.de:8082/~jkico01. In the dissertation Coester uses empirical data from the above mentioned new definition system of the German police. The data represent variables from 214 police records in 2001 as well as 307 victims and 490 offenders.

5. In the Hate Crime Statistics Act hate crimes are defined as "crimes that manifest evidence of prejudice based on race, religion, sexual orientation, or ethnicity, including where appropriate the crimes of murder, non-negligent manslaughter; forcible rape; aggravated assault, simple assault, intimidation; arson; and destruction, damage or vandalism of property" (Hate Crime Statistics Act of 1990, *Pub.L.No.101-275 1990*).

6. The *Deutsches Forum für Kriminalprävention* is a national service and information agency for German, European and international cooperation aimed at ensuring the optimisation of crime prevention by society as a whole. It concept combines a wide range of different approaches to crime prevention including the mobilisation of the co-responsibility and financial commitment of social groups and institutions for and to the cause of prevention; the sensitisationof the general public, public relations work and cooperation with the media; prevention research; the promotion and initiation of prevention schemes and programs; counselling; as well as the active involvement in crime prevention at an European and international level. More information is to be found on the website: www.kriminalpraevention.de

REFERENCES

Banks, J. A. (1988). Ethnicity, class, cognitive, and motivational styles: Research and teaching implications. *Journal of Negro Education, 57*, 452–466.

Bannenberg, B., Rössner, D., & Coester, M. (2005). Empfehlungen der Arbeitsgruppe Primäre Prävention von Gewalt gegen Gruppenangehörige-insbesondere: Junge Menschen. In: B. Bannenberg, M. Coester & E. Marks (Eds), *Kommunale Kriminalitätsprävention. Ausgewählte Beiträge des 9. Deutschen Präventionstages (17 und 18 Mai 2004 in Stuttgart)* (pp. 65–96). Mönchengladbach: Forum Verlag Godesberg.

Bannenberg, B., Rössner, D., & Coester, M. (2006). Hasskriminalität, extremistische Kriminalität, politisch motivierte Kriminalität und ihre Prävention. In: R. Egg (Ed.), *Extremistische Kriminalität: Kriminologie und Prävention* (pp. 17–59). Wiesbaden: KrimZ (KUP-Kriminologie und Praxis, Band 51).

Bender, D. (Ed.). (1996). *Hate crimes*. San Diego, CA: Greenhaven Press.

Bufkin, J. L. (1996). *Toward an understanding of bias crimes and bias groups: A theory of masculinity and power*. Ann Arbor: University of Michigan.

Coester, M. (2003). Nationale und internationale Präventionsstrategien zur Verhütung von Hasskriminalität. *Forum Kriminalprävention, 3*, 3–5.

Coester, M. (2006). Extremismo de derecha y criminalidad por prejuicio en Alemania. In: C. Millán de Benavides (Ed.), *Crímenes de odio*. Cuadernos Pensar en público No.3. Bogota: Altavoz.

Coester, M., & Gossner, U. (2002). *Rechtsextremismus – Herausforderung für das neue Millennium*. Marburg: Tectum Verlag.

Conklin, J. E. (2001). *Criminology* (7th ed.). Boston: Allyn & Bacon.

Dollase, R. (2001). Die multikulturelle Schulklasse-oder: Wann ist der Ausländeranteil zu hoch? *Zeitschrift für Politische Psychologie, 9*, 113–126.

Federal Ministry of the Interior. (Ed.). (1987–2005). *Verfassungsschutzbericht*. Berlin: Federal Ministry of the Interior.

Fuchs, M. (2003). Rechtsextremismus von Jugendlichen. Zur Erklärungskraft verschiedener theoretischer Konzepte. *Kölner Zeitschrift für Soziologie und Sozialpsychologie, 55*, 654–678.

Grattet, R., & Jenness, V. (2001). Examining the boundaries of hate crime law: Disabilities and the dilemma of difference. *The Journal of Criminal Law and Criminology, 91*, 653–697.

Heitmeyer, W. (1994). *Das Gewalt-Dilemma. Gesellschaftliche Reaktionen auf fremdenfeindliche Gewalt und Rechtsextremismus*. Frankfurt a. M.: Suhrkamp.

Heitmeyer, W. (2002). Rechtsextremistische Gewalt. In: W. Heitmeyer & J. Hagan (Eds), *Internationales Handbuch der Gewaltforschung* (pp. 501–546). Wiesbaden: Westdeutscher Verlag.

Howell, J. C., & Hawkins, J. D. (1998). Prevention of youth violence. In: M. Tonry & M. H. Moore (Eds), *Youth violence. Crime and Justice Series* (Vol. 24, pp. 263–315). Chicago: University of Chicago Press.

Jacobs, J. B., & Potter, K. (1998). *Hate crimes. Criminal law and identity politics*. New York: Oxford University Press.

Kazdin, A. E. (1994). Interventions for aggressive and antisocial children. In: L. E. Eron, J. H. Gentry & P. Schlegel (Eds), *Reason to hope. A psychosocial perspective on violence and youth* (pp. 341–382). Washington, DC: American Psychological Association.

Knaack, R., & Hanewinkel, R. (1999). Das Anti-Mobbing-Programm nach Olweus. *Pädagogik*, *51*, 13–16.

Kube, E. (1999). Kriminalprävention-konkrete Ansätze für die Praxis. In: D. Rössner & M. Jehle (Eds), *Kriminalität, Prävention und Kontrolle* (pp. 71–88). Heidelberg: Kriminalistik Verlag.

Lawrence, F. M. (1994). The punishment of hate: Toward a normative theory of bias-motivated crimes. *Michigan Law Review*, *93*, 320–381.

Levin, J., & McDevitt, J. (1993). *Hate crimes: The rising tide of bigotry and bloodshed.* New York, NY: Plenum Press.

Levin, J., & McDevitt, J. (2002). *Hate crimes revisited: America's war against those who are different.* Boulder, CO: Westview Press.

Lösel, F. (1987). Psychological crime prevention: Concepts, evaluations and perspectives. In: K. Hurrelmann, F. X. Kaufmann & F. Lösel (Eds), *Social intervention: Potential and constraints* (pp. 289–301). Berlin: Walter de Gruyter.

McLaughlin, K. A., & Brilliant, K. J. (1997). *Healing the hate: A national bias crime prevention curriculum for middle schools.* Newton, MA: Education Development Center.

Neidhardt, F. (2002). Besprechungsessay. Rechtsextremismus-ein Forschungsfeld. *Kölner Zeitschrift für Soziologie und Sozialpsychologie*, *54*, 777–787.

Neureiter, M. (1996). *Rechtsextremismus im vereinigten Deutschland.* Marburg: Tectum Verlag.

Perry, B. (2001). *In the name of hate: Understanding hate crimes.* New York: Routledge.

Pettigrew, T. F., & Tropp, L. R. (2000). Does intergroup contact reduce prejudice? Recent meta-analytic findings. In: S. Oskamp (Ed.), *Reducing prejudice and discrimination. The Claremont symposium of applied social psychology* (pp. 93–115). Mahawah, NJ: Lawrence Erlbaum.

Riedel, C. (2003). *Situationsbezogene Kriminalprävention.* Frankfurt a. M.: Lang.

Rössner, D., & Coester, M. (2003a). Vorurteilsbedingte Hasskriminalität und ihre Prävention. In: E. Kube, H. Schneider & J. Stock (Eds), *Kriminologische Spuren in Hessen. Freundesgabe für Arthur Kreuzer zum 65. Geburtstag* (pp. 243–255). Frankfurt a. M.: Verlag für Polizeiwissenschaft.

Rössner, D., & Coester, M. (2003b). Der entscheidende Schutz gegen Hasskriminalität ist das Mitgefühl. *Stuttgarter Zeitung*, *59*(June 2), p. 7.

Rössner, D., & Coester, M. (2003c). Die Prävention von Hasskriminalität. *Forum Kriminalprävention*, *3*, 15–17.

Rössner, D., & Coester, M. (2005). Gewalt gegen Fremde: Präventionsmaßnahmen gegen Vorurteilskriminalität. In: K.-H. Meier-Braun & R. Weber (Eds), *Kulturelle Vielfalt. Baden-Württemberg als Einwanderungsland* (pp. 247–260). Stuttgart: Kohlhammer.

Schneider, H. J. (2001). Opfer von Hassverbrechen junger Menschen: Wirkungen und Konsequenzen. *Monatsschrift für Kriminologie und Strafrechtsreform*, *84*, 357–371.

Shaw, M. (2002). *Preventing hate crimes: International strategies and practice.* Online publication: www.crime-prevention-intl.org/publications/pub_3_1.pdf

Slavin, R. A., & Cooper, R. (1999). Improving intergroup relations: Lessons learned from cooperative learning programs. *Journal of Social Issues*, *55*, 647–663.

Stephan, W. G., & Stephan, C. W. (1984). The role of ignorance in intergroup relations. In: N. Miller & M. B. Brewer (Eds), *Groups in contact. The psychology of desegregation* (pp. 229–278). New York: Academic Press.

Tonry, M., & Farrington, D. P. (Eds). (1995). *Building a safer society. Crime and justice series* (Vol. 19). Chicago: University of Chicago Press.

Wallace, H. (1998). *Victimology: Legal, psychological, and social perspectives.* Boston: Allyn and Bacon.

Wasserman, G. A., & Miller, L. S. (1998). The prevention of serious and violent juvenile offending. In: R. Loeber & D. P. Farrington (Eds), *Serious and violent juvenile offenders* (pp. 197–247). Thousand Oaks, CA: Sage.

Wilson, D. B., Gottfredson, D. C., & Najaka, S. (2001). School-based prevention of problem behaviors: A meta-analysis. *Journal of Quantitative Criminology, 17,* 247–272.

Willems, H. (1995). Development, patterns and causes of violence against foreigners in Germany: Social and biographical characteristics of perpetrators and the process of escalation. *Terrorism and Political Violence, 7,* 162–181.

Willems, H. (1997). Jugendunruhen und Protestbewegungen. *Eine Studie zur Dynamik innergesellschaftlicher Konflikte in vier europäischen Ländern.* Opladen: Leske und Budrich.

Willems, H., Würtz, S., & Eckert, R. (1994). *Analyse fremdenfeindlicher Straftäter.* Bonn: Bundesministerium des Innern.

Zigler, E., Taussig, C., & Black, K. (1992). Early childhood intervention. *American Psychologist, 47,* 997–1006.

POLITICAL CRIMES AND SERIOUS VIOLATIONS OF HUMAN RIGHTS: TOWARDS A CRIMINOLOGY OF INTERNATIONAL CRIMES

Stephan Parmentier and Elmar G. M. Weitekamp

1. INTRODUCTION

Some images stick out in the collective memory of mankind and become icons for a whole generation. Among the most forceful images of our generation are the attacks on the World Trade Center in New York and the Pentagon in Washington, on 11 September 2001. These attacks revealed a new face of terrorism at the dawn of the 21st century, with new targets and new means, intended to produce many indiscriminate victims and without any concern for the offenders to save their own lives. Since the dramatic events of September 2001, the academic literature has been flooded with books, articles, and reports about terrorism, Islamic fundamentalism, and new forms of violence, mostly from a viewpoint of political science and law.

Yet, one can wonder if the attack on the twin towers was fundamentally different from the violent attacks on politicians and political targets by the left-wing terrorist groups of the Rote Armee Fraktion in Germany or the Brigate Rosse in Italy in the 1970s and 1980s of the former century. These groups also used violent means against specific targets, with the objective of

Crime and Human Rights
Sociology of Crime, Law and Deviance, Volume 9, 109–144
Copyright © 2007 by Elsevier Ltd.
ISSN: 1521-6136/doi:10.1016/S1521-6136(07)09005-7

creating visibility for their cause, and with the death of many persons as a result. And so was and still is the intention of the guerilla groups in Colombia, Algeria and Sri Lanka, to mention just a few of the last decades. Next to these examples of terrorist activity, old and new, the last quarter of the 20th century has witnessed numerous situations of extreme violence that have generated massive numbers of victims and that have often implicated many perpetrators. The few examples all speak for themselves and have turned the former century, even after the second world war, into one of the bloodiest in human history: the killing fields in Cambodia, the genocides in Guatemala and Rwanda, the ethnic cleansings in the former Yugoslavia, the ethnic-religious conflicts in East-Timor, and the Apartheid regime in South Africa. This is not to speak of the long-lasting conflict between Israelis and Palestinians, the successive civil wars in the Democratic Republic of Congo, the ongoing genocide in Darfur, and the instances of torture and disappearances in many countries, which all continue on a daily basis under our very eyes.

Given the sheer numbers and the deep seriousness of these crimes, and the many offenders and victims implicated in them, it is extremely surprising that they have hardly been the object of criminological research. Why is it that criminology, the discipline *par excellence* that tries to describe and to explain crimes and the behaviour of offenders and victims, has virtually paid no attention to the crimes and the violations of human rights listed above? And, because of their quantitative and qualitative importance, how can these crimes become a central theme of criminological research and teaching in the next decades? These are the two leading questions that have informed this chapter and that will be dealt with in the next paragraphs. To do so, we will first discuss a number of concepts that need clarification, most notably those of political crimes and serious human rights violations; then, we turn to the underwhelming attention for these crimes and these human rights violations in criminology; finally, we try to sketch some areas for further research for the discipline of criminology.

2. POLITICAL CRIMES AND SERIOUS HUMAN RIGHTS VIOLATIONS: IN SEARCH OF A CONCEPTUAL CLARIFICATION

It is clear that the situations listed here all have their own histories and their own specificities, and no single situation can be regarded as identical to another. Despite these idiosyncrasies, however, all situations arguably have at least one element in common, namely that they go beyond the micro level of individuals and individual motivations, and that they are situated at the meso level and the macro level of societies with many – if not all – cases involving ideological motivations. For these specific reasons, they have often been described as political crimes and as serious human rights violations. The distinctions with common or traditional crimes on the one hand and with ordinary human rights violations on the other hand are far from semantic, but they are crucial, not only in the fields of law and politics but also in that of criminology.

2.1. Political Crimes

It can be argued that the categorization of an act as a "political crime" bears huge consequences in a variety of ways. First of all, the qualification is relevant in criminal law, and more specifically in extradition law (Van den Wyngaert, 1980). Several domestic legislations put severe restrictions on the possibilities to extradite suspects of political crimes who have fled to another country to their country of origin, for fear that the persons might be judged and sentenced on political and not just legal grounds. These limitations are also highlighted in an early treaty under the auspices of the Council of Europe, namely the European Convention on Extradition of 1957 (Council of Europe ETS 24). Its Article 3 prohibits the extradition to other states of offenders in respect of political offences as determined by the requested state, and even in respect of ordinary offences when it is believed that the requesting state will prosecute or punish for other reasons (such as race, religion, nationality or political opinion). In 1975, in the heyday of terrorist groups operating in Europe, a protocol to the convention was added, in which the scope of application of political offences was limited (Council of Europe ETS 86). Article 1 of the Additional Protocol stipulates that political offences are not considered to include crimes against humanity as defined in the Genocide Convention of 1948 and in the Geneva Conventions of 1949.

Another area in which the distinction between common crimes and political crimes is relevant is immigration law, and more particularly in asylum law (Hathaway, 2005). The main legal source here is the Refugee Convention of 1951, which prevents persons suspected of having committed political crimes to obtain asylum in another country (United Nations, 1951). Article 1, F (a) mentions that the convention does not apply to persons having committed "a crime against peace, a war crime, or a crime against humanity", followed by the provision that persons having committed "a serious non-political crime outside the country of refuge" are also denied the application of the said convention.

A third area to illustrate the relevance of the distinction between common crimes and political crimes lies in the granting of amnesty, which creates a shield against any further legal action, criminal and civil. These provisions are usually put into place in a context of transitional justice, whereby new regimes have to deal with the legacy of mass abuse by the previous regime and its allies. Even if the reasons for granting amnesty and the specific modalities may differ, some legislation makes amnesty dependent upon the existence of a political crime (Roht-Arriaza & Gibson, 1998). In the case of South Africa, e.g., amnesty could only be obtained for political crimes, not for common crimes, and under the conditions that the applicant provided full disclosure of the facts and expressed remorse in public (Truth and Reconciliation Commission Report, 1998). The fact that this amnesty procedure was part of the Truth and Reconciliation Commission (TRC) process has generated lots of discussion in South Africa (Sarkin, 2004). It does not, however, affect the fundamental point, namely that the distinction between common crimes and political crimes is an important one with far-reaching consequences.

And finally, the distinction is also relevant in the normal criminal justice administrations. In some countries, political crimes are not dealt with by regular courts, but by special courts because of their special character and the risk for abuse. In Belgium, e.g., Article 150 of the Constitution of 1831 provides that political crimes have to be judged by a lay jury, which implies that they are not brought before the ordinary criminal tribunal of first instance or before the Court of Appeals and judged by one or more professional judges, but before the Court of Assizes. This court is set up ad hoc for specific trials of serious crimes, such as murder and attempted murder, and also for political crimes, although in practice it has hardly ever been used for the latter (Alen, 1992).

The above makes clear that it is crucial to come up with a clear understanding and a clear definition of what political offences or political crimes actually are. This is definitely not an easy task, since very little work has been done on political crimes, and the rare attention given to them is fragmented in various disciplines, predominantly political science and law.

2.1.1. Definitions
Let us first turn to some definitional issues. For some authors, political crimes constitute a *contradictio in terminis*, because every crime is necessary

political for two reasons: first, by the very fact that it violates criminal law, which is supposed to contain the fundamental values and norms of any given society and which is produced through a legislative and thus a political process (Hilliard, 2006, p. 300), and second by the fact that the criminal justice process is an arm of government and a prime channel for exercising state power (Allen, 1974). The explicit reference to the notion of "political crimes" or "political offences" in legal instruments, however, clearly indicates that there is some fundamental distinction between crimes that have political dimensions to them and crimes that do not and can therefore be seen as "common crimes" or "ordinary crimes". One such distinction may lie in the intent with which the crime is committed. According to political scientist Schafer, e.g., a political crime is really a "convictional crime", based on the conviction or the motivation of the offender "about the truth and the justification of his own altruistic beliefs" (Schafer, 1977, p. 374). For the "political criminal" violating the law is an "instrumental crime for ideological purposes", which sets him apart from ordinary criminals and also from pseudo-convictional criminal (Schafer, 1977, p. 376).

Not all authors agree with this contention, or rather with the foundation of political crimes on the basis of the intent and the motivation of the offender only. The main problem lies in the purely subjective feature of this intent or this motivation, and how to prove in a legal or judicial procedure that the crime was committed with a particular political intent. Therefore, another approach is based on objective elements that can also be observed by the outside world, such as the context of the act and the actual outcome or the consequences of the act (Van den Wyngaert, 1980, pp. 108–109). If a crime is committed in a political context (e.g. with a political target, or in a situation of political unrest), or if the crime committed produces concrete outcomes of a political nature (e.g. special measures by the government or the parliament, or in a more radical scenario even the change of a regime), then a crime can be called political. Legal scholar Van den Wyngaert has made these distinctions between a subjective and an objective approach to political offences as early as 1980, and has indicated that legal systems may differ in their approach on how to determine the nature of a given offence.

More recently, a mixed approach of subjective and objective elements seems to have gained common ground. The so-called Norgaard principles, named after their drafter who served as the former president of the European Commission on Human Rights, list seven characteristics that can be used to assess if a certain crime can and should be regarded as political or not (Norgaard Principles, 1990). Norgaard drafted his principles at the occasion of the first free elections in Namibia in 1990, where the issue came up which crimes could be categorized as political and could therefore qualify for amnesty, and the same principles have also inspired the amnesty criteria of the TRC in South Africa. The seven principles listed are the following: (1) the motive of the offender; (2) the context in which the offence was committed; (3) the nature of the political objective; (4) the legal and factual nature of the offence; (5) the object and/or objective of the offence; (6) the relationship between the offence and the political objective being pursued; and (7) the question whether the act was committed in the execution of an order or with the approval of the organization, institution or body concerned.

These very different approaches to defining political crimes illustrate at least the elastic nature of the concept. Van den Wyngaert, inspired by the skepticism of the famous international lawyer Lauterpacht, has even coined the concept of political crimes "tautologous" since neither the subjective nor the objective approaches clearly define what is truly "political" about the acts committed (Van den Wyngaert, 1980, pp. 95–96). Without engaging in further debate at this stage, it is worth noting from a criminological perspective that the same skepticism may easily be applied to the notion of common crimes. What constitutes a crime, namely, has no ontological meaning "in se" but solely derives from the fact that particular types of behaviour result in criminal sanctions as imposed by law, and that this is the only way to "recognize" these acts as criminal acts.

2.1.2. Types of Political Crimes

Closely related to the definition of political crimes is a second issue, that of identifying various types of political crimes.

A first typology is based on the nature of the crimes. For Van den Wyngaert there exist "purely political offences" and "related political offences" (Van den Wyngaert, 1980, pp. 105–109). The first category refers to acts that are exclusively directed against the state or the political organization of society, and that are not accompanied by the commission of common crimes (e.g. treason, espionage, conspiracy, collaboration with the enemy, but also acts of passive political dissidence). The second category is completely different and actually comprises common crimes that are assimilated to political offences because of the political purpose they serve (subjective criterion), or because of the political context or the political consequences in which they take place (objective criteria). In trying to simplify matters, it could be argued here that the first category encompasses fundamentally political behaviour that is "criminalized" by means of criminal law, while the second category contains fundamentally criminal behaviour that becomes "politicized" by its intent, context or consequences.

Criminology is host to another two-fold approach, based on the origins of political crimes. Turk was among the first criminologists to deal with political crimes, and the subtitle of his seminal work on *Political Criminality. The Defiance and Defense of Authority* reveals his view on the matter. He suggested two types of political crimes, the first being crimes aimed at defying the (political) authorities, the other meant to defend them (Turk, 1982). This embryonic typology, also based on Roebuck and Weeber (1978), was further developed in the work of Brown, Esbensen and Geis, who have distinguished between two main categories of political crimes: (1) on the one hand, crimes committed by people against the state, designed to protest, change, or bring down the existing establishment; and (2) on the other hand, crimes committed by the state against people, in order "to sanction those who threaten or appear to threaten the establishment (...), or in order to maintain and enhance the existing political and economic systems" (Brown, Esbensen, & Geis, 1991, p. 667). A similar distinction was made by Hagan, although he has turned around the order by first listing "crime by government" and then "crime against government" (Hagan, 1997). The distinction made by Brown et al. was echoed in the work of political scientist Jeffrey Ian Ross, who inspired by the work of Beirne and Messerschmidt, has argued that:

> political crimes consist of crimes against the state (violations of law for the purpose of modifying or changing social conditions) ... and crimes by the state, both domestic (violations of law and unethical acts by state officials and agencies whose victimization occurs inside (a particular country) and international (violations of domestic and international law by state officials and agencies whose victimization occurs outside the U.S.). (Ross, 2003, pp. 3–4)

According to Ross, the crimes against the state can also be called "oppositional crimes" and he lists five classical examples (Ross, 2003, pp. 41–77; Ross, 2005, pp. 1226–1229): (a) subversion ("overthrowing that which is established or existing" and mostly referring to legal but illegitimate actions to undermine democracy); (b) sedition ("incitement of resistance to or insurrection against unlawful authority", e.g. by defamation of the government or single political leaders); (c) treason ("overt acts aimed at overthrowing one's own government or state, or murdering or personally injuring the sovereign ... or their family"); (d) espionage ("secretly obtaining information about another, and typically, hostile country, its military or weaponry"); and (e) terrorism ("a method of combat in which random or symbolic victims become target of violence", and this can be domestically, in a state-sponsored way and internationally). Other authors have added certain types of political crimes to this list, including electoral corruption, civil disobedience and draft dodging, but there is certainly no consensus on these across the board (Ross, 2003, p. 35). For Ross, the crimes committed by the state, can equally be called "non-oppositional crimes", and also "state crimes" (Ross, 2003, pp. 84–86).

Building on the two main origins of political crimes, attention has also been given in criminology to the kind of activities involved in these crimes. Kauzlarich's distinction in the area of state crimes has also proven very useful for the field of political crimes. He has developed a continuum ranging from state crimes of commission (through direct, overt and purposeful action), state crimes of negligence (by disregarding unsafe and dangerous conditions, when the state has a clear mandate and responsibility to make a situation or context safe), and state crimes by omission (through tacit support for organizations whose activities lead to social injury) (Kauzlarich, 2005, pp. 1231–1232). It seems to us that political crimes are predominantly crimes of commission, since they most often require an active stance, either on the part of the state or of non-state actors. This is not to say that omission or negligence can never constitute a political crime.

By way of summary we refer to Ross' attempt to integrate the major concepts on political crimes (Table 1) (Ross, 2003, p. 38).

For sure, all of the above categories are very useful to come to grips with the topic of political crimes, but in our view fail to take into account two major developments in modern-day politics. First of all, the traditional

Table 1. Typology of Political Crimes According to Ross.

Violent/Non-Violent	Oppositional/Non-Oppositional	
	Against the State	By the State (State Crime)
Non-violent	Subversion Sedition Treason Espionage	Corruption Illegal domestic surveillance
Violent	Terrorism Assassination	Police violence Genocide

Source: Ross (2003, p. 38) and slightly adapted by the present authors.

distinction between state agents and non-state actors is very rapidly becoming blurred and various grey zones have emerged (e.g. paramilitary or vigilante groups committing crimes undercover or in their "free" time, or armed opposition groups engaged in criminal activities with state organs to finance their crimes). As a result, state and non-state actors do not only fight each other, but also themselves, which in some countries has generated high levels of intra-group conflicts and crimes (e.g. competition between rebel groups or between organized crime groups, particularly in failing states without strong state apparatus, and sometimes after long periods of authoritarianism). And secondly, a large part of today's political crimes is no longer limited to one national territory, but involves and sometimes even requires an international element for the preparation and execution of such crimes (e.g. the exchange of information or the joint execution of crimes). For these reasons we propose a more extensive typology of political crimes that takes account of the new faces of political crimes, as illustrated in Fig. 2. In our view, societies can be seen as pyramids, with each pyramid containing at least three layers (state apparatus, society organized in non-state groups and associations, and individuals), and the international community is made up of many such pyramids. Following this view, political crimes encompass all criminal activities undertaken by persons in any of these layers against persons or institutions and organizations in any other of these layers, national and international, provided that the crimes are political because of their intention, their context and their consequences. Examples of political crimes include, *i.a.*, the following: individuals and armed groups placing bombs in public places, guerilla groups fighting among themselves, civil society organizations engaged in actions of civil disobedience that may end in violent street protests or the occupation of buildings, state organs upholding competing views on political developments and sliding into criminal activities to fight one another, the police using telephone tapping against so-called terrorist organizations and contrary to criminal law, the military practicing ill-treatment of individual suspects, intelligence services of a state destroying the vital infrastructure of another state, like harbours and airfields, the same intelligence services lending support to opposition groups in another state in order to overthrow that or another government, the police services of one state kidnapping citizens of another state, etc. It is clear that the list is endless and that such conception significantly enlarges the realm of political crimes. However, we like to argue that such large conception precisely accounts for the many complexities related to the new tendencies of fluidity and internationalization in the political and the social field (Fig. 1).

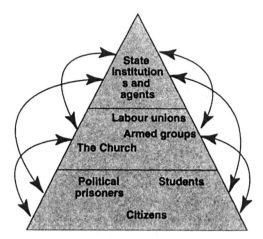

Fig. 1. A New Typology of Political Crimes. *Source:* S. Parmentier and
E. Weitekamp.

2.1.3. Features of Political Crimes

In the light of the foregoing typology, we turn to a third issue, namely the
main features of political crimes. Given the wide variety of political crimes
as illustrated above, it is of course impossible to argue that they all possess
exactly the same characteristics. It is possible, however, to single out some
common features of a large category of political crimes, namely those crimes
involving violent behaviour (the "violent crimes" according to Ross).
Examples of such crimes include terrorism and assassination, disappearances, extra-judicial executions, ethnic cleansing, widespread torture,
systematic rape, destruction of villages, forced removals, mass killings, and
of course genocide, the so-called "crime of crimes". These crimes by nature
are all of an extreme violence, that often goes back to deeply rooted conflicts
in a given society that continue to generate a general "culture of violence".
A second common feature relates to mass victimization, meaning that these
violent crimes are intended to produce large numbers of direct and indirect
victims and also to instill hatred and fear in a society or a segment thereof
(Šeparovic, 1999). In the words of victimologist Fattah, mass victimization
refers to "victimization directed at, or affecting, not only individuals but
also whole groups. In some cases the groups are very diffuse, the members
have nothing or not much in common, and the group is not targeted as a
specific entity. More often, however, the acts of victimization are directed
against a special population" (Fattah, 1991, p. 412). The latter is of course

very clear in the case of genocide, whereby a population is targeted for its distinctive characteristics.

It should be clear that not all types of political crimes share these two main features, as is illustrated by political crimes such as espionage and treason. But it is equally true that a large portion of political crimes, certainly in modern-day relations, is violent in nature and results in many victims.

2.2. Serious Violations of Human Rights

While thus far we have used political crimes and serious human rights violations in one breath, it should be clear that there are some major differences between the two concepts. First of all, in its most fundamental understanding, the difference goes back to the legal framework of reference, because to call an act a "crime" is to make a direct link with a breach of national or international criminal law, while to label an act a "violation of human rights" implies a transgression of national or international human rights law. Further, this difference in the body of law concerned also entails consequences in terms of the responsibility at stake: the former concept namely establishes the principle of the responsibility of individual persons for criminal acts committed, while the latter refers to the responsibility of states for violating human rights. It is therefore of utmost importance to qualify certain acts in an adequate manner. Even more so, because the same act can at the same time constitutes a political crime and a serious violation of human rights.

The notion of "serious" human rights violation is hardly found in international law and international human rights law. Most frequently used is the notion of "gross violations", sometimes in conjunction with the second epitheton "systematic", while other notions that more or less relate to similar realities are "grave violations", "massive violations", "widespread violations" and a "consistent pattern of violations". Many of these terms have originated in the framework of the United Nations, which have traditionally been very concerned with serious cases of violations. The first reference dates back to as early as 1967 in a resolution of the UN Commission of Human Rights on a "Study and Investigation of Situations which reveal a Consistent Pattern of Violations of Human Rights" and the terms subsequently found their way into resolutions of the Human Rights Commission, the Economic and Social Council, and the General Assembly (Medina, 1988; www.unhchr.ch). They also appear in some international treaties, such as the Convention against Torture (Article 20), the Optional Protocol to the Convention on the Elimination of all Forms of Discrimination against Women (Article 8), the African Charter on Human and Peoples' Rights (Article 58) and the General Framework Agreement for Peace in Bosnia and Herzegovina (Annex 6), but without clear definitions. Also the two Special Rapporteurs on the Right to Remedy and Reparation for Victims use the terms "gross" and "gross and systematic" violations of human rights, without further defining them. Rapporteur van Boven preferred instead to provide an exemplary list of actions including "genocide; slavery and slavery-like practices; summary or arbitrary executions; torture and cruel, inhuman or degrading treatment or punishment; enforced disappearance; arbitrary and prolonged detention; deportation or forcible transfer of population; and systematic discrimination, in particular based on race or gender" (Van Boven Report, 1993). In the eyes of Medina, gross and systematic violations imply four elements: (a) quantity (amount of violations), (b) time (present over a longer period of time), (c) quality (type of the rights violated, character of the violations, and status of the victim), and (d) planning (Medina, 1988, pp. 11–16). In our own recent work on reparation for victims, we have come to define "gross and systematic violations" as follows: "those violations of human rights, perpetrated in such a quantity and in such a manner as to create a situation in which the life, the personal integrity or the personal liberty of large numbers of individuals are structurally threatened" (Rombouts, Sardaro, & Vandeginste, 2005, p. 351).

In sum, it has become crystal clear that there is no commonly accepted definition of serious human rights violations in international human rights practice. However, as Sardaro has rightly argued, the types of violations referred to do share a number of common characteristics: "revulsion and moral stigma, infringement of supreme values, intensity of the breach, gravity of the consequences for the victims, deliberate will to breach a norm, and flagrant character of the breach" (Sardaro, 2007). Further, it should be noted that by far the most examples of serious violations implicitly relate to the category of civil and political rights. While this category definitely encompasses very important rights and freedoms, there is in our view no reason why also economic and social rights cannot give rise to serious violations, which may threaten the life, the personal integrity or the personal liberty of people (e.g. policies of poverty and starvation). On the basis of these two conclusions, we have tried to construct a typology of serious violations in Fig. 2, using two main dimensions, the first a qualitative one (the degree of gravity) and the second of a quantitative nature (the level of

Gravity (more grave)

occasional torture and ill-treatment	genocide
individual crimes against humanity	widespread torture
	a pattern of crimes against humanity
	a policy of starvation

Frequency (occasional)   Frequency (widespread)

singular cases of arbitrary detention	a general policy of arbitrary detention
selective repression of freedom	widespread repression of freedom
of expression	of expression

Gravity (less grave)

Fig. 2. A Typology of Serious Human Rights Violations (non-exhaustive list). *Source:* S. Parmentier.

frequency). Of all the violations listed, the most serious human rights violations are found in the upper right corner, where the violations are the gravest and the most widespread. Not coincidentally, this same category of violations has – by and large – developed into the category of "international crimes" as incorporated in the Statute of the International Criminal Court (cfr. infra).

3. THE MISSING LINK: POLITICAL CRIMES AND SERIOUS HUMAN RIGHTS VIOLATIONS AS OBJECT OF CRIMINOLOGICAL RESEARCH

Given the violent nature of many political crimes, the large numbers of victims involved, and the devastating effects on many societies, it is at least surprising if not stunning that these activities have hardly come to the attention of criminology and of criminologists. For criminology is about measuring crime, understanding it, and designing policies and interventions to react to it post factum or to prevent it. While criminology has a very long tradition of research on many forms and types of crime, ranging from juvenile delinquency to white-collar crime and from domestic violence to cyber crime, it has virtually neglected the area of political crimes altogether.

3.1. A Quick Scan of the Existing Literature

For the purposes of this chapter, we have done a small survey of the existing criminological literature without any ambition of being representative, let alone exhaustive, and the harvest has been strikingly poor.

3.1.1. Textbooks, Handbooks and Readers

This is first of all illustrated by the scant attention given in introductory textbooks of criminology in English to the concepts of political crimes, state crimes and human rights violations. One of the most authoritative textbooks, *The Oxford Handbook of Criminology*, does not deal with political crimes at all (Maguire, Morgan, & Reiner, 2002). The four forms of crime analyzed are violent crimes, white-collar crime, the organization of serious crimes (in fact dealing with organized crime), and crime relating to drugs and alcohol. Only in the first section, on violent crimes, some quick attention is given to war crimes and genocide, but only from the viewpoint of attributing responsibility to certain categories of offenders (Maguire et al., 2002, p. 799). Human rights are mentioned very briefly, but they are treated in the context of crime reduction and of the European Convention on Human Rights, and not in the framework of serious human rights violations. Another important textbook, *Criminology* by Sutherland and Cressey, contains no single mentioning of political crimes or human rights, despite being at its tenth edition in 1978 (Sutherland & Cressey, 1978). The same is true with the fifth edition of the textbook by Vold, Bernard and Snipes, which lacks any reference to political crimes, state crime and human rights violations (Vold, Bernard, & Snipes, 2002). Also other textbooks stand out by their complete lack of any references to political crimes and human rights violations (Adler & Laufer, 1993; King & Wincup, 2000; Conklin, 2007).

The references to political crimes, state crimes and human rights violations remain very thinly spread in the existing handbooks and textbooks and only a handful of exceptions have emerged. The oldest reference found is the three-volume work *Crime and Justice*, composed by Radzinowicz and Wolfgang (1977): the first volume contains a piece on "the political criminal" by Schafer (Schafer, 1977, pp. 368–380) and volume two contains an interesting chapter on torture, written by Amnesty International and in fact an excerpt from the first AI Report on Torture of 1975 (Amnesty International, 1977, pp. 221–234). There is, however, no mention of human rights violations or state crime. In the same period, Haskell and Yablonsky devoted a full chapter of their work *Criminology:*

Crime and Criminality to political crimes (Haskell & Yablonsky, 1978). Although their focus was exclusively on the United States, they dealt with a wide variety of examples of political crimes, including the killings of several American presidents, the actions of the Black Panthers, and several forms of political repression by the US state authorities to counter protests during the Vietnam War. They also designed a categorization of political dissent, distinguishing between actions by dissenters and reactions by the authorities (Haskell & Yablonsky, 1978, p. 206). Another noticeable exception in the criminological literature is the full chapter on political crime in the criminological handbook by Brown, Esbensen and Geis. The authors consciously argue that regular textbooks "rarely devote more than cautious passing attention to the issue of political crime, that is, to matters such as treason, assassinations, riots and insurrections, and violations by governments that secretly spy on their own people and seek to undermine the leaders of other nations" (Brown et al., 1991, p. 667). This scant attention, in their view, is due a variety of reasons, including the highly controversial character of political crimes, the fragmentary information about these behaviours, and the elusiveness of the concept itself. Furthermore, two readers in criminology contain some references to political crimes. In their *Criminology Theory Reader* Henry and Einstadter (1998) have included a chapter by Chambliss on state-organized crime (Chambliss, 1998), and McLaughlin, Muncie, and Hughes in their *Criminological Perspectives* (2003) integrated the well-known piece on human rights and crimes of the state by Cohen (Cohen, 2003): interestingly enough, both chapters were reprints of earlier articles published elsewhere. Finally, the most complete references to political crimes, state crime and human rights violations are found in two very recent works that fall somewhat outside of the scope of a textbook or a handbook. The *Encyclopedia of Criminology* of Wright and Miller (2005) in its second volume has the two entries of political crimes against the state and political crimes of the state (by Ross, 2005; Kauzlarich, 2005, respectively), and the *Sage Dictionary of Criminology* composed by McLaughlin and Muncie (2006) contains a two-page entry on political crime (Hilliard, 2006) and less than one-page on state crime by McLaughlin himself (McLaughlin, 2006).

3.1.2. Other Publications
The scant harvest in major handbooks, readers and dictionaries does not imply that there is a total absence of any attention for political crimes, state crime and human rights violations, in criminology or other disciplines.

A few authors have addressed these topics, either in general terms or relating to specific types of political crimes, mostly terrorism and genocide.

First of all, it should be highlighted that the work on political crimes has clear roots in political science. As early as 1979, Ingraham has devoted attention to the field of political crimes in three European countries, France, Germany and Britain (Ingraham, 1979). By looking at a 200-year period (1770–1970), he investigated how political crimes have been defined and dealt with in the legislations of the three countries. His conclusion is both pointing and sobering: "The political nature of the crime depends on the kind of legal response the act evokes from those in authority" (Ingraham, 1979, p. 19). As mentioned before, very influential is the work of Ross, situated on the crossroads between political science and criminology. He continues to be among the very few theorists who have tried to move away from the quagmire of conceptual confusion by coming up with a clear definitional scheme and with a typology of political crimes (Ross, 2003, 2005). To explain these complex forms of crimes, Ross presents a new theory of integrated causes, in fact more of a heuristic model, which looks upon political crime as a complex interplay among four dimensions: individuals who commit political crimes, the situations that presents themselves, the organizational elements that facilitate illegal and deviant behaviour, and the necessary resources (abbreviated as ISOR). His analysis, however, retains a heavy focus on advanced industrialized democracies, such as the United States, at the neglect of less developed countries and conflict-ridden societies, sometimes with an authoritarian leadership (also Tunnell, 1993).

In criminology, a few classics should be mentioned. Turk was among the first criminologists to deal at length with the category of political crimes (Turk, 1982), which for him was the logical consequence of his views about authority as a major source of conflicts in society. In contrast to Dahrendorf and Vold before him, Turk looked upon sources of authority in a broader sense, not only rooted in political power, but also extending to race and ethnicity, gender and age. He argued that the unequal distribution of authority in a given society may lead some individuals and groups to challenge the existing sources of authority, and this may imply committing crime. Likewise, persons, groups and institutions who possess authority want to maintain it and to defend it, which may sometimes lead to criminal acts. Both cases are forms of political crimes, since they relate to "defying" and to "defending" authority in the political sense of the word, as illustrated by the subtitle to his classic book *Political Criminality. The Defiance and Defense of Authority*. Also Chambliss has addressed the phenomenon of crime in a political context, but without calling it political crimes. In fact, Chambliss has demonstrated a life-long interest in the relationship between organized crime, politics and law enforcement (Chambliss, 1998). Starting with his famous research in Seattle and the connections between the top of the legal world (the political elites and the economic tycoons) and the top of the illegal world (the bosses of organized and less organized crime), he has consistently paid attention to the crimes of the powerful, both as individual offenders but also as part of the political and economic complex in any given society. For Chambliss, traditional criminology had systematically neglected this "political economy of crime", and for that reason had not even started to tackle the issue of state-organized crime. By the latter, he means "acts defined by law as criminal and committed by state officials in the pursuit of their job as representatives of the state" (Chambliss, 1998, p. 347). Examples include a state's complicity in piracy, smuggling, assassinations and criminal conspiracies, acting as an accessory before or after the fact, and violating laws that limit its activities. His concept of state-organized crime is thus broader than that of political crime because it also involves crimes that have foremost an economic dimension to them, but on the other hand it is also narrower, because it only relates to crimes committed by state officials and not by other persons or groups in a political context. Yet, there definitely exists a considerable degree of overlap between the two. Finally, with his *States of Denial* Cohen has written a classic in the field of human rights violations and political crimes (Cohen, 2001). Building on his personal experiences in Israel, he has advanced explanations for the strange fact that people and societies as a whole prefer to deny the existence of serious human rights violations that are committed and continue to be committed. His question "how ordinary, even good people, will not react appropriately to knowledge of the terrible" (Cohen, 2003, p. 549) parallels that of the social psychologist Milgram whose famous experiments wanted to find out how ordinary people would behave in terrible ways, in that case by supplying electroshocks beyond the level of safety. Cohen seeks responses in the psychology of denial, the classic "bystander effect", and the well-known neutralization theory of Sykes and Matza. The latter had argued back in 1957 that many offenders look for motivational accounts of their deviant and criminal behaviour in "techniques of neutralization", such as denial of injury, denial of victim, denial of responsibility, condemnation of the condemners and appeal to higher loyalty (Sykes & Matza, 1957). According to Cohen, the same techniques can easily be applied to understand why serious human rights violations or violent political crimes occur in the first place and why they can keep going on.

Furthermore, mention should be made of the criminological work on state crime, which in some cases has come close to focusing on political crimes as well. The early work of Barak on state crimes in America (Barak, 1991), and the research on the state-corporate relationship by Kautzlarich (Kauzlarich, Kramer, & Smith, 1992) and by Kramer (Kramer, Michalowski, & Kauzlarich, 2002) are illustrative of a critical strand vis-à-vis the practices of the American government and its related state agencies in getting involved in criminal activities. It has led Kauzlarich and others to conceptualize a continuum of state complicity, ranging from active explicit involvement (like genocide) to inactive implicit behaviour (like condoning social inequalities) (Kauzlarich, Mullins, & Matthews, 2003). Particular attention should be paid to the two-volume work on *State Crime*, edited by Friedrichs (1998), constituting compilations of articles that explore state crime as the most significant form of crime and an inevitable result of power being concentrated in the hands of the few. As a result, the past century has been characterized by extraordinarily high levels of war, violence and crimes of all types, and states – or those acting on behalf of states – seem to have been complicit in a disproportionate share of such destructive activity. Friedrichs' aims were to understand state crime and its control, and to explore the varieties of state crime and its paradoxical nature, given the fact that the state is also the primary source of both laws that define crime and the institutions of enforcement and adjudication (also Rothe & Friedrichs, 2006).

Besides these general treatises on political crimes, state crimes and human rights violations, it should be noted that an increasing number of researches are dealing with specific forms of political crimes. Terrorism, e.g., has since long been the object of scientific attention, well before the attacks on the Twin Towers have taken place and the ensuing War on Terror has been launched (Laqueur, 1978; Schmid & Crelinsten, 1993; Gearty, 1996). Very recently, Rapoport has published his four-volume overview of terrorism, which starts with the American and the Russian revolutions, continues with the anti-colonial wave after the second world war, to move into the left terrorism of the 1970s in Western Europe, and to end with the newest wave of religious terrorism (Rapoport, 2006; also O'Day, 2004). There is also a considerable literature on genocide, partly historical nature and related to the Holocaust and the second World War, partly relating to more recent examples of genocide (Charny, 1999; Jones, 2004; Totten, 2005; Jones, 2006). Particularly interesting in this vein is the work by Alvarez (2001) who has analyzed the complex dynamics between official authorities and ordinary citizens when it comes to explaining heinous crimes such as genocides around the world. What all these specific studies or case-studies have in common is their issue-oriented approach, and while they are quite meritorious in their own right, they often lack a clear link to political crimes as a category within criminology.

3.2. For a Criminology of International Crimes

Throughout our quick literature overview, it became apparent that situations of serious crimes and mass violence have attracted wide and strong attention from a variety of disciplines, including social and political scientists (Reychler & Paffenholz, 2001) and (criminal) lawyers (Bassiouni, 2002) alike, but that criminology has lagged behind. This academic silence is arguably due to a predominant focus on common crimes at the expense of political crimes, which may be the result of a general lack of attention for all forms of transborder crimes, foreign and international justice, and international relations in general.

However, the turn of the 21st century seem to witness some important changes in this regard. Judging from some publications, the field of criminology is slowly but surely waking up and turning at least one eye to this new field of serious human rights violations. A strong impetus for this was given by the establishment of a number of international criminal justice institutions to deal with massive atrocities, such as the two ad hoc tribunals for the former Yugoslavia (ICTY) and Rwanda (ICTR) in The Hague in the early 1990s, and the permanent International Criminal Court (ICC) after 1998. Also the publicity surrounding non-judicial mechanisms such as truth commissions (Hayner, 2001), notably in South Africa, Peru, and Sierra Leone has raised substantial interest with criminologists to explore new and uncharted territory. Paralleling the establishment of this wide array of institutions, international criminal law has developed the new category of "international crimes" as found in the ICC Statute: genocide, war crimes and crimes against humanity (not to forget the crime of aggression, which still lacks a clear definition). All these developments illustrate the tendency to move away, at least at the international level, from a "culture of impunity" to a "culture of accountability", and its connections with peace and development.

It is therefore no coincidence that, among others, Roberts and McMillan have pleaded for the development of a "criminology of international criminal justice" (Roberts & McMillan, 2003). Taking the example of genocide, they have explored the theoretical and policy dimensions of criminology. As to the first, they suggest to deconstruct the notion of "international crimes" and to look into various cultures of crime causation to explain the commission of such crimes. As to the policy science aspect, with practical lessons for policy-makers, penal administrators and criminal justice professionals, the authors suggest to think outside the legalistic paradigm of international criminal justice in search of other types of legitimacy in other criminal justice systems, to look beyond the individual attribution of guilt and include the organizational context in which such crimes take place, and to widen the concept of justice from a predominantly top-down mode of operation to encompass bottom-up approaches as well. By paying attention to these additional dimensions worthy of critical attention, they argue, criminology both illuminates the penal concerns of international lawyers and opens up important new avenues for further multidisciplinary inquiry. Following the same line of argument is Smeulers, who has strongly advocated the development of a "supranational criminology" to encompass a criminological approach to international crimes and other gross human rights violations (Smeulers, 2006, p. 2; http://www.supranationalcriminology.org):

> Societies and political systems that commit international crimes need to be studied, just like organizations involved in committing the crimes, situations in which such crimes are committed and the dynamics leading to the perpetration if these crimes.

Criminology in her view can make a contribution in six main research areas: (1) defining and conceptualizing international crimes; (2) measuring and mapping international crimes; (3) estimating social costs of international crimes; (4) investigating the causes of international crimes; (5) defining and analyzing ways of dealing with international crimes; and (6) developing preventive strategies in order to prevent international crimes. These six areas in our view refer to three major dimensions commonly referred to for any type of crime: first, conceptualizing and describing criminal behaviour; secondly, explaining crimes and their consequences for individuals, groups and society as a whole; and thirdly, designing criminal policies, to prevent and to repress crimes, and to rehabilitate the victims and offenders involved. In studying this field, Smeulers argues, a clear distinction should be made between ordinary crimes as "crimes of deviance" by offenders breaking the law, and international crimes as "crimes of obedience" whereby law-abiding citizens serve a deviant state and just follow the law (Kelman & Hamilton, 1989). The latter point in our view is quite questionable, since there are many examples of political crimes or gross human rights violations that are not necessarily organized or condoned by the state authorities, but may also be committed by non-state actors operating in states that are more or less governed by the rule of law.

This newest generation of criminologists has also paid attention to specific crimes, particularly to the crime of genocide. Day and Vandiver have reinterpreted older socio-psychological theories of crime causation through the angle of genocide and mass killings in Bosnia and Rwanda. By ignoring the crime of genocide for a long time, criminology in their view has missed enormous opportunities to contribute to this field and to regenerate itself as a discipline (Day & Vandiver, 2000). According to Neubacher, the theory of neutralization techniques of Sykes and Matza applies perfectly to the field of state crimes and to macro crimes in general (Neubacher, 2006). By understanding why ordinary people use various forms of neutralization to rationalize their horrendous behaviour, we can avoid the trap of categorizing all of them as delinquent individuals and can link the individual and the political level. Also Woolford has strongly argued in favour of a "critical criminology of genocide", not by simply applying the existing criminological frameworks and notions but by developing a new and flexible criminological approach. Such approach, he argues, should at the same time be reflexive, critical and responsible (Woolford, 2006). This echoes the pleas of sociologist John Hagan for a "public sociology of crime" (Hagan, 2003). From another angle, Jamieson has edited a special journal issue of *Theoretical Criminology* on War, crime and human rights (Jamieson, 2003). Since criminologists have often failed "to explore the potentially pertinent literatures that deal directly with the reality of war and its sequellae", the various contributing authors look into issues of torture, political violence and the state's monopoly of power.

Finally, in our own work on transitional justice, we have tried to describe and to analyze situations of mass victimization under authoritarian rule and in post-conflict situations and various strategies – judicial and non-judicial – to address them from an interdisciplinary perspective, including criminology (Parmentier, 2003). Because of the focus on legacies of mass abuse, it should be mentioned that the concept of transitional justice is increasingly stretched to cover periods of democracy as well, e.g. the abuses against the First Nations in Canada and the aboriginals in Australia. One particular strand of our work is the focus on restorative justice in post-conflict situations, with the objective of testing the possibilities and limits of some restorative justice principles that were developed in the sphere of common or traditional crimes (Christie, 2001; Parmentier, 2001; Weitekamp, Parmentier, Vanspauwen, Valiñas, & Gerits, 2006; www.restorativejustice.org). Through case-studies on South Africa, Bosnia/Serbia and Colombia, we have tried or are trying to combine theoretical and empirical approaches to transitional justice. In the longer run, it may lead us to assess the potential of a "restorative diplomacy of peace" as coined by Braithwaite (Braithwaite, 2002, pp. 169–171).

4. DEALING WITH INTERNATIONAL CRIMES IN TRANSITIONAL OR POST-CONFLICT SITUATIONS

While the previous paragraphs have provided a short review of the criminological literature on political crimes and serious violations of human rights, the last part of this chapter will focus on situations of post-conflict and try to highlight the relevance of criminological research in such context. The main question is how criminology can come to grips with the many difficult issues that emerge after gross and massive violations of human rights, mostly committed for political reasons, have taken place in a particular country? Debates about such international crimes committed in the past usually take a start during times of political transition, which is when societies are moving away from an autocratic regime in the direction of more democratic forms of government. At that time, the new elites are openly confronted with the fundamental question on how to address the heavy burden of their dark past. This question was posed in most countries of Latin America in the 1980s, in all countries of Central and Eastern Europe in the 1990s, and in several countries in Africa and Asia in the last decade.

In the older legal and the social science literature, this problem is known as the question of "dealing with the past" (Huyse, 1996). In this chapter, we prefer two notions that are broader and more neutral at the same time, and which we will use interchangeably: (1) one is "transitional justice" (Kritz, 1995), in some literature understood as "the study of the choices made and the quality of justice rendered when states are replacing authoritarian regimes by democratic state institutions" (Siegel, 1998, p. 431), and in more recent documents viewed as "the full range of processes and mechanisms associated with a society's attempts to come to terms with a legacy of large-scale past abuses, in order to ensure accountability, serve justice and achieve reconciliation" (United Nations, Security Council, 2004, p. 4); (2) the other notion is that of "post-conflict justice", presented as comprising two related meanings, one referring to "retributive and restorative justice with respect to human depredations that occur during violent conflicts" (in other words mostly dealing with the past), the other referring to "restoring and enhancing justice systems which have failed or become weakened as a result of internal conflicts" (in other words geared towards the future) (Bassiouni, 2002, p. xv). Although these two notions are not identical, and although they are not without conceptual problems, they seem to catch best the kinds of situations and the kinds of problems associated with the commission of international crimes.

The overwhelming majority of publications on transitional justice and post-conflict justice is concerned with analyzing and evaluating various strategies and mechanisms for dealing with the international crimes of the past, including the criminal prosecution of offenders before a national or international tribunal or court, civil procedures to claim damages for victims, lustration and vetting policies to oust collaborators with the former regime from their post, truth commissions to sketch a general picture of the violations and the crimes, and policies of granting amnesty to perpetrators. While these studies are extremely important and worthwhile, it is in our view advisable to conduct a prior exercise, namely to first investigate the key issues that come up when societies are facing their dark past, and to discuss the main challenges related to them. By doing so, it will be much easier to understand the contribution of each of the strategies and mechanisms mentioned above, and to design new ones whenever appropriate.

What are then the key issues that new regimes are facing in their pursuit of justice? In an earlier publication, it was argued that four issues stand beyond doubt and can therefore be considered key issues or core issues: searching the truth about the past, ensuring accountability for the acts committed, providing reparation to victims, and promoting reconciliation in society (Parmentier, 2003). Inspired by our own recent research work in Bosnia, we wish to add two more key issues, namely dealing with the trauma of the victims, and building trust among all parties. We will briefly review all six key issues and indicate what contribution criminology could make to further investigate them.

4.1. Searching the Truth about the Past

A first key issue to be addressed by the new elites is how to bring the truth about the past to the forefront, and give it some form of credit. Unearthing the truth is an important exercise, not only because individuals wish to know what has happened to their beloved ones, but also because societies have an interest in being aware of the patterns of serious human rights violations that have existed in the past. Establishing the truth is also a necessary, though not automatic, step towards some form of acknowledgement of past abuses, either by individuals or by society (Schotsmans, 2005). Moreover, it is essential if society at one point wishes to construct a form of collective memory about the legacy of an often horrendous past (Amadiume & An-Naim, 2000; Czarnota, 2001).

However, the truth is never unequivocal and always multifaceted, for which reason it is not an exercise without major challenges. In trying to disentangle some of this complexity, the South African Truth and Reconciliation Commission (TRC) has made the distinction between four notions of truth (TRC Report, 1998, pp. 110–114): (1) the factual or forensic truth, meaning the evidence obtained and corroborated through reliable procedures; (2) the personal and narrative truth, meaning the many stories that individuals told about their experiences under Apartheid; (3) the social or dialogue truth, established through interaction, discussion and debate; and (4) the healing and restorative truth, meaning the truth that places facts and their meaning within the context of human relationships. According to the Commission, every type of truth has its own value and its own procedures to reach it.

It is clear that criminology can play an important role in this process of truth seeking. First of all, it can contribute to the various notions of truth, e.g. by developing new techniques and interpretations of forensic procedures, by creating forums in which victims can discuss their experiences, and by exploring the possibilities of bringing victims and offenders together to confront their painful past. Secondly, and at a more theoretical level, criminology can contribute to mapping the crimes of the past and their origins, e.g. by reinterpreting the rich body of existing criminological theories about the sociological and the psychological causes of crime, but also by developing new theoretical frameworks to better understand political crimes, serious human rights violations, and the characteristics of perpetrators and offenders.

4.2. Ensuring Accountability of Offenders

The second key issue in a transitional or post-conflict situation is how to make sure that the offenders can be called to account for the crimes committed. The accountability of the perpetrators is an equally important aspect for new regimes, first of all to respond to the idea that "justice be done", and thus to re-establish the moral order of the victims and of society as a whole. But it is also important for political reasons, namely to reaffirm the ideals of the "rule of law" and human rights, and thereby to strengthen the fragile democracy. Both elements contribute to breaking through the thick walls of impunity and to move to a "culture of accountability" (Minow, 1998).

Of course, the challenges are never far off (Huyse, 1996). A first challenge relates to the type of offenders that can and should be called to account: are they only those who executed the orders – and those who assisted them in doing so –, or do they also include the heads and the planners of the human rights violations? what about the so-called "bystanders", who did not actively participate in committing the crimes, but nevertheless remained passive and silent when they were committed, and may even have watched them taking place? and if some of these bystanders have benefited from the political or economic consequences of the crimes, should they be called to account for that? A second challenge deals with the type of accountability (Kritz, 1996). Victims, supported by other sectors of society, most often call for criminal prosecution, relying on the legal argument that there exists "a duty to prosecute in international human rights law" (Orentlicher, 1991). Criminal prosecution of offenders, however, is not without problems. This is partly due to the substantial capacity that is required of a judicial system – both national and international –, taking into account the demanding rules of due process and human rights; but also because criminal prosecution may endanger the new democracy, due to the fact that the old political and military elites may still possess real power and be inclined to use it accordingly (Huyse, 1996); and even because the local population may have very divergent views about trying its leaders (Hagan, 2003). Confronted with these many problems, also other types of accountability can be envisaged, such as claims for civil damages under national tort law, lustration or vetting policies of a predominantly administrative nature whereby institutions and organizations are "purified" of persons having collaborated with the former regime (Nanda, 1998), and also forms of political accountability that may entail tangible consequences for proven offenders through non-legal means, e.g. by exposure in the media or in public debates.

The role of criminology is potentially very extensive here as well. First, and drawing on the many studies on criminal justice systems around the world, it can analyze the many bottlenecks that may exist for the police and the justice administration on the road to criminal prosecution of offenders, thereby making the distinction between national and international systems, and providing recommendations to overcome these hurdles. Moreover, and from a wider point of view, it can analyze the strengths and weaknesses of a criminal justice approach compared to other approaches of accountability, civil, administrative or political, and it can suggest new avenues to enlarge the scope of accountability mechanisms outside of the courts. Finally, criminology can also increase our understanding of the motivations of direct and indirect offenders, and of bystanders and beneficiaries, and suggest ways to deal with these complex issues of involvement, complicity and accountability (Balint, 2007).

4.3. Providing Reparation for Victims

A third key issue, that has gained increasing attention over the last decade, is the problem how to repair the victims of international crimes for the harm inflicted upon them during periods of violent conflict or otherwise. Using the "reparative justice" approach (Mani, 2002) and designing concrete reparative measures is a rapidly emerging development in order to address, and even to undo, some of the injustices of the past (De Greiff, 2006). Following the adoption of the Basic Principles and Guidelines on the Right to a Remedy and Reparation, by the General Assembly of the United Nations in 2005, the concept of reparation is now to be understood as encompassing various aspects, including the restitution of goods, financial compensation, rehabilitation through social and medical measures, satisfaction and symbolic measures, and guarantees of non-repetition of the crimes committed. All of these measures can be individual or collective (De Feyter, Parmentier, Bossuyt, & Lemmens, 2005).

Despite, and maybe because of, these recent developments important challenges have become visible (Vandeginste, 2003). A first one is about the entity to assume the responsibility for reparation measures, in other words, who is the duty-bearer of reparations, the perpetrators themselves, the former elites, or the agencies of the new regime, and what can be the role of the bystanders who benefited? Furthermore, how can the right to reparation for victims effectively be enforced, through a general government policy or through individual administrative or judicial actions? Finally, not to be neglected is the problem of "victim competition", whereby individual victims or victim associations start to compete amongst themselves for the scarce resources that are available at a given moment (Chaumont, 1997). All of these elements are crucial if the right to reparation is to become a reality, more than just wishful thinking or even a utopia.

For the discipline of criminology, reparation for victims of political crimes and serious human rights violations poses new challenges as well. Although it has a very limited tradition in evaluating existing compensation and reparation policies at the national level, criminology can of course extend its focus and its methodology to the sphere of international crimes, to study and to evaluate the existing schemes and to recommend improvements. Moreover, it can also go deeper in the analysis of the key concept of "harm" inflicted, partly by asking victims directly through empirical work how they have experienced their victimization and what their attitudes and opinions about reparation and redress may be.

4.4. Promoting Reconciliation in Society

A fourth core issue in post-conflict settings relates to the need of reconciling the various communities and sectors of society that have been part of the conflict, in order to reconstruct the previously existing relationships or to construct new ones if necessary. The question is thus how a country or a society, that has been conflict-ridden for a long time, and has produced numerous victims, can regain some form of social cohesion, which is absolutely essential for its future development? The issue of reconciliation after violent conflict is gaining increasing attention in theory and practice (Bloomfield, Barnes, & Huyse, 2003; Daly & Sarkin, 2006).

If the preceding issues already pose big challenges, the issue of reconciliation might be even more difficult. First of all, there is a conceptual problem as the notion means many different things to many different people. Again the South African TRC has shed some light on this complex notion, by distinguishing four different levels of reconciliation: (1) the individual level of coming to terms with a painful truth, e.g. after exhumations and reburials of beloved ones; (2) the interpersonal level of specific victims and their perpetrators; (3) the community level, when addressing the internal conflicts inside and between local communities; and (4) the national level, by focusing on the role of the state and non-state institutions (TRC Report, 1998). Particularly the passages on reconciliation have allowed the TRC to make the link with the notion of restorative justice, which is broadly interpreted in its Report as "restoring civil and human dignity" for all South Africans, victims and perpetrators alike (TRC Report, 1998, pp. 125–131). The Peruvian Truth and Reconciliation Commission has enlarged this notion of reconciliation by projecting it to three different fields: (1) political reconciliation, to reconstruct the ties between the state and the society; (2) social reconciliation, to end the divisions in civil society triggered by the violence and the dictatorship; and (3) interpersonal reconciliation, to reconstruct the ties and relationships within communities and social groups (Peruvian Truth and Reconciliation Commission, 2003). A second major challenge relates to the ideological use of the "re-conciliation" discourse. Many commentators have suggested that violent conflicts and human rights violations disrupt a balanced situation that existed in the past, and that reconciliation actually means going back to that past. However, it is very doubtful whether this retrospective approach is relevant in situations of long-lasting divisions in society, whereby certain groups such as indigenous peoples or the poor have been completely excluded from participation, and whereby going back to the past would mean a confirmation of long-time inequalities. In those circumstances, it is preferable to speak of the importance of "conciliation" or "construction" for the future.

Given the difficulties attached to reconciliation in transitional justice, criminology may provide a unique contribution in this regard. First of all, on a conceptual level, it can clarify the multiple dimensions of "reconciliation", particularly through empirical research with specific target groups or with the population at large, thereby demystifying the frequent ideological use of reconciliation. Moreover, it can study and evaluate the existing initiatives and practices, whether process or outcome oriented, that are designed to bring victims and perpetrators together and particularly look into their long-term effects towards reconciliation. Finally, on a more theoretical level, criminology can test the general applicability of the principles of restorative justice in cases of political crimes and serious human rights violations. To do so, it has at its disposal a rapidly growing body of research on the new paradigm of restorative justice as developed in the sphere of common or traditional crimes.

These four key issues of transitional or post-conflict justice can be grouped together in a heuristic model, which we have previously called the TARR model (truth, accountability, reparation and reconciliation) (Fig. 3). This model is inspired by the writings of the left realists in criminology of the early 1990s, who have developed a similar framework for the analysis of crime and its various components (state-society-offender-victim) (Lea, 1992, p. 69).

4.5. Additional Key Issues: Dealing with Trauma for Victims and Building Trust in Society

As suggested before, the TARR model is an open and flexible one and can (and should) be adapted to new insights. One of these insights stems directly from our current research on mass victimization and restorative justice in the Balkans, in which we are looking into actual and possible practices of

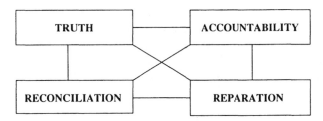

Fig. 3. TARR Model of Key Issues in Transitional or Post-Conflict Situations (Truth-Accountability-Reparation-Reconciliation). *Source:* S. Parmentier (2003), based on Lea (1992, p. 69).

restorative justice and peace-making, with the objective of testing the applicability of restorative justice principles as developed for common crimes in situations where political crimes and serious human rights violations have taken place. Part of this research has included a nation-wide quantitative survey in Bosnia in 2006, asking our respondents to explain what types of victimization they have encountered during the conflict of the 1990s, and what strategies to address the legacy of the past they consider appropriate, hereby referring to the four key issues listed above (truth-accountability-reparation-reconciliation). Although we are still analyzing the data of the 855 respondents in more detail, it has already become clear that two crucial elements have emerged, namely dealing with trauma for victims, and building trust among individuals and communities. Given the importance of these two issues in transitional or post-conflict situations, we hereby suggest to refine the existing TARR – I model by adding both issues into an upgraded TARR – II model.

Let us have a quick look at these two additional issues. First of all, we argue that it would be a big mistake to assume that after violent conflicts have come to an end, people can just go on with their lives as before. The enormous suffering encountered during the conflict, and at the time of the often horrendous violations or the crimes, produce very significant levels of trauma that continue to exercise a strong impact in any post-conflict situation (Schotsmans, 2005). This is illustrated by the many physical and psychological problems of individuals when trying to resume their daily activities, but also by the many tensions and difficulties in communities and society at large to discuss the past and to deal with it. Dealing with trauma is therefore a top priority, foremost for the direct victims of the crimes, but also for persons who may not have directly experienced harm. The second and corollary key issue is that of trust. In order for individuals to be able to resume their life and their activities, and for society to move on, some level of trust with oneself and the surrounding context is of paramount importance. The absence of trust or the low levels of trust may strongly endanger any initiative or practice, any strategy or approach to deal with the past and to construct the future in a post-conflict or transitional situation. It goes without saying that criminology can strongly contribute to understanding both issues better. For this purpose, it can build on extensive existing research about trauma and trust as experienced by victims and communities dealing with ordinary or common crimes, e.g. in situations of death row (Volf, 1996; Beck, Britto, & Andrews, 2007) and also in the context of restorative justice (Zehr, 1990).

It seems to us that both additional issues, dealing with trauma and trust building, are not only important in their own right, but that they may also have a direct impact on each of the four key issues mentioned above. This is illustrated in Fig. 4, which also suggests more clearly that there exists no special sequence between the six components and that the order of addressing them may vary depending on the time, the country and the circumstances at stake.

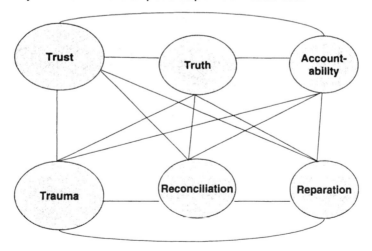

A Restorative Justice Model for Post Conflict Situations by Elmar G. M. Weitekamp and Stephan Parmentier 2007

Fig. 4.   TARR – II Model of Key Issues in Transitional or Post-Conflict Situations   (Trauma-Trust-Truth-Accountability-Reparation-Reconciliation).   *Source:* E. Weitekamp and S. Parmentier.

5. CONCLUDING REMARKS: TOWARDS A CRIMINOLOGY OF INTERNATIONAL CRIMES

In this contribution, we have studied political crimes and serious human rights violations from the angle of criminology. Although criminology portrays itself as the main academic discipline to describe and to explain all forms of crime, it is striking that the overwhelming majority of its work is concentrated on crimes called common or traditional because they are incorporated in common or traditional criminal law. Our literature review has made clear that crimes with a political component to them, either because of the intent of the offender, or of the object or the context in which they take place, have very rarely been addressed. Examples included "older" political crimes such as treason, espionage and civil disobedience, as well as "newer" forms such as terrorism, torture, disappearances, genocide. The latter forms are also known as serious violations of human rights, although they lack a clear definition in international human rights law. They have, on the other hand, in the last decade become incorporated in international criminal law as international crimes. Several of these crimes involve many perpetrators, produce massive numbers of victims, and therefore have a strong impact on individuals and on society alike.

For that reason, it is even more surprising that criminology has only paid very scant attention to them. Part of the explanation may lie in the methodological difficulties of researching such crimes, but another aspect squarely touches upon the very sensitive nature of political crimes and serious human rights violations, which are often directly linked to the activities of state organs and non-state actors with considerable power and influence. The latter aspect may also have an impact on the possibilities for funding research on such crimes.

At the same time, it is crystal clear that the criminological attention for international crimes is rapidly gaining ground in recent years. The potential for criminology as an academic discipline is indeed vast and wide. This is illustrated through our discussion of post-conflict situations, not only by looking at the various strategies and mechanisms to deal with legacies of past human rights abuses, but also by focusing on a number of key issues that new regimes cannot escape to address. In doing so, we have also enlarged our own conceptual framework, so as to include six key issues, i.c. trauma, trust, truth, accountability, reparation and reconciliation. Each of these issues entails many challenges, and to address them goes far beyond the limits of one particular discipline. It is our strong belief that criminology, with its unique interdisciplinary approach to criminalization, criminal behaviour, and criminal policies and institutions, is particularly fit to explore this largely uncharted "terra incognita".

SOURCES OF INFORMATION

Books and Reports

Adler, F., & Laufer, W. (Eds). (1993). *New directions in criminological theory*. New Brunswick/London: Transaction Publishers.

Alen, A. (Ed.). (1992). *Treatise on Belgian constitutional law*. Deventer: Kluwer Law and Taxation.

Allen, F. (1974). *The crimes of politics. Political dimensions of criminal justice*. Cambridge: Harvard University Press.

Alvarez, A. (2001). *Governments, citizens and genocide: A comparative and interdisciplinary analysis*. Bloomington: Indiana University Press.

Amadiume, I., & An-Naim, A. (Eds). (2000). *The politics of memory. Truth, healing and social justice*. London: Zed Books.

Amnesty International. (1977). Report on torture. In: L. Radzinowicz & M. Wolfgang (Eds), *Crime and justice* (2nd ed., 3 vols, Vol. 1, pp. 221–234). New York: Basic Books.

Barak, G. (1991). *Crimes by the capitalist state: An introduction to state criminality*. Albany, NY: SUNY Press.

Bassiouni, C. (Ed.). (2002). *Post-conflict justice*. Ardsley: Transnational Publishers.

Beck, E., Britto, S., & Andrews, A. (2007). *In the shadow of death: Restorative justice and death row families*. Oxford: Oxford University Press.

Bloomfield, D., Barnes, T., & Huyse, L. (Eds). (2003). *Reconciliation after violent conflict. A handbook*. Stockholm: International Idea.

Braithwaite, J. (2002). *Restorative justice and responsive regulation*. Oxford: Oxford University Press.

Brown, S., Esbensen, F.-A., & Geis, G. (1991). *Criminology. Explaining crime and its context*. Cincinnati, OH: Anderson Publishing Co.

Charny, I. (Ed.). (1999). *Encyclopedia of genocide* (Vols. 2). Santa Barbara, CA: ABC-CLIO.

Chaumont, J. (1997). *La concurrence des victimes*. Paris: Edition de la Découverte.

Cohen, S. (2001). *States of denial: Knowing about atrocities and suffering*. Cambridge: Polity Press.

Conklin, J. (2007). *Criminology* (9th ed.). Boston: Pearson.

Daly, E., & Sarkin, J. (2006). *Reconciliation in divided societies. Finding common ground*. Philadelphia: University of Pennsylvania Press.

De Feyter, K., Parmentier, S., Bossuyt, M., & Lemmens, P. (Eds). (2005). *Out of the ashes. Reparation for victims of gross and systematic human rights violations*. Antwerp: Intersentia.

De Greiff, P. (Ed.). (2006). *The handbook of reparations*. Oxford: Oxford University Press.

Fattah, E. (1991). *Understanding criminal victimization*. Scarborough, CA: Prentice Hall Inc.

Friedrichs, D. (Ed.). (1998). *State crime* (Vol. 2). Aldershot: Ashgate/Dartmouth.

Gearty, C. (Ed.). (1996). *Terrorism*. Aldershot: Dartmouth.

Hagan, F. (1997). *Political crime: Ideology and criminality*. Boston, MA: Allyn and Bacon.

Hagan, J. (2003). *Justice in the Balkans. Prosecuting war crimes in the hague tribunal*. Chicago: University of Chicago Press.

Haskell, M., & Yablonsky, L. (Eds). (1978). *Criminology: Crime and criminality* (2nd ed.). Chicago: Rand McNally.

Hathaway, J. (2005). *The rights of refugees under international law*. Cambridge: Cambridge University Press.

Hayner, P. (2001). *Unspeakable truths. Confronting state terror and atrocity*. New York: Routledge.

Henry, S., & Einstadter, W. (Eds). (1998). *The criminology theory reader*. New York/London: New York University Press.

Ingraham, B. (1979). *Political crime in Europe. A comparative study of France, Germany and England*. Berkeley, CA: University of California Press.

Jones, A. (Ed.). (2004). *Genocide, war crimes and the West*. London: Zed Books.

Jones, A. (2006). *Genocide. A comprehensive introduction*. London/New York: Routledge.

Kelman, H., & Hamilton, V. (1989). *Crimes of obedience. Towards a social psychology of authority and responsibility*. New Haven: Yale University Press.

King, R., & Wincup, E. (Eds). (2000). *Doing research on crime and justice*. Oxford: Oxford University Press.

Kritz, N. (Ed.). (1995). *Transitional justice: How emerging democracies reckon with former regimes* (Vols. 3). Washington: US Institute of Peace.

Laqueur, W. (1978). *Terrorism*. London: Weidenfeld and Nicolson.

Maguire, M., Morgan, R., & Reiner, R. (Eds). (2002). *The oxford handbook of criminology* (3rd ed.). Oxford: Oxford University Press.

Mani, R. (2002). *Beyond retribution. Seeking justice in the shadows of war*. Cambridge: Polity Press.

McLaughlin, E., Muncie, J., & Hughes, G. (Eds). (2003). *Criminological perspectives. Essential readings* (2nd ed.). London: Sage.

McLaughlin, E., & Muncie, J. (Eds). (2006). *The Sage dictionary of criminology* (2nd ed.). London: Sage.

Medina Quiroga, C. (1988). *The battle of human rights. Gross, systematic violations and the inter-American system*. The Hague: Martinus Nijhoff.

Minow, M. (1998). *Between vengeance and forgiveness. Facing history after genocide and mass violence*. Boston, MA: Beacon Press.

O'Day, A. (Ed.). (2004). *Dimensions of terrorism*. Ashgate: Aldershot.

Radzinowicz, L., & Wolfgang, M. (Eds). (1977). *Crime and justice* (2nd ed., Vols. 3). New York: Basic Books.

Rapoport, D. (Ed.). (2006). *Terrorism. Critical concepts in political science* (Vols. 4). London: Routledge.

Reychler, L., & Paffenholz, T. (Eds). (2001). *Peace-building. A field guide*. Boulder, CO: Lynne Rienner Publishers.

Roebuck, J., & Weeber, S. (1978). *Political crime in the U.S.* New York: Praeger.

Ross, J. I. (2003). *The dynamics of political crime*. New York: Sage.

Sardaro, P. (2007). *Serious human rights violations and remedies in international human rights adjudication*. Doctoral dissertation in Law. Leuven: Faculty of Law, K.U. Leuven.

Sarkin, J. (2004). *Carrots and sticks: The TRC and the South African amnesty process*. Antwerp: Intersentia.

Schmid, A., & Crelinsten, R. (Eds). (1993). *Western responses to terrorism*. London: Frank Cass.

Sutherland, E., & Cressey, D. (1978). *Criminology* (10th ed.). Philadelphia, PA: J.B. Lippincott.

Totten, S. (Ed.). (2005). *Genocide at the Millennium*, Vol 5 of the Series Genocide. A Critical Bibliographic Review. New Brunswick/London: Transaction Publishers.

Truth and Reconciliation Commission of Peru. (2003). *Final Report* (Vols. 9). Lima: Comision de Verdad (www.cverdad.org.pe).

Truth and Reconciliation Commission of South Africa. (1998). *Report* (5 Vols, Vol. 1). Cape Town: Juta Publishers.

Tunnell, K. D. (1993). *Political crime in contemporary America. A critical approach.* New York: Garland Publishing.

Turk, A. (1982). *Political criminality. The defiance and defense of authority.* Beverly Hills/London: Sage.

Van den Wyngaert, C. (1980). *The political offence exception to extradition.* Antwerp: Kluwer.

Vold, G., Bernard, T., & Snipes, J. (Eds). (2002). *Theoretical criminology* (5th ed.). New York/Oxford: Oxford University Press.

Volf, M. (1996). *Exclusion and embrace.* Nashville: Abingon Press.

Wright, R., & Miller, J. M. (Eds). (2005). *Encyclopedia of criminology* (Vols. 3). Routledge: New York/London.

Zehr, H. (1990). *Changing lenses. A new focus for crime and justice.* Scottdale, PA: Herald Press.

Articles in Books and Journals

Balint, J. (2007). Dealing with international crimes: Towards a conceptual model of accountability and justice, Paper presented at the Expert Meeting "Towards a Criminology of International Crimes", Maastricht University, April 12–15.

Chambliss, W. (1998). Towards a political economy of crime. In: S. Henry & W. Einstadter (Eds), *The criminology theory reader* (pp. 346–362). New York/London: New York University Press.

Christie, N. (2001). Answers to atrocities. Restorative justice in extreme situations. In: E. Fattah & S. Parmentier (Eds), *Victim policies and criminal justice on the road to restorative justice. Essays in honour of tony peters* (pp. 379–392). Leuven: Leuven University Press.

Cohen, S. (2003). Human rights and crimes of the state: The culture of denial. In: E. McLaughlin, J. Muncie & G. Hughes (Eds), *Criminological perspectives. Essential readings* (3rd ed., pp. 542–560). Sage: London.

Czarnota, A. (2001). Law as Mnemosyne married with Lethe. Quasi-judicial institutions and collective memories. In: E. Christodoulidis & S. Veitch (Eds), *Lethe's law: Justice, law and ethics in reconciliation* (pp. 115–128). Oxford: Hart Publishing.

Day, L. E., & Vandiver, M. (2000). Criminology and genocide studies: Notes on what might have been and what still could be. *Crime, Law and Social Change, 34,* 43–59.

Hilliard, P. (2006). Political crime. In: E. McLaughlin & J. Muncie (Eds), *The Sage dictionary of criminology* (2nd ed., pp. 300–302). London: Sage.

Huyse, L. (1996). Justice after transition: On the choices successor elites make in dealing with the past. In: A. Jongman (Ed.), *Contemporary genocides* (pp. 187–214). Leiden: PIOOM.

Jamieson, R. (Ed.). (2003). *Special Issue: War, crime and human rights of Theoretical Criminology* (Vol. 7, pp. 259–405).

Kauzlarich, D. (2005). Political crimes of the state. In: R. Wright & J. M. Miller (Eds), *Encyclopedia of criminology* (Vols. 3, pp. 1231–1234). Routledge: New York/London.

Kauzlarich, D., Kramer, R., & Smith, B. (1992). Toward the study of governmental crime: Nuclear weapons, foreign intervention and international law. *Humanity and Society, 16,* 543–563.

Kauzlarich, D., Mullins, C., & Matthews, R. (2003). A complicity continuum of state crime. *Contemporary Justice Review, 6,* 241–254.

Kramer, R., Michalowski, R., & Kauzlarich, D. (2002). The origins and development of the concept and theory of state-corporate crime. *Crime and Delinquency, 48,* 263–282.

Kritz, N. (1996). Coming to terms with mass atrocities: A review of accountability mechanisms for mass violations of human rights. *Law and Contemporary Problems, 59,* 127–152.

Lea, J. (1992). The analysis of crime. In: J. Young & R. Matthews (Eds), *Rethinking criminology. The Realist Debate* (pp. 69–94). London: Sage.

McLaughlin, E. (2006). State crime. In: E. McLaughlin & J. Muncie (Eds), *The Sage dictionary of criminology* (2nd ed., p. 303). London: Sage.

Nanda, V. (1998). Civil and political sanctions as an accountability mechanism for massive violations of human rights. *Denver Journal of International Law and Policy, 26,* 391.

Neubacher, F. (2006). How can it happen that horrendous state crimes are perpetrated? An overview of criminological theories. *Journal of International Criminal Justice, 4,* 787–799. Symposium Nuremberg Revisited 60 Years on.

Orentlicher, D. (1991). Settling accounts: The duty to prosecute human rights violations of a prior regime. *Yale Law Journal, 100,* 2537–2615.

Parmentier, S. (2001). The South African truth and reconciliation commission. Towards restorative justice in the field of human rights. In: E. Fattah & S. Parmentier (Eds), *Victim policies and criminal justice on the road to restorative justice. Essays in honour of Tony Peters* (pp. 401–428). Leuven: Leuven University Press.

Parmentier, S. (2003). Global justice in the aftermath of mass violence. The role of the international criminal court in dealing with political crimes. *International Annals of Criminology, 41,* 203–224.

Roberts, P., & McMillan, N. (2003). For criminology in international criminal justice. *Journal of International Criminal Justice, 1,* 315–338.

Roht-Arriaza, N., & Gibson, L. (1998). The developing jurisprudence on amnesty. *Human Rights Quarterly, 20,* 843–885.

Rombouts, H., Sardaro, P., & Vandeginste, S. (2005). The right to reparation for victims of gross and systematic violations of human rights. In: K. De Feyter, S. Parmentier, M. Bossuyt & P. Lemmens (Eds), *Out of the ashes. Reparation for victims of gross and systematic human rights violations* (pp. 345–503). Antwerp: Intersentia.

Ross, J. I. (2005). Political crimes against the state. In: R. Wright & J. M. Miller (Eds), *Encyclopedia of criminology* (Vols. 3, pp. 1225–1230). Routledge: New York/London.

Rothe, D., & Friedrichs, D. (2006). The state of criminology of state crime. *Social Justice, 33,* 147–161.

Schafer, S. (1977). The political criminal. In: L. Radzinowicz & M. Wolfgang (Eds), *Crime and justice* (2nd ed., 3 Vols, Vol. 1, pp. 368–380). New York: Basic Books.

Schotsmans, M. (2005). Victims' expectations, needs and perspectives after gross and systematic human rights violations. In: K. De Feyter, S. Parmentier, M. Bossuyt & P. Lemmens (Eds), *Out of the ashes. Reparation for victims of gross and systematic human rights violations* (pp. 105–133). Antwerp: Intersentia.

Šeparovic, Z. P. (1999). Victims of war crimes. In: J. van Dijk, R. van Kaam & J.-A. Wemmers (Eds), *Caring for crime victims: Proceedings of the 9th international world symposium on victimology* (pp. 271–286). Monsey: Criminal Justice Press.

Siegel, R. (1998). Transitional justice. A decade of debate and experience. *Human Rights Quarterly, 20*, 431–454.

Smeulers, A. (2006). Towards a criminology of international crimes. *Newsletter Criminology and International Crimes, 1*(1), 2–3 (www.supranationalcriminology.org).

Sykes, G., & Matza, D. (1957). Techniques of neutralization. *American Sociological Review, 22*, 664–670.

Vandeginste, S. (2003). Reparation. In: D. Bloomfield, T. Barnes & L. Huyse (Eds), *Reconciliation after violent conflict. A handbook* (pp. 145–162). Stockholm: International Idea.

Weitekamp, E., Parmentier, S., Vanspauwen, K., Valiñas, M., & Gerits, R. (2006). How to deal with mass victimization and gross human rights violations. A restorative justice approach. In: U. Ewald & K. Turkovic (Eds), *Large-scale victimization as a potential source of terrorist activities. Importance of regaining security in post-conflict societies* (pp. 217–241). Amsterdam: IOS Press.

Woolford, A. (2006). Making genocide unthinkable: Three guidelines for a critical criminology of genocide. *Critical Criminology, 14*, 87–106.

Other

Council of Europe, European Treaty Series (ETS). Strasbourg: Council of Europe (*www.coe.int*).

Norgaard Principles. (1990). Reproduced in the South African *Government Gazette* of 7 November 1990.

United Nations. (1951). Convention relating to the status of refugees (*www.unhchr.ch*).

United Nations, Security Council. (23 August 2004). *The rule of law and transitional justice in conflict and post-conflict societies.* Report of the Secretary-General to the Security Council, S/2004/616.

Van Boven Report. (1993). *Study concerning the right to restitution, compensation and rehabilitation for victims of gross violations of human rights and fundamental freedoms.* UN Doc. E/CN.4/Sub.2/1993/8.

Website

www.supranationalcriminology.org (Academic network on the criminology of international crimes, University of Maastricht, Amsterdam).

PART II:
HUMAN RIGHTS AND JUSTICE

HUMAN RIGHTS AND POLICE DISCRETION: JUSTICE SERVED OR DENIED?

Jack R. Greene

The safety of the people shall be their highest law

– Cicero, De legibus, 3.3

1. INTRODUCTION

It is perhaps a paradox that policing civil society is at its core the imposition of the state into private matters, but generally at the will of the populace. The police walk a delicate line in civil societies, as they at once represent the visible presence of the law and the capacity of the state for social regulation and the use of force, while at the same time drawing their legitimacy from the very populace they police – at least in democratic societies (see Bayley, 1975; Manning, 2003). This balance between state authority and individual or human rights is at times strained by police actions. Police discretion is conditioned by many factors imbedded in individual circumstances and how social "facts" are presented and perceived. However, discretion can be seen as a mechanism through which state rights and human rights are often reconciled, if reconciled at all. This is in part due to the observation that policing worldwide, as undertaken as a state function, both protects and restrains human behavior. The choices the police make in the exercise of

Crime and Human Rights
Sociology of Crime, Law and Deviance, Volume 9, 147–169
Copyright © 2007 by Elsevier Ltd.
All rights of reproduction in any form reserved
ISSN: 1521-6136/doi:10.1016/S1521-6136(07)09006-9

their discretion either sustain or detract from the human condition and consequently from human rights as broadly construed. When police act within the limits of their civic mandate, their *authority* not their *power* is exalted. When police power exceeds their granted authority their *legitimacy* is often called into question. Balancing civic legitimacy and state intervention often rests on the choices made by the police, who wield considerable discretion in choosing between the means and ends of law enforcement and of social regulation (Tyler, 2001; Tyler & Huo, 2002).

How the use of police discretion intersects with human rights is the broad subject of this chapter. Most particularly, the range of what are considered "coercive" police actions that most affect human rights is considered. Our consideration here first focuses on thinking about the police in their broader political context, most especially as their actions either facilitate or impede the exercise of individual and collective liberty. This chapter is most particularly focused on democratic policing, as policing in totalitarian regimes is largely based on *fear* rather than social or community consensus. Policing most clearly intersects with human rights by way of the various actions taken by the police that affect free and open human movement and discourse. The most easily observable tensions between policing and human rights are associated with police actions such as arrest and taking persons into custody, the taking of statements (and how those statements are taken) that may have criminal implications for those making the statements and who are in custody, and the use of physical restraint, extreme or lethal force. Each is briefly considered below, but first preceded by a discussion of the overarching rationale for policing and its implications for human rights. Also considered here is the facilitating role that police discretion can have on human rights.

Police discretion is taken here to involve the choices and decisions police make in pursuit of their institutional objectives and as found in their daily routine activities (see, Manning, 1977); that is, providing a safe and secure environment within which civil society functions. Discretion involves police "making law", or at least "making law come alive". Choices in the application of the criminal sanction begin first with police action typically taken in an interpersonal or community setting (see, Black, 1976). How those decisions shape the quality of justice and public perceptions of the police and the legal system are also considered.

In the end the safety of the people is indeed their highest end, and the police are charged with formally providing that safety. Of course, many segments of society contribute to the reality and perception of safety, but it is the police who are the most visible agents of social control, law enforcement, protection and restraint in civil society. It, therefore, follows that on matters of individual and community safety the public will ultimately judge the police. And, as a consequence, human rights as construed in democratic societies, particularly those rights associated with personal freedom, liberty, and justice before the law, will also be accordingly judged, most particularly in regard to police actions that support or diminish those rights.

2. POLICING LIBERTY AND HUMAN RIGHTS

Liberty is doing whatever the laws permit ... A government may be so constituted, as no man shall be compelled to do things to which the law does not oblige him, nor forced to abstain from things which the law permits. (Montesquieu (1748 [1777], *The Spirit of Laws*)

In democratic societies, and what are now called emerging democracies, civic concern seeks a balance between social regulation and social empowerment. Under democratic assumptions, the aims of government are to provide a climate that facilitates and encourages a wide spectrum of social actions and behaviors that conform to broad legal principles and structures that have shared meaning and which are generally consensually held. But even within the broad parameters of legal consensus there are actions and behaviors that challenge conventionally held beliefs, and that pose some "risk" or "threat" to the body politic. So, civil policing seeks to regulate human conduct within a legal consensus, which is likely in flux. The shift from liberal justice policies to neo-conservative ones, and counter shifts toward "local" or community-based policies in the span of 30 to 40 years attests to considerable flux in legal consensus (see, Stenson & Edwards, 2003). Moreover, even when such consensus is indeed in flux, policing must at least appear congruent with the broad legal principles governing that society, even when such actions ultimately limit social or individual liberty. This is the case if the institution of policing is to be civically accepted and supported.

Simply put, the status quo is always changing and, from the perspective of social control, informal and formal institutions are also adapting their influences on social behaviors, changing definitions of acceptable and unacceptable behavior, as well as methods to address what is deemed unacceptable. For the police this requires making adjustments to law enforcement and social regulation in light of shifting mores, norms and laws. For example, changes in attitudes toward social groups such as newly arrived immigrants can result in increased police surveillance of, or increased community hostility toward, these groups. Conversely, as public attitudes toward certain behaviors shifts so too will police actions and interventions that previously addressed socially accepted or rejected such behaviors. Enforcement of "vice" laws, for example, has clearly ebbed and flowed in the course of history, some behaviors criminalized and decriminalized over space and time, and enforcement practices adjusted accordingly.

Ultimately, however, the actions taken by police in democratic societies must support social (collective) and personal liberty. Freedoms of speech, assembly, religion and or the rights of minority interests, whether they are social or political, are seen as the essential elements of human rights, and indeed of the pursuit of liberty (see, Mill, 1869). So too are rights associated with standing before the law, as an accused and as a victim. That the police are the visible manifestation of the law in society they ultimately represent a liberating or repressive law by how they regulate social conduct.

Casting police decision-making and hence discretion as a matter of detracting from human rights has long standing in Western societies, where concern for government over regulation and indeed oppression has perhaps been most visible and vocal. Seeing police discretion used in support of human rights is of more recent origin (see, Alderson, 1979). Such a position interprets policing as fundamental to free and open discourse protecting the human rights of all to participate fully in society. As policing becomes more "pluralized", that is broadening the array of government agents and organizations that have a "policing" function while also incorporating a "policing" functionality and perspective from non-governmental actors (Jones & Newburn, 2006, pp. 1–11) assuring that human rights are a "first principle", not the last consequence is imperative. Use of police discretion in support of human rights can potentially represent a fundamental shift in emphasis in a 21st century characterized by a wider recognition of human rights deficit across the world. To do this however, policing will need to focus on how police discretion is currently exercised, and what forces constrain or detract from the police embracing fully a human rights agenda.

3. A NOTE ON NON-DEMOCRATIC POLICING AND POLICE DISCRETION

While not the subject of this chapter, policing occurs in many political contexts, some of which are not democratic. In such contexts policing as discussed here fails to be connected to human rights, except in their violation. Democratic policing first and foremost must conform to the rule of law. That is to say, for the police, the enforcement of the law is constrained by the legal process itself, and for the police to be seen as effective and lawful, their actions must conform to the spirit and letter of the law (Tyler, 2001). Police torture, the murder of the civil population by the police, police tolerance of internal sectarian violence and similar cultural and community atrocities do not conform with any notions of the "rule of law", thus placing the police in these circumstances outside legal and civic boundaries. Even in states where religious law is strictly enforced, the police draw their legitimacy from staying within the boundaries of legal and civic consensus on that law.

Totalitarian regimes that use the police to enforce eras of fear and violence escape the idea of a civil police altogether; that, is serving as a trusted civil guard, generally separated from the military, and concerned with domestic social regulation most associated with crime and social behavior, as well as civil order. In such regimes the rule of law is generally suspended or non-existent, and the populace ruled by fear of the police and indeed of the government itself. Under such circumstances "policing" is a hollow concept, rather replaced with the repressive maintenance of the political regime at all costs, including the human costs associated with the degradation of human rights. Police actions that participate in or condone sectarian violence, which have been widely reported in the media recently in the Middle East for example, dilute respect for civil processes and associate the police with social and religious terrorism. In such instances the government has failed, and the loss of human rights is most evident.

Regimes characterized by internal political violence, including the broad label of civil war, where the police support or directly use political violence, also escape any notion of policing viewed as a socially and legally mediating force in a society characterized by legal and social consensus. Where and when the police act in these ways, human rights are inevitably trampled, often in the extreme. In these circumstances there is neither a clear sense that the overarching government works, nor the executive branch within which the police function. Such governmental systems failures (including those of the police) move us from considerations of civil policing to considerations of political crime, genocide, and the abrogation of human rights, often in the name of repressive ideologies or regimes.

Perhaps more disturbing are police actions that routinely happen in places where the façade of civil process and democracy is represented as being present (see, Chevigny, 1995). Where the police are lawless, there is no law, and, of consequence, no civil or human rights. And in regimes and at times where the police act in ways that introduce political and social violence, or condone it on the part of others, then "policing" as it is considered here does not exist. Democratic policing requires lawfulness, and civic acceptance of the police as a mechanism of social regulation. Having said this, even within civil societies, characterized as democratic, the police must be vigilant to support and not detract from human rights.

The United Nations Universal Declaration of Human Rights (1948) contains some 30 Articles that outline the breath and scope of human rights accorded all peoples. In its Preamble the Declaration calls for "... recognition of the inherent dignity and the equal and inalienable rights of all members of the human family is the foundation of freedom, justice and peace in society". In organizing the 30 Articles that elaborate these human rights, the United Nations specifically calls out several that are police or justice system focused. Of most attention here is Article 29, Section 2,

> In the exercise of his rights and freedoms, everyone shall be subject only to such limitations as are determined by law solely for the purpose of securing due recognition and respect for the rights and freedoms of others and of meeting the just requirements of morality, public order and the general welfare in a democratic society.

Human rights then are those that are supported by duly constituted governments that regulate human conduct in ways that conforms to the rule of law, and which support the dignity and social inclusion of all. The United Nations Universal Declaration of Human Rights focuses some 10 of its Articles[1] on matters pertaining to personal security and recognition before the law. These 10 UN Articles have substantial implication for how the police function in civil society. Moreover, enacting a style of policing which is consonant with the UN Declaration on Human Rights requires that police use their discretion to uphold the moral and legal dignity of all. In point of fact most Western and indeed many other countries have adopted similar constitutions or provisions that elevate human rights as a national ideal and proscription. Whether the rhetoric and the reality correspond in many parts of the world remains an open question.

4. POLICE DISCRETION AND HUMAN RIGHTS

> For the middle class, the police protect property, give directions and help old ladies. For the urban poor, the police are those who arrest you. (Michael Harrington, *The Other America*, 1962)

The police, of necessity, are given broad powers to regulate human conduct. In its variation in application the discretion given to the police is at once expected and abhorred. Discretion is expected (indeed well accepted) if the variation works in the favor of the social or legal norms the police enforce. And, of course police discretion is also well accepted by the individual if the outcome of its application is favorable to that individual. Discretion is abhorred and often challenged to the extent that it produces variations in outcomes for individuals who are engaged in similar behaviors, and, consequently is seen as biased. This is especially the case when the outcomes appear to vary by group status not the behaviors in question.

In either case (accepted or decried) the police are granted leeway in making legal decisions about the imposition of the criminal sanction. "Black Letter Law" or law as written does not clearly govern the interactions of police and community members, except in some *ex post facto* way. Rather, a "law in action" model most aptly describes such interactions; the law is taken into consideration among many social and cultural variables and values arising from the interactions themselves, including but not restricted to their legal severity (see, Black, 1980). Indeed police discretion is often seen as the product of a complex interaction of legal and extra-legal factors that shape legal outcomes. More recently use of such discretion is also tied to major shifts in justice system philosophies, particularly in the West (see, McLaughlin & Murji, 2001).

In its use police discretion has at times and in places been seen as a tool of elite politics used mainly for the surveillance of the underclass. Such assessments of the police have considerable support in social history, both historically and in contemporary society. From their onset the police in Britain and later in the US, and other Western societies were suspect (Miller, 1977). In the Americas, particularly in the central and southern regions – but also in the US and North America, the police have been associated with considerable state violence and the active deprivation of human rights. Moreover, private vengeance in the Americas has often been beyond the control of the police, leading to inter-group hostility and violence. As Chevigny concludes:

> The comparison has shown a correlation between the sociopolitical structure of the places and the level of violence by the police; the departments represent and reproduce the relations in the social order. Where, for example, the order is one in which respect for rights is weak and private vengeance is not well controlled, the police tend to act with arbitrary violence. (Chevigny, 1995, p. 249)

So, police exercise discretion, which has implications for public and private violence as well as respect for civil and human rights. Where social norms devalue respect for rights, so too are police actions likely to also devalue these rights. Understanding police exercise of discretion requires placing the police in the social and political contexts within which they function. Even when the police are placed in political and social milieus that support human rights it does not follow that the police will embrace a human rights facilitating role. Rather, given the nature of crime control, much effort to date even within democracies, is focused on preventing police violations of human rights, rather than having the police embrace a proactive human rights agenda.

5. WHAT DOES IT MEAN – USE OF POLICE DISCRETION IN SUPPORT OF HUMAN RIGHTS?

A central feature of the modern state according to Marx is the state's monopoly over the legitimate use of force (see, Avineri, 1968). Moreover, how the citizens perceive the state's exercise of force conditions the legitimacy citizens accord the state. As the police are one of two visible arms of state exercise of force (the military being the other), how the police exercise this capacity so too conditions the legitimacy accorded the police, and ultimately the legal system as well.

Acknowledging that the police exercise considerable discretion in interpreting social facts and then choosing among criminal sanctions does not mean that such decisional latitude will support or even recognize human rights, however. In fact, there is considerable historic and contemporary evidence that police discretion has more often represented violations of human rights, as we commonly understand them. Such violations are often consistent with local mores, customs and indeed law; supporting an argument that the police appear first bound by local cultural and social constructions and then by legal constructions. Human Rights Watch issued its World Report 2007, outlining the continued trampling of human rights in virtually all regions of the world. Much of the criticism involves failure of governments to protect their people, or recent immigrants, from internally generated violence – something that the police are expected to in part address. Historically, in many parts of the world policing has been shaped by the social and legal cultures of many societies. Preserving law and order within any of these societies has more often been associated with maintaining the status quo, even when doing so depreciated the value of human rights. Religious intolerance, cast distinctions, the treatment of recent immigrants or asylum seekers, and attitudes toward women and children has shaped police discretion in ways that has not supported human rights ideals. Police condoning sectarian violence, hate crimes directed toward "out groups" including recent immigrants or those seeking relief from political oppression or war, the trade of women and children into bondage for labor or the sex trade, the mutilation of young girls and women, and even murder associated with maintaining family honor, are all illustrations of behaviors that police choose to tacitly (and at times overtly) support these human rights violations in the use of their discretion (see, Human Rights Watch, World Report issues), most particularly in failing to intervene.

In function civil policing carries with it an expectation that human rights violations by the police will be controlled. Moreover, in addition to controlling their own actions and behaviors, civil police are also expected to provide safety and security for the community – thereby preventing human rights violations of others as well. So the proscription for civil policing is to prevent harm from others, while doing no harm in the exercise of police discretion. To realize such a reorientation of civil policing to affirm and support human rights requires a brief examination of the problem areas where policing worldwide appears to fail on matters of assuring human rights. The areas briefly considered below included police arrest practices, the taking of statements from those in custody and the use of lethal force.

5.1. Arrests and Custody

Police taking persons into custody, usually through a process of arrest, represents state actions that most directly confront notions of individual sovereignty and liberty. Arrest by the police is the most direct confrontation to liberty and hence to human rights. In its Universal Declaration of Human Rights (1948) the United Nations specifically enjoined governments from depriving people of their liberty and security, subjecting them to torture or cruel treatment, denying them equal recognition before the law, or subjecting them to arbitrary arrest (Articles 3, 5, 6, and 9). Such proscription is foremost focused on the actions of the police who often are the state's representatives engaged in the arrest and detention of individuals.

The arrest and detention of people by the police often without charges or legal oversight has been a continuing problem worldwide. Detention arrests made by the police have often been associated with repressing political speech or government protest (see, Human Rights Watch, 2007; Amnesty International, 2007). Such detentions call into question, police use of their legal discretion to arrest for behaviors, or attitudes that are not unlawful, and which are seen as protected human rights. In the first three weeks of 2007 Amnesty International issued calls for urgent action against police detention arrests and abductions in Thailand, Syria, Tunisia, Iran, Greece, Egypt, and the USA (Guantanamo) (Amnesty International, 2007, www.amnesty.org).

Such calls in the previous month (Amnesty International, 2006) included
Belgium, Yemen, Pakistan, the Congo, and Mexico. The concern raised by
Amnesty International and other human rights organizations often calls for
inquiry into police arbitrary arrest, the detention of political dissidents, and
incommunicado detentions including those made by the USA as part of its
conflict with Iraq and Afghanistan. In South America police have also been
associated with large-scale arrest, detention and purges of individuals in
Argentina, Brazil, and Peru for example (see, Chevigny, 1995, for example).
And of course, police enforced arrests and detention of large numbers of
people at times of political upheaval in Southeast Asia, the Balkans, parts of
Africa, and the Middle East in both distant and contemporary history are
widely recorded (Human Rights Watch, 2007). Police use of their arrest and
discretion powers to systematically purge unpopular political dissent, or
groups marginalized on the basis of religious or social beliefs are clear and
flagrant violations of human rights. But such practices can also occur within
countries that emphasize their commitment to civil and human rights. While
aggregate statistics do not exist across or even within cities, lawsuits settled for
false arrest and imprisonment in the US are thought to be staggering. Most
recently, in the US, 33 of the 50 US states have active litigation stemming
from concerns with racial profiling (www.racialprofilinganalysis.neu.edu),
most commonly defined as police stopping persons on the basis of their
membership in racial groupings, rather than as a result of probable cause to
believe that these persons committed a crime. Such concerns have included
police traffic stops and arrests as well as profiling now associated with
terrorism. This has resulted in a call for "bias-free policing" by the
International Association of Chiefs of Police (2006), headquartered in the US.

When the police exercise their discretion to deprive persons of their liberty
they do so within the context of human rights. Balancing the rights of the
state for the legitimate exercise of authority with the rights of individuals
suspected of criminal or other illegal behaviors, frames the question of
police arrest as a matter of human rights. Such a recognition calls for police
restraint in the use of arrest where appropriate.

5.2. Interrogations and the Taking of Criminal Statements

Police actions that are focused on in-custody interrogations or the taking of
criminal statements from suspected offenders create an important need to
assure that human rights are upheld in these instances as well. This has
become even more pronounced in a "security conscious" world. UN and

other conventions prohibit the use of torture on those detained and being questioned by the police.

In the US preventing the use of police force to coerce confessions from those in police custody has been a continuing struggle, but one largely accomplished. Nonetheless, Chevigny suggests that the use of tasers or stun guns by the police in field settings are "sometimes used to inflict pain" (1995, p. 133), rather than just to subdue suspects, thereby raising the specter of human rights violations. As the world witnessed the beating of Rodney King by the Los Angeles police it was clear that the police were punishing a person they could control. Such violations have occurred in several US cities, generally associated with the get tough, "zero tolerance" policies of large cities like New York.

In Central and South America, Chevigny (1995) documented considerable use of torture routinely applied in police in-custody interrogations. Amnesty International in a survey conducted in 2000 indicated that it uncovered reports of torture in more than 150 countries (www.amnestyusa/org/stoptorture). "In more than 70, they were widespread or persistent and in more than 80 countries, people reportedly died as a result".

Most recently US conduct of a war in Iraq revealed military police misconduct and torture at two facilities where such behaviors were widely reported – Abu Ghraib and Guantanamo. In fact, as the world, and most particularly the US, has moved from providing safety to the "war on terrorism" concern with international conventions overseeing torture and the ill treatment of detainees has surfaced with increasing regularity. As Amnesty International reports:

> The USA ratified the International Covenant on Civil and Political Rights in 1992 under the first President Bush and the Convention against Torture in 1994 under President Clinton. To each treaty, the US attached a number of conditions, including that it considered itself bound by the prohibition on cruel, inhuman or degrading treatment only to the extent that it matched existing US law. During at least the first four years of "war on terror" detentions, Justice Department lawyers took the position that because of these reservations the USA had no treaty obligation on cruel, inhuman or degrading treatment with respect to foreign nationals held in US custody overseas (including Guantánamo). (2006, p. 1)

Such reports of police mistreatment of persons in their custody have been filed for countries in Africa, South America and Asia. And, as governmental concern for addressing domestic and international terrorism has risen across the world, so too have complaints about those taken into government custody, typically by the police.

5.3. Use of Force and Physical Restraint

At its core policing is the lawful application of coercion or force in civil society (Bittner, 1970). Policing is the only civil occupation charged with the use of state force in the regulation of the public, and as such the coercive powers of the police are always a bit suspect in democratic societies. Police use of force is continually at the core of concern with how "out groups", often defined by race and ethnicity, are treated. In democratic societies police use of force often involves a question of the proportionality of police response between minority and majority communities. Where the police are seen as acting within the restraint of the law, their institutional legitimacy is enhanced. All too often, however, police abuse of force occurs in inter-actions with marginalized or disenfranchised communities where tensions between the police and the public are perhaps the greatest.

Police use of lethal force has been the subject of considerable inquiry. In the Western world this has often been cast as excessive use of force by the police, while in parts of South America, Asia, and Africa, police wholesale use of lethal force has been documented in its impact on these societies. Chevigny (1995) reviews literature from Brazil, Argentina, and in Mexico City and documents persistent patterns of police use of lethal force – police killings – at astounding levels. China's televised use of police and military force against unarmed civilians in Tiananmen Square in 1989 was well documented and graphic. Studies of police use of excessive force in Northern Ireland (Amnesty International, 1988; Ellison & Smyth, 2000), the US (Skolnick & Fyfe, 1993), Brazil, Argentina and Mexico City (Chevigny, 1995), among many, continue to call police use of lethal force into question. As a matter of human rights, this may be the area of greatest concern in the international community.

What structures police use of discretion for positive or negative purposes? Research on the police has suggested that the structures, cultures and work environments of the police have a profound impact on police use of discretion. If we are to broaden police awareness of their role in facilitating and supporting human rights, then we should look to those forces that ultimately have great impact on police use of discretion.

6. POLICE CULTURE AND ORGANIZATION AS IMPEDIMENTS TO SUPPORTING HUMAN RIGHTS

There are many discussions about why the police fail to fully embrace human rights in the exercise of their discretion. For many years the structures and cultures of police organizations, as well as the nature of police work have been associated with an insular model of policing that separates the police from the public, often sustaining negative public interactions and police use of violence (see, Skolnick, 1994; Skolnick & Fyfe, 1993). For example, Skolnick (1994) suggested that the police develop a "working personality", which is shaped by the danger that they may have to encounter, the secrecy often associated with police operations and investigations and the efficiencies demanded of the police by the public.

Policing is also described as an occupation that distances itself from the body politic as a way of avoiding the paradoxes it often confronts (Center for Research on Crime and Justice, 1975). That is to say, as the police have often come from the very classes they most directly police (lower and working class), creating distance between their class interests and those often defined by political elites has resulted in police adoption of the trappings of "legal formalism" and "professionalism", which enable the police to distance themselves, socially and ideologically, from those policed.

Police culture also been suggested as negatively influencing police views of the public, and has been studied worldwide. What is perhaps most interesting are the similarities in police cultures that appear to exist over time and places. And, while police culture is indeed not monolithic, it exhibits several common features. Reiner (1992, pp. 111–129) identified several features of police culture, which include cynicism, machismo and often-racist attitudes, strong within group solidarity among officers, and support for conservative politics. These findings have been replicated in the US and elsewhere, and while most agree that there are multiple cultures in policing stemming from rank (Reuss-Ianni, 1983), level of organization (Manning, 1989), or functional work assignment (Chan, 1992), there is considerable agreement that the work cultures of the police do not evenly support democratic values.

Such cultural underpinnings can also be shaped by the police organization, either reinforcing or negating the effects of culture. In his assessment of policing in the Americas, for example, Chevigny suggests that:

> Within the bounds of the politics of the city, the police can, to choose the extremes, emphasize regularity and law or act as delegated vigilantes. The characteristics of departments can encourage the use of violence; thus, for example, departments that represent themselves as similar to military forces, as the military police in Sao Paulo and the Los Angeles police have done, will use violence as an instrument of control much more than police who represent themselves clearly as part of civil government. (1995, p. 250)

Today there is an increasing adoption of several aspects of military organization by the police. Such a militarization of the police, perhaps, offers a more cynical posture in the discussion of policing for human rights. The rise of paramilitary teams, such as Special Weapons and Tactics Units (SWAT), in police agencies has often led to the rhetoric and practices of military operations within civil policing circles. For example, Kraska and Kappler (1997) suggest that the rapid rise of military-like units in civil policing in the US, as well as their expansion of activities, has led to a normalization of such units within civil policing. Such normalization they argue postures civil policing and the problems they address as military problems and responses. Andreas and Nadelmann (2006, p. 225) suggest that in a post September 11, 2001 world there is increased international criminalization of transnational activity, and that as a result, "[t]he policing face of the state is becoming more and more prominently displayed, with its gaze extending beyond national borders". Such extended international criminalization in their view is increasingly homogenizing police cultures across the world.

Human rights in a "security conscious" and "risk adverse" world have become a central issue for concern in the 21st century. As governments have embraced the ideology and practices of "war on terrorism", concern for civil and human rights violations has concomitantly increased. Increased concern for security in "risk society" (Beck, 1992) continues to fuel more conservative justice policies (Garland, 2001) including the discretionary practices of the police. Such conservatism, it might be argued, erodes police concern for human rights.

The nature of police work also shapes police attitudes and values as well. In many ways the police develop "perceptual shorthand", which are cautious and conservative in nature and, which anticipate danger and potential violence. Support from fellow officers, a must in a dangerous world, also helps to maintain police solidarity. Public questioning of police behaviors and their aggregate effectiveness also shapes police attitudes and beliefs about the level of support they receive from the public. Taken together, such work-based influences are considerable on policing, often further isolating the police from the public.

Changes in police discretion that support human rights as a first principle will have to confront the ideologies, cultures, structures, and working environments of the police. Evidence suggests that these factors shape the police officers "working personalities", including how decisions and discretionary choices are made. Without attention to what might be considered the fundamental drivers of police decision-making, outside the criminal law, refocusing the police as facilitating human rights will likely be difficult.

7. CIVIL POLICING RECONSIDERED

A civilization is to be judged by its treatment of minorities. (Mohandas K. Gandhi, 1993)

Civil policing in democratic societies has continually struggled with balancing institutional effectiveness with legitimacy. Moreover, policing worldwide has often involved oversight of minority interests in the face of majority concerns or demands. How the police respect minority interests is of great concern in democratic societies and those who are evolving toward democratic processes.

In recent years the Western World has come under great fear of terrorism. Since September 11, 2001 democratic policing throughout the world has faced serious challenges, the most significant of which is balancing civic concern with "security" with maintaining institutional legitimacy. Under reaction to security concerns poses risk for the police and the community. As all terrorism is "local" the police cannot legitimately distance themselves from such civic concern (see, Riley, Treverton, Wilson, & Davis, 2005).

By contrast, some of the approach to the new security world order can be cast as "moral panic" (Cohen, 1972), where the overreach of the police fuels public concern for individual liberty and the accountability of the state. The community will generally not condone a lackluster police response to terrorism, nor will an over zealous approach to terrorism be condoned either.

The world's focus on terrorism casts the police in an intrusive intelligence-gathering role that potentially erodes their civic support. Local police "spying" on the citizenry is fraught with concern and complaint (see, Greene, unpublished). Essentially policing at the local level is most seen as legitimate when it responds to local crime, preventing or mitigating such behavior. Under such norms, social agreement on criminal behavior (generally cast) has more civic consensus than does agreement on what the precursors of terrorism might be. Absent such agreement, the police must intrude into social behaviors and attempt to address what might be considered the symbols of potential terrorism often leading to charges of violations of human rights.

Reorienting the police toward a human rights perspective will require a multi-faceted approach involving selection, training, evaluation and daily accountability through supervision, and connection with the broader communal goals of society. Such an approach is possible if we learn from the large scale "experiment" that has been associated with community policing and its derivatives being conducted for nearly 20 years around the world.

8. USING POLICE DISCRETION TO SUPPORT HUMAN RIGHTS: AN ALTERNATIVE PERSPECTIVE

Of course the converse of what has been previously argued here is equally the case. That is, the police in function, role and outcome can indeed be organized to support and further human rights by using their discretion in ways that embrace human rights as a first principle. As a first principle, policing would embrace the philosophy and practice of maintaining respect for individual dignity and equality before the law. Decision- and policy-making organized in such a manner could provide a broad agenda for the police in democratic societies; that is, how to increase human capital, while maintaining social order and respect for the law. Recent approaches to reorganize policing around community-focused outcomes might provide an organizing model for "human-rights" oriented policing in the future.

While the coercive role of policing remains even in democratic societies, it does not follow that the police operate only in a coercive posture. The argument that the police at their core are a state-legitimized tool for the use of force ignores the broader legitimacy that they draw from their communities expectations about what the police will and will not do (see, Tyler & Huo, 2002).

8.1. Community Policing

In fact, through the 1990s and into the 21st century policing in many countries embraced philosophies, principles and practices that can actually further human dignity and human rights. These philosophies, practices, and programs are grouped under the broad heading of "community policing". While community policing has had "mixed results" in relation to its impact on crime and social disorder in the US (see, Roth, 2000; Roth, Roehl, & Johnson, 2004), it has had great import for police legitimacy as its programs have been especially focused on improving the transparency of police decisions and actions. Such transparency helps to improve public acceptance of the police thereby increasing their institutional legitimacy. As suggested by Mastrofski and Greene (1993, p. 81), at least four subsystems of police accountability are potentially affected in the adoption of a community policing organizational and delivery model. First, legal systems (civil, criminal, and administrative) and their institutions are potentially affected by a COP model in that emphasis on civil and human rights comports well with the legal principles promulgated by such systems. Rather than having an adversarial relationship (control through oversight) with the police, a shift toward COP emphasizing human rights can facilitate a more complementary oversight process, fraught with less conflict and distrust. Second, the internal policies, rules, regulations and the like of police agencies can also be shaped by a COP emphasis that stresses human rights, in that, congruence among the goals and practices of the police agency itself is likely to reduce role conflict for officers. Often officers must choose a role, either emphasizing community contact, problem solving or strict law enforcement. And, while each as a place in modern-day policing, the historical choices often pitted the police organization and its personnel (law enforcement focus) against the public (order maintenance focus). Third, workgroups within the police as well as those external to police agencies are potentially affected by a shift to the philosophy and practices of community policing. Workgroups shape a considerable amount of police behavior; their refocusing on broader social service and human rights norms can go a long way in setting an internal culture that supports the incubation of such a change in the ends of policing (see, Rosenbaum & Wilkinson, 2004). Moreover, external groups seeking police professionalism and broader standards of "good practice" for policing can draw from the principles and practices of COP to help assure transparency and lawfulness of police decisions and actions. Fourth, and perhaps the source of the prior three subsystems is community tolerance of the police and acceptance of policing as a legitimate source of social control. Of course this is the source of police rightful authority in the first instance, and links clearly with democratic principles and the uplifting of human rights.

Under the auspices of community and problem-oriented policing, the police have come to embrace community input and see themselves not only as the purveyor of law, but also as a catalyst for social change that reduces violence and social disorder problems in discrete community settings. Community and problem oriented policing tacitly embrace a communitarian view of social life (see, Etzioni, 1993). That is to say policing that has a community or problem focus often includes a community voice helping to shape the dimension of the problem, as well as assessing the appropriateness of the police response.

Community and problem oriented policing came about in the US and UK first largely in response to two complaints: police inefficiency and police unlawfulness. The police were adrift from their constituent, and in separating from the community lost institutional legitimacy. Community and problem oriented policing were advanced in part to overcome the general feeling that police actions had "no effect", and when they did they were at considerable variance from community standards of lawfulness, fairness and decency (see, Greene, 2000). Despite the potential application of community policing to a broadened police role that explicitly supports human rights, the question can be asked: "Is community policing compatible with the Rule of Law?" (see, Mastrofski & Greene, 1993). We see no inherent conflicts between community policing and the rule of law, but questions remain about how much the community can be involved in setting police standards of practice, and how community influence in policy and decision-making can be structured. To be sure, at one extreme community policing could devolve into vigilantism when majority community norms seek the repression of minority interests. But, opening the police to a broader communication with the community, other social service agencies and governmental agencies that the police have heretofore avoided can greatly enhance police horizontal integration, thereby improving service (see, Greene, unpublished).

Perhaps one question that can be raised in relationship to policing and human rights is whether the police in adopting a human rights perspective (through a COP orientation) become "soft on crime?" Much of the latter half of the 20th century has shifted the justice apparatus of many western nations toward more and more conservative stances regarding individual behavior and justice system practices. Since the late 1980s, policing in Western societies has been continually seen as strengthening its role as a repressive agent of social control, and part of a larger process of class segregation that results in the police focusing their efforts on the underclass and out-groups. Such a model of the justice system has been exported throughout the world, reinforced by the "global war on terrorism".

David Garland (2001) suggested that most especially in the US, England, and Australia a "culture of control" has emerged via the government, legislators and supported by a public sense and fear of crime and insecurity. Justice system philosophies and practices have shifted from a progressive and liberally focused crime control agenda found principally in the first half of the 20th century to justice philosophies and practices that embraced populist sensibilities, have become considerably more punitive (less proportionate) in orientation, have abandoned concepts imbedded in the "welfare-state", rather adopting neo-conservative ideologies emphasizing, and what Garland calls "supply-side" criminology (2001, p. 129), "shifting risks, redistributing costs, and creating disincentives". Collectively such changes have resulted in a broad "get tough" emphasis at all stages of the justice process.

The COP and POP movements worldwide can, perhaps, be cast as interventions designed to re-legitimize the police in the face of public criticism and skepticism of police commitment to constitutional governance, the rule of law and human rights. This is not to argue that community policing is a panacea for police violation of human rights. Studies of community policing in other parts of the world (see, Brogden & Nijhar, 2005), as part of the global movement that COP now represents, also reveal significant short-comings in application and effect. Accountability processes will need to be in place and made visible and accessible to the public. However, models of criminal justice that are now emerging as "community centered", potentially return civil law enforcement to a more liberalized and less punitive model than currently exists (McLaughlin & Murji, 2001). Should this occur it is likely that there will be greater civil and cultural pressure for the police to embrace a model of civil law enforcement that embraces human rights.

8.2. An Illustration: Family and Domestic Violence

One illustration of how police can support and enable human rights is visible in efforts to stem family and domestic violence. The Council of Europe, for example, has identified such violence as a violation of human rights. In the "Blueprint of the Council of Europe Campaign to Combat Violence against Women, including Domestic Violence" (Task Force to Combat Violence Against Women, 2006, p. 1) the Council indicates:

> Violence against women is a violation of human rights, the very nature of which deprives women of their ability to enjoy fundamental freedoms. It often leaves women vulnerable to further abuse and is a major obstacle to overcoming inequality between women and men in society. Violence against women is a detriment to peace, security and democracy in Europe.

Such a recognition led to the Council's Campaign, which aims to (1) increase awareness that such violence is a human rights violation, (2) build the political will of member states to provide adequate resources (including police interventions) to address violence against women, and (3) develop additional legislation addressing such violence. Such measures have been extended into other forms of family violence including elder and child abuse.

These interventions typically focus on raising awareness as a process to affect the use of discretion by the police and other service providers. Whereas in many cultures and at many times violence within the family has been overlooked by the police, in favor of families settling their own disputes or in keeping with cultural norms that often disfavor women, children or elders, now casting such violations as matters of human rights creates obligations for police to use their discretion in light of broader human rights standards. In the case of violence against women and children such shifts in police understandings, priorities and commitment to human rights issues have taken root in many western countries. Amnesty International in its Report for 2006 calls for increased protection for women, particularly in intimate settings (2007). They

> ... emphasized the duty of governments to intervene to adequately protect, respect, promote and fulfill women's human rights. [Amnesty International] produced reports documenting domestic violence in a number of countries including Afghanistan, Guatemala, Gulf Cooperation Council countries, India, Iraq, Israel and the Occupied Territories, Nigeria, the Russian Federation, Spain and Sweden. Reports were also issued on the impact of guns on women's lives, and on women, violence and health.

Police adoption of a response to the battering of women, children, and elders, as well as the sale of women and children in to forced labor or the sex industry, can indeed become a model of human rights policing envisioned here. Adoption of such philosophies and practices is also consistent with numerous conventions that prohibit such behavior throughout the world.

9. A CONCLUDING NOTE

This paper has briefly examined the nexus of the exercise of police discretion with human rights. This is a complicated intersection even in democratic societies because the police do indeed exercise considerable latitude in regulating human conduct. Calls for "zero-tolerance" policing made in the US and elsewhere have often demonstrated that such approaches produce as many problems as they solve, most particularly in the human right arena. Incidents associated with "zero tolerance" suggest that the social and institutional legitimacy of the police suffers under such approaches, particularly in disaffected communities, where ironically the police need the support of the community, perhaps the most.

Some form of community-oriented policing has been proffered here as a medium for improving police and community interactions and hence the institutional legitimacy of the police. Of course such legitimacy attained through community or other forms of policing must include concern for supporting human rights. And it is not argued here that community policing is the panacea for improving human rights through police decision-making. In fact there are many who see community policing as but a façade constructed by the police to mystify their larger repressive role on society.

Nonetheless, there is some evidence that experience with forms of community-oriented policing has improved relations between the police and minority communities, often those whose civil and human rights are most fragile and vulnerable. Through experimentation in community and related forms of policing the police have increased their horizontal integration into local communities, local government structures and with the private sector. Much of this is attributable to the emphasis on building partnerships for crime prevention. Such horizontal integration has resulted in the police being better linked with other sectors of local government, the private sector and with community agencies, each of which has an interest and capacity for preventing crime, but within the rule of law. This foundation might become an important platform for expanding the police role and use of discretion in supporting human rights.

NOTE

1. Articles 3 through 5 focus on rights associated with personal security including arrest situations, and Articles 6 through 12 focus on rights associated with due process before the law.

REFERENCES

Alderson, J. (1979). *Policing freedom*. Plymouth, UK: Macdonald and Evans.

Amnesty International. (1988). *United Kingdom: Northern Ireland: Killing by security forces and "supergrass" trials*. London: Amnesty International.

Amnesty International. (2006). *United States of America. Five years on "the dark side" – A look back at "war on terror" detentions*. London: Amnesty International.

Amnesty International. (2007). *Amnesty international report 2006 – The state of the world's human rights*. London: Amnesty International.

Andreas, P., & Nadelmann, E. (2006). *Policing the globe: Criminalization and crime control in international relations*. Oxford: Oxford University Press.

Avineri, S. (1968). *The social and political thought of Karl Marx*. Cambridge: Cambridge University Press.

Bayley, D. H. (1975). The police and political development in Europe. In: Ch. Tilly (Ed.), *The formation of nation states in Western Europe* (pp. 328–379). Princeton, NJ: Princeton University Press.

Beck, U. (1992). *Risk society*. Translated by Mark Ritter. London: Sage.

Bittner, E. (1970). *The functions of police in modern society*. Washington, DC: US Government Printing Office.

Black, D. (1976). *The behavior of law*. New York: Academic Press.

Black, D. (1980). *Manners and customs of the police*. New York: Academic Press.

Brogden, M., & Nijhar, P. (2005). *Community policing: National and international models and approaches*. Devon, UK: Willan Publishing.

Center for Research on Crime and Justice. (1975). *The iron fist and the velvet glove: An analysis of the US police*. Berkeley, CA: Center for Research on Criminal Justice.

Chan, M. (1992). *Policing in a multi-cultural society: A study of the New South Wales police.* Final Report to the New South Wales Police Service. Sydney: New South Wales Police Service.

Chevigny, P. (1995). *Edge of the knife: Police violence in the Americas.* New York: The New Press.

Cohen, S. (1972). *Folk devils and moral panics.* London: Mac Gibbon and Kee.

Ellison, G., & Smyth, J. (2000). *The crowned harp: Policing Northern Ireland.* London: Hurst.

Etzioni, A. (1993). *The spirit of community: Rights, responsibilities and the communitarian agenda.* New York: Crown Publishers, Inc.

Gandhi, M. K. (1993). *An autobiography: The story of my experiments with truth* (Trans.). Boston: Beacon Press.

Garland, D. (2001). *The culture of control: Crime and social order in contemporary society.* Oxford: Oxford University Press.

Greene, J. R. (2000). Community policing in America: Changing the nature, structure and function of the police. *Criminal justice 2000* (Vol. 2, pp. 299–370). Washington, DC: National Institute of Justice, US Department of Justice.

Greene, J. R. (unpublished). Community policing and terrorism: Problems and prospects for local community security. In: B. Forst, J. R. Greene & J. Lynch (Eds), *Security and justice in the homeland: Criminologists on terrorism.*

Harrington, M. (1962). *The other America: Poverty in the United States.* New York: Macmillan.

Human Rights Watch. (2007). *World report 2006.* New York: Human Rights Watch.

International Association of Chiefs of Police. (2006). *Protecting civil rights: A leadership guide for state, local, and tribal law enforcement.* Gaitherburg, MD: International Association of Chiefs of Police.

Jones, T., & Newburn, T. (Eds). (2006). *Plural policing: A comparative perspective.* New York: Routledge.

Kraska, P. B., & Kappler, V. E. (1997). Militarizing American police: The rise and normalization of paramilitary units. Reprinted. In: V. E. Kappler (Ed.), *The police and society: Touchstone readings* (pp. 463–480). Prospect Heights, IL: Waveland Press.

Manning, P. K. (1977). *Police work: The social organization of policing.* Cambridge, MA: MIT Press.

Manning, P. K. (1989). Occupational culture. In: W. G. Bailey (Ed.), *The encyclopedia of police science* (pp. 472–475). New York: Garland.

Manning, P. K. (2003). *Policing contingencies.* Chicago, IL: University of Chicago Press.

Mastrofski, S. D., & Greene, J. R. (1993). Community policing and the rule of law. In: D. Weisburd & C. Uchida (Eds), *Police innovation and control of the police* (pp. 80–102). New York: Springer Verlag.

McLaughlin, E., & Murji, K. (2001). Lost connections and new directions: Neo-liberalism, new public managerialism, and the 'modernization' of the British police. In: K. Stenson & R. Sullivan (Eds), *Crime, risk and justice: The politics of crime control in liberal democracies* (pp. 104–121). Devon, UK: Willan Publishing.

Mill, J. S. (1869). *On Liberty.* London: Longman, Robert and Green.

Miller, W. (1977). *Cops and bobbies: Police authority in New York and London, 1830–1870.* Chicago: University of Chicago Press.

Montesquieu. (1748[1777]). In: T. Nugent (Trans.), *The Spirit of the Laws* (Vol. 1). London: J. Nourse.

Reiner, R. (1992). *The politics of the police* (2nd ed.). Hemel Hempstead: Harvester Wheatsheaf.

Reuss-Ianni, E. (1983). *Two Cultures of Policing: Street Cops and Management Cops.* Brunswick, NJ: Transaction Publishers.

Riley, K. J., Treverton, G. F., Wilson, J. M., & Davis, L. M. (2005). *State and local intelligence in the war on terrorism.* Santa Monica, CA: Rand.

Rosenbaum, D., & Wilkinson, D. (2004). Can police adapt? Tracking the effects of organizational reform over six years. In: W. G. Skogan (Ed.), *Community policing: Can it work?* (pp. 79–108). Belmont, CA: Thompson/Wadsworth.

Roth, J. A. (Ed.) (2000). *National evaluation of the COPS program – Title 1 of the 1994 crime Act.* Washington, DC: National Institute of Justice, US Department of Justice.

Roth, J. A., Roehl, J., & Johnson, C. C. (2004). Trends in community policing. In: W. G. Skogan (Ed.), *Community policing: Can it work?* (pp. 3–29). Belmont, CA: Thompson/Wadsworth.

Skolnick, J. (1994). *Justice without trial: Law enforcement in a democratic society* (3rd ed.). New York: Macmillan.

Skolnick, J., & Fyfe, J. J. (1993). *Above the law; Police and the excessive use of force.* New York: Free Press.

Stenson, K., & Edwards, A. (2003). Crime control and liberal government: The 'Third Way' and the return to the local. In: K. Stenson & R. R. Sullivan (Eds), *Crime, risk and justice: The politics of crime control in liberal democracies* (pp. 68–86). Devon, UK: Willan Publishing.

Task Force to Combat Violence Against Women. (2006). *Blueprint of the council of Europe campaign to combat violence against women, including domestic violence* (Report number (EG-TFT). 8, rev. 3). Strasbourg: Council of Europe.

Tyler, T. (2001). Public trust and confidence in legal authorities: What do majority and minority group members want from the law and legal institutions? *Behavioral Sciences and the Law, 19,* 215–235.

Tyler, T., & Huo, Y. J. (2002). *Trust in the law: Encouraging public cooperation with the police and courts.* New York: Russell Sage Foundation.

RESTORATIVE JUSTICE AND HUMAN RIGHTS

Ann Skelton

1. INTRODUCTION

1.1. The Search for a Definition of Restorative Justice

Defining restorative justice has proved to be a challenge for restorative justice writers. This is partly because the concept is a contested one, and partly because restorative justice writers prefer to keep the parameters broad to allow for further development of the concept. Johnstone and Van Ness (2006) have identified three basic conceptions that proposed definitions of restorative justice usually incorporate. The first of these is "encounter", which focuses on the importance of a meeting at which stakeholders discuss the crime, what contributed to it, and its aftermath. In restorative justice processes, the victim, offenders and other interested parties discuss the crime in a fairly informal setting, and that process helps them come to terms with what happened. The second conception is described as "reparative". From this perspective, restorative justice must provide some sort of redress either directly to victims or more broadly to communities. "Transformation" is the third conception. This is concerned with mending damaged relationships. It can deal with relationships between individuals, but can also deal with social injustices such as racism or sexism.

The field of restorative justice has been powerfully influenced by concepts and practices of indigenous justice (Skelton, 2005). In fact, Johnstone has

Crime and Human Rights
Sociology of Crime, Law and Deviance, Volume 9, 171–191
Copyright © 2007 by Elsevier Ltd.
ISSN; 1521-6136/doi:10.1016/S1521-6136(07)09007-0

argued that in order to obtain a comprehensive understanding of restorative justice, it is necessary to "engage with accounts of its use in historical societies and in contemporary indigenous communities" (Johnstone, 2002, p. 10).

This chapter will deal specifically with human rights in restorative justice processes, as compared with the application of human rights in the mainstream criminal justice system. The application of restorative justice at the macro level such as truth commissions is dealt with elsewhere in the book. In this chapter the risks that restorative justice may pose to human rights is explored, as well as some ideas about how those risks might be managed. It is further proposed that the discourse about rights needs to be broadened beyond the Western legalistic focus on individual rights.

1.2. Is the Protection of Human Rights Necessary in Restorative Justice Systems?

Although restorative justice processes appear to be less punitive than the mainstream criminal justice process, it must be borne in mind that restorative justice processes do have consequences. Barnett has pointed out that "as the punitive characteristic of criminal justice measures is diminished, so too is the perceived need for strong procedural protection" (Barnett, 1980, p. 119). Johnstone (2002) is of the view that advocates for restorative justice tend to neglect procedural protection for suspects, and even view formalistic procedural rules as a stumbling block to achieving restorative outcomes. This may be because many proponents of restorative justice see restorative justice processes as being non-punitive, focused on restitution and reparation, similar to a civil law compensation claim. Johnstone warns that this approach is dangerous, because in most systems the wider context against which restorative justice operates is essentially one of crime and punishment. The process is organised around a "crime" or "offence". The terms "offender" and "victim" are used, and the police or prosecutors are often involved. An offender who fails to fulfil his or her obligations is likely to end up back in the criminal justice system.

1.3. A Restorative Justice Perspective on the Evolution of Human Rights in Criminal Justice

A popular, though not uncontroversial theory (Daly, 2002; Johnstone, 2002) posited by some restorative justice writers is that restorative justice is not a discovery but a rediscovery. The theory is based on the idea that if Western people look back far enough into their collective history they will find a time when disputes belonged to the people and restitution, rather than retribution, was the normal resort (Christie, 1977; Jacob, 1977; Zehr, 1990; Bianchi, 1994; Van Ness & Heertderks Strong, 2006). Such a historical reassessment provides a demonstration of how rights protection for suspects developed in Western legal systems. Following the invasion of Britain by the Normans the monarchy gradually took over the role that had previously been occupied by the victim, as crimes became offences against the crown (Jacob, 1977). This method of dealing with crime developed into the criminal justice system we know today in which the State and the suspect are the sole parties. The imbalance of such a system, the might of the monarch or the State on the one side and the puny individual on the other, led the system to gradually develop protections for suspects (Skelton & Sekhonyane, 2006). This was necessary, largely because the consequences of such a system are harsh. These protections came to be referred to as the principles of a fair trial, and later, due process rights. This chapter will explore the standard protections that exist in the criminal justice system, as well as broader human rights issues, and consider what implications restorative justice has for the rights of both victims and offenders.

2. RIGHTS THAT THE CRIMINAL JUSTICE SYSTEM AIMS TO PROTECT

2.1. The Right to a Fair Trial

The principles of a "fair trial" or "due process" include legal principles that protect the suspect, which are common to all Western legal systems, irrespective of whether the procedure is adversarial or inquisitorial, as both have been influenced by the ideology of enlightenment (Damaska, 1975). The principles of a fair trial are included in international instruments, Bills of Rights, statutes and common law.

A person charged with a crime has the right to a public trial by a competent and impartial court. The right to remain silent is a key element, and it is linked to the rule that the accused is presumed innocent until proven guilty. The suspect has a right to be present and to participate at the trial, and should have adequate notice and time to prepare. The state has a legitimate power to apply sanctions for breaches of the law, but sentences should not be cruel, inhuman or degrading, and should be proportionate to the crime (Akester, 2003). Any judicial decision which affects a defendant's rights should be open to review, and there should be mechanisms to apply for appeal from the decisions made by the court. The concepts of "autrefois aquit, autrefois convict" and "double jeopardy" arise from the principle that a person must not be tried twice for the same offence. The adversarial system rests on the idea that the "opponents" in the court should be equally placed, thus the defendant has a right to be placed on an equal footing with the prosecutor. It is therefore considered a right to be legally represented in a criminal trial.

2.2. The Development of Victims' Rights

The fair trial principles focus on the defendant, but in the past 25 years the rights of victims have come to the fore. Strang (2001) record how the victim movement developed differently in different parts of the world. They describe the model that developed in the United States as a rights-based one, whilst the European model has focused more on providing support for victims, and this may be linked to the differences in the adversarial and inquisitorial approaches to criminal justice.

The victims' rights movement has concentrated on reforming laws and procedures that are disadvantageous to victims, such as cautionary rules that prejudice victims, particularly women and children, and which weaken the impact of their evidence. The victim's rights movement has also fought for the right of victims to be provided with information about their cases. The victim rights movement has lobbied actively for greater participation in the criminal justice process and their successes are seen in procedural and legislative breakthroughs regarding victim impact statements. The rights of victims to participate at the sentencing stage are controversial, as some fear that their subjectivity may tip the scales heavily against the offender. Ashworth, for example, says that crime is a matter for "public interest" and that this goes beyond whether the victim considers that action should be taken against the offender, or how the offender should be punished (Ashworth, 2002). He cites the New Zealand court of appeal case of R v Clotworthy (1998) 15 CRNZ 651 (CA) and the UK case of R v Nunn [1996] 2 Cr App R(S) 136 as examples of cases that have found that victims should not be involved in sentencing. R v Clotworthy was a case in which a young man had stabbed another man in an uncharacteristic outburst whilst drunk. The trial court had referred the case to a restorative victim-offender mediation process. The victim and the offender had agreed that it would serve no purpose for the offender to go to prison, but that the offender should pay compensation to the victim so that he could have plastic surgery to repair the scar he had sustained. On appeal, the Court overturned the sentence that had been based on the agreement reached at the restorative justice process, and replaced it with a period of three years imprisonment.

Referring to R v Nunn, Ashworth presents the "just deserts" view that the victim's involvement in sentencing is problematic, whether they are vindictive or merciful. In this case the defendant had been sentenced to four year's imprisonment for causing the death of a close friend by dangerous driving. When Nunn's appeal against sentence came before the court, the court had before it written statements by the victim's mother and sister, saying that although they recognised the need for some punishment, their own grief was being increased by the thought of the defendant having to spend four years in prison. They mentioned in their statements that the victim's father and brother took a different view. The court dismissed the appeal, and had the following to say:

> [T]he opinions of the victim, or the surviving members of the family, about the appropriate level of sentence do not provide any sound basis for reassessing a sentence. If the victim feels utterly merciful towards the criminal, and some do, the crime has still been committed and must be punished as it deserves. If the victim is obsessed with vengeance, which can in reality only be assuaged with a very long sentence, as also happens, the punishment cannot be made any longer by the court than would otherwise be appropriate. (Cited in Ashworth, 2002, p. 588)

Braithwaite has pointed out that cases such as these prove that "the retributive presumption tends to be empirically wrong" (2002a, p. 161). What Braithwaite means by this is that there is a general presumption, promoted by just deserts theorists, that victims will demand more punishment than the courts consider to be appropriate. In fact, the emerging jurisprudence has shown that victims more often demand less than the court deems appropriate.

3. RISKS ENCOUNTERED IN RESTORATIVE JUSTICE PROCESSES

3.1. Possible Risks to Victims

The risks to the rights of victims within restorative justice processes include coercion to participate, threats to personal safety through participating, offender-biased proceedings and a lack of information about what to expect from proceedings. Restorative justice processes may leave victims without a remedy if there is a failure by offenders to follow through on agreements, especially with regard to restitution. Given the value placed on restitution by victims (Umbreit, Coates, & Vos, 2001) this kind of failure may result in overall distrust in the potential of these processes to respond to victims' particular needs. One of the attractive aspects of restorative justice is that restitution or compensation can be dealt with in the same forum as the offence. There has been minimal discussion about the victim's right to bring civil proceedings being compromised by taking part in a restorative justice process. Can we ask victims of crime to forfeit their right to use the civil process as a pre-requisite to participating in a restorative justice process? If we do not do so, what about the risk to offenders who may be asked to pay compensation through a restorative justice process and later be sued through the civil process (Skelton & Frank, 2004)? It is clear that legislated mechanisms are necessary to manage these risks, and such regulations are already in place in some jurisdictions.

3.2. Risks to Suspects

3.2.1. The Risk of Being Coerced to Acknowledge Responsibility
The acknowledgement of responsibility by the offender is usually a pre-requisite to participation in restorative justice processes. It may be argued that this effectively removes the presumption of innocence and the right to silence from the suspect. A possible response to this concern is that the suspect is voluntarily relinquishing these rights in order to benefit from the restorative justice option. However, the voluntariness of such decisions may be called into question. It depends on how the options are put to the suspect. This problem of the risk of coercion is not unique to the situation where suspects are offered the opportunity to participate in a restorative justice process, however. Many formal criminal justice processes offer options such as police cautioning and plea bargaining, and when accepting such an opportunity the suspect gives up the rights to be presumed innocent and to remain silent in order to benefit from being diverted or by receiving a reduced sentence. The solution appears to lie in reducing the risk of coercion, through the proper training of the officials who are responsible for putting the option to the accused.

3.2.2. Legal Representation

Whilst some restorative justice processes do allow parties to have legal representatives present, there are indications that lawyers who have not been trained in mediation or restorative justice tend to hinder rather than help the process. Braithwaite (2002b, p. 566) points out that restorative justice is intended "to transcend adversarial legalism", and he therefore does not support a legal right of the accused to be represented by a lawyer at such proceedings, although he considers it reasonable to allow suspects to seek the advice of a lawyer on whether they should participate in the programme. However, a useful model has emerged in New Zealand, where youth advocates assist young people in family group conferences. They are specially selected and trained for this work, and therefore they assist with the process whilst ensuring rights protection (Morris, Maxwell, & Robertson, 1993).

3.2.3. Double Jeopardy

A fair trial includes the right not to be tried twice for the same offence. This is known as double jeopardy, or as "autrefois acquit, autrefois convict". The risk of double jeopardy in restorative justice may arise where an offender complies with the agreement to a certain point, and then fails to complete all the terms of the agreement. Warner (1994) points out that this situation is not true double jeopardy, because it does not involve having previously been convicted of a crime. Nevertheless there is a risk, because the offender may have done months of community service, or paid over a substantial sum of money, only to find herself back in the criminal justice system when she breaches the conditions towards the end of the period. Warner gives an example of legislation that prevents the outcome of the mediation being presented back to court. This approach, however, may leave the victim with no remedy.

3.2.4. The Risks of "Net Widening"

Criminal justice reformers generally recognise that efforts to find alternatives to the criminal justice system sometimes have the unintended consequence of drawing a larger number of people into the new processes, resulting in "net widening". Net widening can appear in different guises. Cases where there is insufficient evidence to sustain a conviction may end up being "dumped" on the restorative justice pile, along with petty cases that the prosecution considers not worth taking to trial, school cases that could have been dealt with in school and family issues that could have been dealt with in the family. However, a restorative justice approach may consider that solving conflicts in schools or neighbourhoods whilst these are still "small" amounts not only to peace-making but also to peace-building, thus contributing effectively to crime prevention (Skelton & Sekhonyane, 2006).

3.2.5. Risks to Child Defendants

Due to their lack of experience children are highly suggestible, and are more likely to be coerced into making false admissions to avoid "more trouble". Dumortier (2003) has recorded research that indicates that children are often excluded from mediation due to their inability to pay material reparation, and that once in a process they may concede agreements that they cannot in reality fulfil. Haines (1998) has warned against a situation in which a child is "upbraided" by a room full of adults. When dealing with child offenders, special care must be taken to ensure that the process does not result in domination, or in outcomes that are disrespectful or humiliating. Morris (2002) has pointed out that these risks are minimised if the child is properly supported throughout the process.

3.2.6. Outcomes

The principle of proportionality is a major factor in deciding on a particular sentence in a criminal trial. Warner (1994) asserts the "just deserts" perspective that in a criminal trial a sentence cannot be increased beyond a limit appropriate to the severity of the offence, neither on the grounds of possible future offending, nor on the grounds of the need to treat the offender. However, these kinds of considerations may tend to influence outcomes of restorative justice processes.

Just deserts theorists and restorative justice theorists generally agree that there is a need to set upper limits in sentencing or outcomes. Their disagreements arise in the area of lower limits. Just deserts theorists would generally insist that proportionality must be maintained, and there are limits below which the sentence must not go. Restorative justice theorists would argue that if the participants in the process decide that there should be no punishment, such an outcome is acceptable (Braithwaite, 2003).

Another concern relates to disparities in outcomes. Restorative justice outcomes may be outside the range of penalties usually imposed by courts. Thus there is a risk that not only will there be internal inconsistency in restorative justice outcomes, but in addition there will be disparity between restorative justice outcomes and court outcomes for similar offences. In most criminal justice systems, if a convicted person is of the view that his or her sentence is disproportionate to the offence, or if it is not consistent with sentences in similar cases, a remedy lies by way of an application for leave to appeal. This option is not always available in restorative justice processes.

4. BROADER HUMAN RIGHTS ISSUES

4.1. Social Justice

A critique often levelled at restorative justice has been its inability to resolve questions relating to social justice (White, 2000). This question looms large when assessing the rights of participants in restorative justice interventions. Economic, social and racial inequalities are deepening globally. It is likely that the rights of those who are disempowered, excluded and vulnerable due to these inequalities will be at risk in restorative justice processes. Whilst it is not suggested that the criminal justice system is any better an arbiter of these social justice concerns (Ashworth, 2002), the broader ambitions of restorative justice dictate that these concerns be brought to the centre of the discourse relating to both theory and practice (Skelton & Frank, 2001).

4.2. Power Imbalances

Researchers and observers have raised many concerns relating to the effects of power imbalances that frustrate the intentions of restorative justice interventions (Daly, 2002; Dumortier, 2003). These disparities, arising from differences such as race, class, culture, age and gender pose a substantial threat to the protection and promotion of rights in restorative justice programmes. Razack (1994, pp. 907, 910) has observed that "community has not been a safe place for women" and that "culture, community and colonialisation can be used to compete with and ultimately prevail over gender-based harm". Mbambo and Skelton (2003) have raised concerns about children suspected of crimes in South African communities being victimised, sometimes violently, by communities that are angry about crime. Issues of race and culture play themselves out in different, though equally problematic ways (Umbreit et al., 2001).

Given the power imbalances discussed above, coercion and the degree of voluntariness remain a concern (Zehr, 1990; Boyes-Watson, 2000). The assumption that coercion disappears once there is consent to participate in a restorative justice process is dangerous and denies the nuances relating to power that are present in all human interactions (Skelton & Frank, 2004).

5. PROTECTION OF RIGHTS IN NON-STATE FORMS OF JUSTICE

Informal justice systems or non-State forms of justice are those that do not rely on or are not linked to the formal justice system. Skelton and Sekhonyane (2006) have divided these into three categories: firstly, in some countries with indigenous populations, traditional or customary courts are still part of informal systems to which people take their disputes directly, rather than going to the police; secondly, in some countries there are popular forums that have been modelled on traditional systems, but have grown out of a lack of faith in the colonial or imposed systems (Penal Reform International, 2001); thirdly, there are instances when communities take the law into their own hands and mete out punishments, which are not restorative.

In the first category, it must be noted that the existence of non-State forms of justice in many communities pose a different set of challenges than those presented by restorative justice processes linked to the criminal justice system. African traditional courts, for example, often do not follow the principles of a fair trial. In such systems a person is often presumed guilty until proven innocent and the right to remain silent is not recognised. The patriarchal nature of traditional society means that the justice system is sometimes prejudicial towards women and children (Bennett, 1999; Tshehla, 2005).

On the other hand, the practice of these traditional courts can be described as restorative in many respects (Elechi, 2004). Through the traditional court system, the perpetrator must apologise to the victim and compensate for stolen or damaged property either by restitution, or by repairing damage, or paying for losses. When Lesotho piloted their restorative justice approach in rural villages it took root very quickly, largely due to the fact that elements of restorative justice already existed in the traditional justice practices (Qhubu, 2005).

With regard to the second category of non-State forms of justice, Ashworth (2002) identifies two countries, Northern Ireland and South Africa, as examples where the legitimacy of the State and its apparatus had suffered a serious collapse, giving rise to non-State forms of justice (Mc Evoy & Mika, 2002; Schärf & Nina, 2001). The failure by the State to provide legitimate systems and the failure of many States to deal with social inequalities are acknowledged as reasons why many restorative justice advocates call for the State to play a residual rather than prominent role in the criminal justice process. However, Ashworth (2002) is of the view that the State should maintain control over crime and punishment, and one of the reasons he advances for this is that human rights must be protected. His rationale is that values such as impartiality, proportionality and consistency are of vital importance to human rights protection, but that in restorative justice they are in tension with other values such as participation, involvement of the victim and empowerment. Strang and Braithwaite (2001, p. 13) summarise the balance needed:

> We come to see the restorative justice agenda not as a choice between civil society and state justice, but as requiring us to seek the most productive synergies between the two.

The third type of non-State justice arises where high levels of crime and the resulting fear have caused many communities to administer harsher measures (Mistry et al., 2004). This coupled with the perceptions that the criminal justice system is weak, has seen the rise of vigilante activity in some countries. Some communities in South Africa, tired of crime in their areas and feeling that the police and courts have failed to curb the scourge, are taking the law into their hands, assaulting and even killing suspected criminals. From media reports and research conducted by a number of civil society organisations and academics, there is a general consensus that vigilantism exists because the state fails to provide security for the people, especially the poor and marginalised. The other argument advanced heavily, is that the criminal justice process is perpetrator friendly. Proponents of vigilantism argue that criminals get off lightly because sentences are lenient and bail is granted easily, and they therefore feel it is justified when communities take action to remedy this weakness in the criminal justice.

It is important when considering non-State forms of justice to separate out those that are restorative in nature from those that are not. Traditional justice systems are generally restorative, although they may fail to include women and young people adequately and in some cases may use corporal punishment. Whilst the systems do not hold up to a critique of due process rights protection that Western legal practitioners expect from the criminal justice system, the processes are generally protective and healing and aim at restoring harmony in communities.

The second category of community driven alternatives to justice that operate independently of the criminal justice system are less steeped in tradition and are more likely to allow full participation of women and young people. In the South African Community Peace Programme, for example, it has been noted that women are at the forefront of the peace-making and peace-building work (Roche, 2002). This programme has its own code, part of which states that those involved will abide by the rights set out in the South African Constitution (Shearing, 2001). Similarly, the restorative justice alternatives in Northern Ireland have developed their own sets of standards for rights protection. The history of non-State forms of justice in South Africa, however, demonstrates that people's courts can become a negative force, particularly in times of conflict, and can ultimately lean towards the third category, vigilantism.

Sachs has observed, in the foreword to a book on non-State forms of justice in South Africa, that

> [T]here can be neither an in-principle acceptance nor a categorical rejection of this Other law ... The Other law would function not outside of or in opposition to the constitutional realm, but in the spaces acknowledged by the Constitution itself. (Schärf & Nina, 2001, p. vi)

6. STANDARDS SETTING

6.1. Standards: A Dangerous Debate?

Braithwaite has captured some of the dangers of standardisation in the following quotation:

> While it is good that we are now having debates on standards for restorative justice it is a dangerous debate. Accreditation for mediators that raises the spectre of a Western accreditation agency telling an Aboriginal elder that a centuries old restorative practice does not comply with the accreditation standards is a profound worry. We must avert accreditation that crushes indigenous empowerment. (2002b, p. 565)

Braithwaite also voices a concern that standardisation may inhibit innovation, as we are still learning how to do restorative justice well. However, he concedes that there is some practice that is so obviously bad that we do need to act to eliminate it. He gives the example of a family group conference in Australia that required a boy to publicly wear a tee-shirt bearing the words "I am a thief". Braithwaite concludes that such practices may be an even greater threat to restorative justice than overly prescriptive standards.

Notwithstanding these concerns, the setting of standards both internally (within the project or programme) and at a national or even international level has now become part of restorative justice discourse (Van Ness, 2003).

6.2. The UN Basic Principles on Restorative Justice

At the eleventh session of the UN Commission on Crime Prevention and Criminal Justice, Canada put forward a resolution that encourages countries to draw from Basic Principles on the Use of Restorative Justice Programmes in Criminal Matters in developing and implementing restorative justice. The Commission approved the resolution, and the Basic Principles may be seen as guidelines to assist States and organisations in their work. The principles were developed by a UN expert group on restorative justice, drawing on previous recommendations and existing guidelines developed by practitioner groups (Van Ness, 2003).

Section II of the Principles is headed "Use of restorative justice programmes" and includes the following principles:

- Restorative justice programmes should be generally available at all stages of the criminal justice process;
- Restorative processes should be used only with the free and voluntary consent of the parties. The parties should be able to withdraw such consent at any time during the process. Agreements should be arrived at voluntarily by the parties and contain only reasonable and proportionate obligations;
- All parties should normally acknowledge the basic facts of a case as a basis for participation in a restorative process. Participation should not be used as evidence of admission of guilt in subsequent legal proceedings;
- Obvious disparities with respect to factors such as power imbalances and the parties' age, maturity or intellectual capacity should be taken into consideration in referring a case to, and in conducting a restorative justice process;
- Where restorative justice processes and/or outcomes are not possible, criminal justice officials should do all they can to encourage the offender to take responsibility vis-à-vis the victim and affected communities, and reintegration of the victim and/or offender into the community.

Section III of the Basic Principles has the title "Operation of restorative justice programmes". Guidelines and standards and fundamental safeguards should be applied to restorative justice programmes and processes, and these include the parties' right to legal advice before and after the restorative justice process, parties being fully informed of their rights and protection from being induced by unfair means to participate. Confidentiality of the proceedings is flagged as a principle, with the discussions not to be disclosed subsequently, except with the consent of the parties. Judicial discharges based on restorative justice agreements should preclude prosecution on the same facts.

The Basic Principles include guidelines on what should happen when the parties fail to reach agreement, and when there is failure to implement an agreement that has been made. The remainder of the Basic Principles deal with the recruitment of facilitators and guidelines for how they should carry out their functions, as well as the continuing development of restorative justice programmes, the promotion of research on and evaluation of restorative justice programmes.

International and regional standards are not specific to the particular country context. Therefore the possibility of standards being set in a more detailed manner in individual countries is also a consideration. This is sometimes done through legislation, or through codes of conduct. The more prescriptive such standards become, however, the more there is a danger that they begin to destroy the essence of what restorative justice sets out to achieve.

7. RIGHTS AND VALUES

The Universal Declaration of Human Rights adopted in 1948 by the United Nations General Assembly was the first attempt to universalise human rights. Rights that are universal do not all enjoy the same standing, however. Some rights, such as the right to life and the right to human dignity, are inalienable or entirely non-derogable. The South African Constitution, for example, prizes the values of human dignity, equality and freedom above all others, and these three values, in addition to being in the list of rights themselves, are also used as values to test the other rights contained in the Bill of Rights. It is apparent, therefore, that there is some congruity between rights and values. The right to human dignity has proved to be a touchstone for the interpretation of the South African Bill of Rights, and the interesting thing about this value is its applicability across both Western and African legal systems.

Braithwaite (2003) has offered a list of values relevant for restorative justice, which he divides into three different categories. The first list he describes as constraining values, which are fundamental procedural safeguards that take priority where any serious sanction is at risk. They include empowerment, honouring legally specific upper limits on sanctions, respectful listening, equal concern for stakeholders, accountability, appealability and respect for the fundamental human rights specified in international instruments. A second group of restorative justice values are proposed by Braithwaite (2002a), which he describes as "maximizing standards", meaning that they should be promoted and encouraged. These values relate to healing and restoration. They include very basic kinds of restoration such as returning property, and more abstract ones such as the restoration of dignity, compassion, social support and the prevention of future injustice. The third group of standards are described as "emergent standards". They are remorse over injustice, apology, censure of the act, forgiveness of the person, and mercy. Unlike the second category, participants should not be actively encouraged to bring these standards to the fore; they should simply be allowed to emerge. Braithwaite recognises the usefulness of the UN standards, which he describes as "top-down". However, he stresses the importance of "bottom-up value clarification". Those working at local level must consider how to ensure effective quality assurance and accountability in restorative justice. This can be done by taking a list of values, such as those Braithwaite has proposed, and beginning a debate about the standards to which they want their programmes to conform.

8. BROADENING THE DISCOURSE AROUND HUMAN RIGHTS

The recognition of the need for human rights protection has become part of developing restorative justice practice. The criminal justice system emphasis on due process rights is, however, a rather narrow construct of rights. It is possible to give up the right to be presumed innocent through acknowledging responsibility and have one's human rights remain intact. Indeed, human rights such as dignity and equality may be enhanced through acknowledging responsibility in a restorative justice process, notwithstanding concerns about the limitations of restorative justice to deal with issues of social justice and power differentials.

Humbach (2001) has offered a fresh perspective on rights. He is of the view that depersonalised rights and rules cannot mediate the intricacies of interactions amongst human beings. Humbach refutes the idea that justice is achievable through the protection of individual rights. He believes that what we should be striving for is "a justice of right relationships". He contrasts this with the justice of rights, which he characterises as "a justice of entitlements". A justice of right relationships, on the other hand, arises out of the human attachments and connections that people form.

> At its core, the justice of right relationships is the intrinsic good that inures to persons
> who live in interaction with others whose fundamental concern is to maintain the quality
> and mutual worth of their relationships, instead of insisting on their rights. (2001, p. 42)

Feminist writer Carol Gilligan (1982) has found that whereas men tend to favour a justice ethic, women tend to place a higher value on relationships and to have an ethic of caring for others. She argues that whereas boys will usually resolve a dilemma by acting alone to do the right thing, girls try to solve such dilemmas through discussion and considering the effects of solutions on relationships. Fulani (1994) has subjected Gilligan's work to a critique, in which she finds that Gilligan has fallen into the trap of viewing dilemma resolution through a Western morality code. Fulani suggests that the entire idea of morality is a Western patriarchal construct. Women are less impartial, less utilitarian and are less likely than men to make decisions based on abstract principles.

The way forward may lie in broadening the discourse around rights (Skelton & Frank, 2004). The confines of the due process conceptualisation of rights will tie the field down to providing a mirror of the standard criminal justice process. Human rights encompass a broader view but are still, as reflected in international instruments, based on a very individualised approach. In countries that have a history of indigenous conflict resolution a more communitarian approach to rights is evident (Skelton & Sekhonyane, 2006).

In a stinging critique of the Western model of human rights, Maka Mutua (2002) argues that the entire human rights enterprise mistakenly misrepresents itself as a final, inflexible truth. The idea is promoted that advancement is inexplicably linked to a utopian world based on human rights. In Mutua's view, the entire corpus of human rights, though well intentioned, is a Eurocentric formula for the recolonisation of non-Western societies and peoples through a set of norms based on cultures, norms and practices that are based on liberal thought and philosophy. Mutua argues that, if the human rights endeavour is to succeed, it must be separated out from what he sees as a "civilising crusade" by the Western world aimed at "non-Europeans". He calls on the peoples of Asia, Africa and the Pacific to promote indigenous non-European traditions to involve themselves in the deconstruction of the Western perspective of human rights, and to reconstruct a new idea of human rights based on a multi-cultural approach.

In an essay on the ethics and values needed for peace in the 21st century, Campbell also asserts that the world has been organised according to the views of Western male leaders who have relied on conceptions such as the importance of the individual as espoused by John Locke, the free market as propounded by Adam Smith, and the survival of the fittest as described by Charles Darwin. Campbell suggests that it may be possible to provide alternatives to this approach of maximising self interest by focusing on other values such as peace, reconstruction and reconciliation (Campbell, 2002).

In essence, this alternative perspective rests on the moral ethic of collective unity. Whilst Western ideation is premised on individualisation, African ideation is based on a theory of collective living, which finds voice in a number of key African concepts (Skelton & Sekhonyane, 2006). The philosophy of *ujamaa,* used by Julius Nyerere to describe the kind of life he believed Tanzanians should live. This was a simple life in which people lived in harmony with their close families. Wealth belonged to the family as a whole, and no one could use wealth as a way of dominating others. "We want the whole nation to live as a family", was how Nyerere explained the idea. He recognised that this approach was akin to socialism, but he used the term *ujamaa* because he wanted to root the concept of socialism in the African philosophy of collectivism, and because he wanted to be sure that no-one would act as "master over servant" in the system that he was promoting (Nyerere, 1998, p. 78). The importance of people living together at the same level, recognising differences but not allowing domination or discrimination was further illustrated by Nyerere in his promotion of the concept of *ndugu,* meaning brotherhood or sisterhood. In South Africa it has been argued that the ethic of collective unity is captured in the concept of *ubuntu* (Tutu, 1999; Mokgoro, 1998).

African philosopher (Gyeke, 1998) asserts that a communitarian ethos underpins African social structures. He believes that although the general thrust of this ethos emphasises duties towards the community, it does not do so to the detriment of individual rights, the existence and value of which should be recognised by the community. Restorative justice theorists and practitioners may need to move beyond the focus on the individual which characterises the Western approach to human rights, and begin an evaluation of the rights of the individual within a more communitarian approach (Skelton & Frank, 2004).

9. CONCLUSION

Restorative justice writers differ in their opinions about the importance of rights protection. There are those who are of the view that due process rights need to be strictly enforced in restorative justice processes and programmes, whilst others take the position that such an approach is not

necessary, and may even hinder or impede restorative justice outcomes.
It has been observed that

> [I]n an attempt to be sensitive to human rights protection, restorative justice
> practitioners appear to be getting drawn into a confined discourse about due process
> rights, in which restorative justice processes are being expected to provide the same
> protections as courts. The protections relating to due process were designed to deal with
> the specific dangers inherent in the criminal justice trial process, particularly adversarial
> trials. It is not particularly logical, therefore, that the rules designed for those processes
> must be mirrored in restorative justice processes. (Skelton & Frank, 2004, p. 209)

This chapter has aimed to show that there are different ways of looking at
rights, and that these different ways should be factored into the debates about
how to ensure human rights protections within restorative justice practice.
It may be necessary to resist a Eurocentric or Western conceptualisation of
human rights, and instead to construct new ways of thinking about the
protection of people going through restorative justice processes. Human
rights, as conceptualised by the Western world, is not a panacea. Indigenous
peoples have taught much to the field of restorative justice, and their call
for a more communitarian and less legalistic approach to rights protection is
to be heeded.

REFERENCES

Akester, K. (2003). *Restorative justice, victim's rights and the future.* Available at
    www.restorativejustice.org.uk/article1.html
Ashworth, A. (2002). Responsibilities, rights and restorative justice. *British Journal of
    Criminology, 42,* 578–595.
Barnett, R. (1980). The justice of restitution. *American Journal of Jurisprudence, 25,*
    117–132.
Bennett, T. W. (1999). *Human rights and African customary law.* Cape Town: Juta.
Bianchi, H. (1994). *Justice as sanctuary.* Bloomington: Indiana University Press.
Boyes-Watson, C. (2000). Reflections on the purist and maximalist models of restorative justice.
    Contemporary Justice Review, 3, 441–451.
Braithwaite, J. (2002a). In search of restorative jurisprudence. In: L. Walgrave (Ed.),
    Restorative justice and the law (pp. 150–167). Cullompton: Willan Publishing.
Braithwaite, J. (2002b). Standards for restorative justice. *British Journal of Criminology, 42,*
    563–577.
Braithwaite, J. (2003). Principles of restorative justice. In: A. von Hirsch, J. Roberts,
    A. Bottoms, K. Roach & M. Schiff (Eds), *Restorative justice and criminal justice:
    Competing or reconcilable paradigms* (pp. 1–20). Oxford: Hart Publishing.
Campbell, H. (2002). The ethics, qualities and values necessary for leadership and peace in the
    twenty-first century. In: G. Wildschut (Ed.), *Emerging African leadership: Opportunities*

and challenges for peace and development. Cape Town: Desmond Tutu Leadership Academy.

Christie, N. (1977). Conflicts as property. *British Journal of Criminology, 17*, 1–15.

Daly, K. (2002). Restorative justice: The real story. *Punishment and Society, 4*, 55–79.

Damaska, M. (1975). Structures of authority and comparative criminal procedure. *Yale Law Journal, 84*, 480–532.

Dumortier, E. (2003). Legal rules and safeguards within Belgian mediation practices for juveniles. In: E. Weitekamp & H.-J. Kerner (Eds), *Restorative justice in context: International practice and directions* (pp. 197–207). Cullompton: Willan Publishing.

Elechi, O. (August 8–12, 2004). Human rights and the African indigenous justice system. A paper presented at the 18th International Conference of the International Society for the Reform of Criminal Law, Montreal. Available at http://www/isrd.org/papers

Fulani, L. (1994). Moving beyond morality and identity. In: E. Burman (Ed.), *Deconstructing feminist psychology* (pp. 140–158). London: Sage.

Gilligan, C. (1982). *In a different voice: Psychological theory and women's development.* Cambridge, MA: Harvard University Press.

Gyeke, K. (1998). Person and community in African thought. In: P. Coetzee & A. Roux (Eds), *The African philosophy reader* (pp. 317–336). London: Routledge.

Haines, K. (1998). Some principled objections to a restorative justice approach to working with juvenile offenders. In: L. Walgrave (Ed.), *Restorative justice for juveniles: Potentialities, risks, and problems for research* (pp. 93–113). Leuven: Leuven University Press.

Humbach, J. (2001). Towards a natural justice of right relationships. In: B. Leiser & T. Campbell (Eds), *Human rights in philosophy and practice* (pp. 41–61). Dartmouth: Ashgate.

Jacob, B. (1977). The concept of restitution: A historical overview. In: J. Hudson & B. Galaway (Eds), *Restitution in criminal justice* (pp. 45–62). Lexington: Lexington Books.

Johnstone, G. (2002). *Restorative justice: Ideas, practices, debates.* Cullompton: Willan Publishing.

Johnstone, G., & Van Ness, D. (Eds). (2006). *Handbook of restorative justice.* Cullompton: Willan Publishing.

Mbambo, B., & Skelton, A. (2003). Preparing the South African community for implementing a new restorative child justice system. In: L. Walgrave (Ed.), *Repositioning restorative justice* (pp. 271–283). Cullompton: Willan Publishing.

Mc Evoy, K., & Mika, H. (2002). Restorative justice and the critique of informalism in Northern Ireland. *British Journal of Criminology, 42*, 534–562.

Mistry, D., Burton, P., Du Plessis, A., Leggett, T., Louw, A., & Van Vuuren, H. (2004). *National victims of crime survey.* Pretoria: South Africa.

Mokgoro, Y. (1998). Ubuntu and the law in South Africa. *Buffalo Human Rights Law Review, 4*, 15–24.

Morris, A. (2002). Critiquing the critics: A brief response to critics of restorative justice. *British Journal of Criminology, 42*, 596–615.

Morris, A., Maxwell, G., & Robertson, J. (1993). Giving victims a voice: A New Zealand experiment. *The Howard Journal*, 304–321.

Mutua, M. (2002). *Human rights: A political and cultural critique.* Philadelphia: University of Pennsylvania Press.

Nyerere, J. (1998). Leaders must not be masters. In: E. C. Eke (Ed.), *African philosophy: An anthology* (pp. 77–80). Oxford: Blackwell Publishers Ltd.

Penal Reform International. (2001). *Access to justice in sub-saharan Africa.* London: Penal Reform International.

Qhubu, N. (March 14–17, 2005). The development of restorative justice in Lesotho. Unpublished paper presented at the Association of Law Reform Agencies for Eastern and Southern Africa Conference, Cape Town. Available at http://www.salrc.org.za

Razack, S. (1994). What is to be gained by looking white people in the eye: Culture, race and gender in cases of sexual violence. *Signs: Journal of Women in Culture and Society, 19*, 894–923.

Roche, D. (2002). Restorative justice and the regulatory state in South African townships. *British Journal of Criminology, 42*, 514–532.

Schärf, W., & Nina, D. (2001). *The other law: Non state ordering in South Africa*. Cape Town: Juta.

Shearing, C. (2001). Transforming security: A South African experiment. In: H. Strang & J. Braithwaite (Eds), *Restorative justice and civil society* (pp. 14–34). Cambridge: Cambridge University Press.

Skelton, A. (2004). For the next generations: Remaking South Africa's juvenile justice system. In: E. Doxtader & C. Villa-Vicencio (Eds), *To repair the irreparable: Reparation and reconstruction in South Africa* (pp. 211–223). Claremont: David Philip.

Skelton, A. (2005). *The influence of the theory and practice of restorative justice in South Africa with special reference to child justice*. Unpublished doctoral thesis. University of Pretoria, Pretoria.

Skelton, A., & Frank, C. (2001). Conferencing in South Africa: Returning to our future. In: A. Morris & G. Maxwell (Eds), *Restorative justice for juveniles: Conferencing, mediation and circles* (pp. 103–120). Oxford: Hart Publishing.

Skelton, A., & Frank, C. (2004). How does restorative justice address human rights and due process issues? In: H. Zehr & B. Toews (Eds), *Critical issues in restorative justice* (pp. 203–214). Monsey: Criminal Justice Press Willan Publishing.

Skelton, A., & Sekhonyane, M. (2006). Human rights and restorative justice. In: G. Johnstone & D. Van Ness (Eds), *Handbook of restorative justice* (pp. 580–597). Cullompton: Willan Publishing.

Strang, H. (2001). The crime victim movement as a force in civil society. In: J. Braithwaite & J. Strang (Eds). *Restorative justice and civil society*. Cambridge: Cambridge University Press.

Tshehla, B. (2005). *Traditional justice in practice: A Limpopo case study*. Pretoria: Institute for Security Studies.

Tutu, D. (1999). *No future without forgiveness*. London: Rider.

Umbreit, M., Coates, R., & Vos, B. (2001). In: A. Morris & G. Maxwell (Eds), *Restorative justice for juveniles: Conferencing, mediation and circles* (pp. 121–144). Oxford: Hart Publishing.

Van Ness, D. (2003). Proposed basic principles on the use of restorative justice: Recognising the aims and limits of restorative justice. In: A. von Hirsch, J. Roberts, A. Bottoms, K. Roach & M. Schiff (Eds), *Restorative justice and criminal justice: Competing or reconcilable paradigms* (pp. 157–176). Oxford: Hart Publishing.

Van Ness, D., & Heertderks Strong, K. (2006). *Restoring justice: An introduction to restorative justice* (3rd ed.). Cincinnati, OH: Lexis/Nexis and Anderson Publishing.

Warner, K. (1994). Family group conferences and the rights of the offender. In: C. Alder & J. Wundersitz (Eds), *Family conferencing and juvenile justice: The way forward or misplaced optimism?* (pp. 142–152). Canberra: Australian Institute of Criminology.

White, R. (2000). Social justice, community building and restorative strategies. *Contemporary Justice Review, 3*, 55–72.

Zehr, H. (1990). *Changing lenses: A new focus for crime and justice.* Scottdale, PA: Herald Press.

CASES REFERRED TO:

R v Clotworthy (1998) 15 CRNZ 651 (CA).
R v Nunn (1996) 2 Cr. App. R (S) 136.

THE ZWELETHEMBA MODEL: PRACTICING HUMAN RIGHTS THROUGH DISPUTE RESOLUTION

Jan Froestad and Clifford Shearing

1. INTRODUCTION

In this paper we look to activities of people living primarily in informal housing within South Africa to explore how they have thought about articulating and protecting the sorts of values thought of as human rights. The concept of human rights has meaning within these collectivities even though they may never have encountered a professional human rights discourse. For example, even though the vast majority of South Africans have never read the South African Constitution they know that it exists and that it protects human rights. Similarly most South Africans have an idea as to what sorts of values are referred to by human rights even though they may not be able to articulate what these are and may not endorse all or some of these values. In short, human rights exist as part of South Africans' life world.

In what follows we consider how groups of South Africans who practice a dispute resolution process (that has come to be called the Zwelethemba model) articulate and practice human rights within in the context of the processes this model promotes. We do so to explore how looking to the practices of ordinary people might contribute to our understanding of what human rights mean in the day-to-day circumstances of peoples lives and to

Crime and Human Rights
Sociology of Crime, Law and Deviance, Volume 9, 193–214
Copyright © 2007 by Elsevier Ltd.
All rights of reproduction in any form reserved
ISSN: 1521-6136/doi:10.1016/S1521-6136(07)09008-2

see how these meanings might be articulated with the meanings given to human rights within professional discourses. Our primary purpose is to consider how such an articulation might contribute to debates taking place amongst professionals within contemporary human rights discourses. That is, our objective is to see what, if anything, a bottom-up perspective might contribute to contemporary debates about human rights.

2. HUMAN RIGHTS DISCOURSE(S)

Discourses on human rights have been conceived as the last grand narrative (Alves, 2000), characterized as an international communication about human freedom and dignity that can be thought of signalling an emergent or "overlapping consensus" about justice and core human values in a world of doctrinal fragmentation and insecurity (Donnelly, 2001). One consequence of this, it has been argued, is that "the language of universal rights has been seized by the oppressed and excluded as a weapon in the fight for freedom and dignity" (Goodhart, 2003, p. 959). This claim is not without its critiques and many scholars have expressed reservations about the continued value of human rights as a source of freedom, critique and reinvention.

In *The End of Human Rights*, Douzinas maintains that the human rights discourse has been loosing its value as an inspirational source of human emancipation as it has been used to constitute to a language that strengthens state powers and expert knowledge (Douzinas, 2000). Baxi (2002) argues that the human rights discourse is being hijacked by powerful groups and that, as a consequence, it is being uncoupled from the suffering and needs of the poor and the oppressed (see also Twining, 2006). Similarly Guilhot (2005) argues that human rights, through a process of "professionalization" and "technical specialization", has been translated into a language of state administration and institutions. These arguments identify human rights as a resource that can be mobilized in a variety of ways for a variety of purposes. The challenging question, that these and other observers raise, is how to uphold the "critical intent" of human rights. Central to this challenge is how human rights as a resource may be mobilized by the poor and oppressed. This, Guilhot argues, requires linking the discourse to perceptions of injustice (see also Erman, 2005). Utilizing the distinction between life-world and system (Habermas, 1988, 1997) Fortman argues that human rights have become a system of:

> Intergovernmental and nongovernmental centres, compliance and complaints procedures with commissions, committees and courts of law, training programmes and academic

training courses, often quite removed from the life-world perspectives. (Fortman, 2001, p. 7)

Likewise Stammers (1995, pp. 506–507) argues that this discourse is now almost exclusively tied to states – there is now "little more space for thinking about human rights in any other way". As a consequence private economic powers often evade human rights protections. It is also argued that this top-down way of thinking about human rights is elitist and disabling, constraining the potential for popular mobilization by directing any mobilization that does occur towards the state (*Ibid.*, p. 507). The question is what other spaces can be constituted and used. In criticizing the statist orientation Stammers argues that it:

> Must be superseded by a reconstructed notion of human rights, systematically grounded and understood to challenge existing power relations – a notion of human rights that enables, rather than disables, those whose voices are currently stifled by the dominant western discourses on human rights, both liberal and social democratic. (*Ibid.*, p. 508)

The question that is posed is: What can be done to uphold the critical content of human rights? As argued by Fitzpatrick (2006, p. 15) the "political" element of rights inheres, at least partly, from the ability rights have to go beyond their existent content. Rights have shown a capacity to be something other than what they were intended to be. This in-determinant, "vacuous" or "abstract" character of rights has made them susceptible to occupation by effective powers. In making this point Guilhot (2005) documents how the US, under republican rule, transformed the human rights discourse into a mechanism of domination and aggression, tying it to its foreign policy of exporting "democracy". While human rights used to function as external standards held up against government, especially as a guard against an imperialistic foreign policy, today they have been instrumentalized as weapons to legitimate aggressive interventions. Chandler (2001) underscores how the human rights-based approach to humanitarian aid has undermined earlier humanitarian values such as universality and neutrality and has constructed humanism as an ambiguous concept "capable of justifying the most barbaric of military actions" (*Ibid.*, p. 698). In a similar vein Forsythe (2005) notes how humanitarian arguments were used by the US to legitimate the invasion of Iraq.

The growth and expansion of an international network of human rights NGOs has frequently been interpreted as "a quiet revolution" spawning the emergence of international civil society (Otto, 1996). However, Smith, Pagnucco, and Lopez (1998) draw attention to important dividing lines within such networks as Southern NGOs have to work with substantially less access to resources than Northern ones. Mertus (1999) questions the democratic status of the NGOs and argues that many of them operate in ways that may threaten local autonomy. Guilhot (2005) points to the fact that traditional forms of NGO activism have to a large extent been transformed because, in order to be successful, international networks have increasingly been professionalized through lawyers, political scientists, media specialists and public relations experts.

This literature calls for a social science and political practice that is more committed to a change from below. This may well require forms of decentralization operating to some extent outside of state and corporate power and that link to international efforts to deepening democracy and human rights (Fields & Narr, 1992). According to Donnelly (2001) the key to human rights progress in the coming decades lies in creating more creative and effective efforts by a multitude of agencies – states, citizens, and other national and international actors. Freeman (1994) emphasizes the need to conceptualize human rights in a manner that is flexible enough to allow space for the very human creativity it seeks. Langlois (2002) sees the human rights discourse as a tool for co-operation, providing a forum that will permit multi-cultural traditions of justice to find expression. The call here is for greater and more varied forms of participation that give life to human rights. Preis (1996) makes the point that underlying the "progressive" assumptions of many human rights texts, is the often subterranean assumption that development must emanate from centres of powers, such as states or international interests, through a staged process. What is needed, he argues, is better knowledge of human rights as actual existing practices, which accords priority to an understanding of human rights within everyday life (*Ibid.*, pp. 13–15).

What Preis and other scholars suggest is the importance of de-stabilizing the dominant human rights discourse; to move it out of its statist and legalistic orientation in ways that open it up to a plurality of voices – especially the marginalized. Again a similar question arises: How can new practices be developed that confront such challenges in human rights? In raising this and similar questions the issue put on the table is how to contribute to finding the spaces that enable human rights to continue to express emancipatory possibilities. How can the poor and the oppressed better use human rights possibilities to promote their emancipation?

In what follows we will explore which insights might be drawn in responding to these questions from the practices of poor South Africans who participate in a process of dispute resolution that harnesses human rights values, as they are locally conceived as tools in the construction of peaceful existences. While these processes were not developed explicitly to address the questions raised above, they are certainly relevant to them, and they can be read as addressing elements of the debates we have just reviewed. We turn now to briefly outline these processes.

3. THE ZWELETHEMBA MODEL

Zwelethemba is the name of the urban area in the vicinity of Cape Town, in which the processes to be outlined were developed as a model for resolving local disputes in the townships (see Johnston & Shearing, 2003 for a fuller discussion of this development). The Zwelethemba – a Xhosa word that means country or place of hope – model creates a set of sustainable processes for resolving local disputes by using local resources. These resources are mobilized through a deliberative process constituted through the gathering together of local people who are invited through deliberation to develop a plan of action that will reduce the likelihood of the dispute continuing. This deliberative work is facilitated by local residents who constitute themselves as Peace Committees. Peace Committees vary considerably in size but are usually made up of between 10 and 20 people. In some of the areas were the model is operating (some 20 at the time of writing) Peace Committees operate along side state institutions (particularly police) that refer disputes to them and that receive cases from them. Peace Committees deal with a wide range of cases. The following break down of 13,544 cases processed from February 2000 to end of December 2006 provides an indication of the range of issues handled. Money lending was an aspect of the dispute in nearly half of all cases (47%) and other kinds of property offences nearly as often (43%). Domestic violence occurred as an issue in 21% of all cases, assaults in 15% and substance abuse in 10%. Approximately one forth of all conflicts arose as disputes among neighbours. Sixty four percent of the participants at the peace gatherings were women. Exit interviews conducted from 1998 to date show that approximately 95% of all participants experience the peacemaking process as very fair and an equal percentage that the gathering had improved the matter a lot. Average resolution time for a dispute was 2.7 days and 98% of the implicated reported that they thought the dispute was resolved quickly enough.

A key feature of the activity is that it is highly regulated. There are several features to this regulatory environment – a code of practice, procedures for facilitating deliberative forms, review sessions, exit interviews with persons attending gatherings and community surveys. This set of regulatory tools seeks to promote values associated with human rights, both civil and political rights and economic, social and cultural rights.

In the following paragraphs, we draw on the results of a recent study of the activities facilitated by Peace Committees (that used both observational and interview methods) to explore the questions within the human rights debates we canvassed briefly above.

4. RECONCILING UNIVERSAL RIGHTS WITH LOCAL NORMS

In 1947 the American Anthropological Association issued a statement rejecting the idea that the Declaration of Human Rights had universal application, asserting that "rights of Man in the Twentieth Century cannot be circumscribed by the standards of any single culture" (for a more recent discussion, see Pollis, 1996). Notwithstanding the influence of this position, a number of scholars have recently begun to look for ways of rescuing the idea of universal values. In trying to do so, the challenge has been to steer a path between strong versions of both universalism and particularism (Twining, 2006). In developing this line of thought Perry (1997) and Tilley (2000) distinguish between different versions of the relativist argument. Tilley demarcates methodological contextualism (the position that every custom, belief, or action must be studied in the context of the culture in which it occurs) from the claim of ethical or moral relativism, holding that any event or action can only be properly judged or appraised from within the normative context of the culture within which it arises. Radical relativism leads to absurdities, such that to morally criticize the norms of one's own culture is by necessity a wrong or ridiculous act. In challenging radical relativism he notes how some moral statements, like "torturing children, only for the fun of hearing them screaming is wrong" (*Ibid.*, p. 529) are difficult to reject from any cultural perspective. As Perry argues, claiming that cultural contexts are relevant "is a far cry from claiming that nothing, no act or failure to act, is bad and nothing is good for every human being" (Perry, 1997, p. 482; see also Fields & Narr, 1992, p. 20 and O'Manique, 1990, pp. 482–83).

Freeman (1994) in canvassing this issue distinguishes between those who emphasize contingency, construction and relativity, and those who try to locate objective foundations for human rights in reason or morality.

His own position is to see human rights as contingent, while at the same time insisting that core human rights values, like well-being and freedom, are not arbitrary, because they are respected across a wide range of cultures (see also Donnelly, 2001).

Others have sought to re-conceptualize how the universal character of human rights relates to the particularities of diverse collectivities. Langlois (2002), for example, argues that the concept of human rights does not make sense without a reference to universalism. The problem for him is that current discourses are often dominated by the moral and political interests embedded in Western concerns. A solution for Langlois would be to understand human rights as "a proposal for the rules under which people who pursue diverse goals in a complex, rapidly changing and highly inter-dependent world might hope to live in dignity and peace" (*Ibid.*, p. 495).

4.1. Zwelethemba-Reconciling the Universal and the Contextual

These are similar to the debates that took place in the formation of the Zwelethemba process. These debates were embodied in a process of trial and error experimentation. A major concern during this process was the fact that participatory forms of governance within local South African communities have had a very chequered history, sometimes producing limited change and sometimes being hijacked for repressive ends. In response regulatory structures were developed that drew upon popular understandings of human rights. These debates look to general values as constraints that would regulate the way in which local knowledge and capacity were mobilized. While local knowledge and capacity should be given much reign in problem-solving, it should not, it was felt, reign supreme. Central to the regulatory constraint that the model embeds is a set of steps (rules) that structure the deliberative processes in ways that give all participants "rights" to be heard as well as a set of over arching values (seen as having wide community support) in the form of a code of practice. "Universalism" was introduced into this code through a reference to the South African constitution and to South African law. The code requires respect for law and the constitution. Within the model this code constitutes, and is seen as constituting, a "constitutional framework" that guides and limits what takes place locally. It establishes a language and meanings that are used in constituting "cases" and in developing resolutions. At this level of practice the universal and the local are seen as usually complementary. The universal here, however, is not understood as universal values that South Africans through the processes that had founded a new South Africa had embraced. The assumption was there had been and would continue to be deliberative processes at the state level that canvassed and then endorsed proposals for values that would be treated by South Africans as universal in Langlois' sense. The universal here was seen as a product of a democratic state that had the support of local people and local collectivities. The universal-local distinction was constituted as a distinction between multiple deliberative forums (from general forums such as the national parliament all the way down to very local forums such as peace gatherings) with more general forums, both setting the frameworks for and trumping more local ones.

In the case of this process Peace Committees constitute themselves deliberately as having no adjudicative power or coercive powers, arguing that these are properly powers that only belong to state processes and state officials. For them, acting ways that respected the human rights of persons meant respecting state sovereignty in these realms, a classic Hobbesian position. What the processes of the model seek to do is to carve out a space for the local level, in which rights endorsed by deliberative forums at the state level, can be mobilized effectively to enhance democratic self-direction. This means that local people develop plans for creating peace in their lives that enable the voices of the poor and the marginalized to shape courses of action. Within the Zwelethemba model rights have a meaning within nested deliberative forums that promote self-direction.

One of the features of the code linking the universal with the particular is its argument that out of deliberative engagements – that draw on notions of deliberative democracy – dispute resolutions must be sought. These deliberations are structured to promote a future orientation that sees members of the Peace Committee acting as facilitators, rather than as judges, of local engagement. The key right mobilized within these processes is the equal right of every participant to democratic engagement. The character of these nested processes is illustrated in the following comments by Peace Committee members:

> ...Yes, I have the experience now. But I must still be able not to work as a judge. I must ask the questions that contribute to the solution, but I must remember not to be a judge. I have some questions to ask, like, "What do you think that the Peace Committee can do for you". And the second question, digging the root cause, we can ask is "What do you think caused this to happen..."[1]

> And we also ask the disputants; How do you think we [the participants at the Gathering] can deal with this, how can we help you?, so that we will have their input...[2]

4.2. Promoting Self-Direction

The Zwelethemba model uses general values that shape its regulatory architecture to promote spaces in which local knowledge (and values endorsed locally) can be mobilized to promote self-direction. In accomplishing this, the model encourages disputants, and others mobilized to assist in dispute resolution, to constitute spaces in which they can take charge of their lives directly – this is seen as "deepening democracy". One way to do this is by encouraging disputants to find consensual resolutions that will avoid disputes being transferred to state forums where resolutions will be imposed.

By way of illustration consider the following dispute involving a conflict between a married couple and the wife's brother and his girlfriend. The older sister of the siblings attended the gathering constituted to pursue a resolution. The married couple had allowed the brother to live in a dwelling in the backyard of their house with his girlfriend. For sometime their co-existence had not been peaceful. In particular, conflicts had arisen over the use of shared facilities. The unmarried couple used the main house for water and for toilet facilities. This had become a source of much irritation that lead to one conflict after another arising. Both couples had, it was claimed at the gathering, "spread rumours" about partners "sleeping around". The conflict had escalated into verbal and physical abuse – the wife of the married couple reported the incident to the police, who in turn referred the case to the Peace Committee. This referral took place within an arrangement whereby the local police recognized the Peace Committee as promoting forums for consensual resolutions that would avoid the necessity of having a resolution sought and imposed through criminal justice processes.

After an initial exploration of the incidents that led to the abuse, a Committee member drew attention to the norms of Xhosa culture as a way of building a platform around which to build a consensual resolution:

> The things you said about affairs are things that are said about single people, people who are not married, not to a married woman. This is a married woman, what you did was wrong running to her husband and telling him what she did. This is your sister, no matter what. I had a sister who just passed away, she used to curse at me and say I am a priest of the devil, but I never hit her, not even once. I used to live in her backyard ... I never answered her back because, really, it was her house.

Those present accepted this set of norms as applicable and ones to be drawn upon in establishing a resolution. The brother, however, argued that the problem lay not with the values but with the living arrangements which were the source of the conflict. This was agreed. The Peace Committee in pursuing a resolution pointed to the availability of a municipal housing office where the dispute could be taken. If taken to these authorities it was argued they may well loose control of the resolution and may have to live with an imposed solution. This mobilization of Galanter's (1981) "shadow of the law" promotes the self-direction while at the same time pointing out that this could only take place so long as more universal norms were respected. In this case, it was the norm that non-state resolutions had to be consensual rather than imposed. In promoting self-direction they affirmed the law and its prescriptions, in particular those concerning the legitimate use of coercion. In responding to this encouragement to embrace self-direction the brother apologized to his sister. Further discussion revealed that the brother had already taken action to move out and that a "shack" had been erected on a site in another informal settlement. The gathering ended with a mutual acknowledgement of "mistakes" and with a Committee member inviting the wife to call on them again if the abuse continued. In making this invitation the Committee member referred to the fact that if self-direction failed, other state operated forums that could impose resolution might have to be engaged. She referred specifically to seeking a protection order from the courts.

This example confirms the model's recognition that deliberative forums are nested and that different forums have different characteristics and different implications for the way in which the value of self-direction is realized. If self-direction is recognized as a human right the Peace Committees can be seen as negotiating the terrain of nested forums to promote it.

5. RECONCILING TENSIONS WITHIN THE FAMILY OF HUMAN RIGHTS

A significant arena of debate within human rights discourses has been the extent to which development – economic, social and cultural rights – is recognized within the family of universal human rights. However, most scholars agree that there has been relatively little practical success in getting these "rights" included as genuine universal human rights – something incidentally that the South African constitution formally does. It is indicative that the relation between the human rights discourse and the prestigious Millennium Development Goals project of the United Nations (UN) is described by Alston (2005) as "ships passing in the night". In his view, neither the human rights nor the development communities have embraced this linkage with enthusiasm or conviction. Human rights continue to be debated

mostly at large international conferences and monitored by the UN Human Rights Commission, while development policies are still formulated and implemented by completely different institutions (Sano, 2000). Human Rights NGOs, having a significant voice within the human rights discourse during the last couple of decades, continue to focus almost exclusively on civil and political rights. Skogly (2002) proposes that the main reason that the UN and the human rights community continues to neglect economic and social human rights is that their violations are by far most frequently experienced by poor people. Poor people have been left out in the drafting and implementation of the instruments designed to protect such rights.

A link between development and rights has indeed been forged, but this has taken through the linkage of aid from wealthy nations to the willingness of host nations to support and promote the established conception of human rights as centred on civil and political rights (Skogly, 1990). This approach to rights has been linked within some of the rights literature to structural adjustment programmes promoted by international agencies such as the World Bank and the International Monetary Fund as both sets of initiatives prioritize "northern" concerns over those of the "global south". This has led to arguments from the "South" that southern regions should be wary of adopting policies in any arena that does not arise out of and resonate with their own concerns (Udombana, 2000). Mary Robertson (2004), the UN High Commissioner for Human Rights from 1997 to 2002, argues for the link between economic, social and cultural rights and practices that promote decision-making processes that include the poor and the marginalized.

In arguing along these lines, Felice (2004) questions the possibility of this happening as long as decisions on what should count as human rights are left to forums in which states are the principal players. Similarly Wellman (2000) argues for finding institutional mechanisms that will permit the inclusion of a plurality of actors, knowledges and institutions that extend beyond states. This requires institutional arrangements at various levels to facilitate this. In promoting this, Yamin (2005) proposes a search for innovative strategies in human rights which moves out of the entrenched dichotomy between the public and the private, identifies how power can be devolved to different groups, communities and individuals through their participation in decision-making forums that provide for an authentic transfer of power from the state, and establish forms of collaboration between traditional human rights communities and a broad range of other groups and social movements (*Ibid.*, pp. 1232–1239).

The motivation for the development of the Zwelethemba model lies in a similar interest in building institutional arrangements outside of state

institutions that would promote participatory decision-making. Therefore, we now turn once again to this set of processes and their implications for shifting beyond an understanding of rights that is constructed around political and civil rights.

At the heart of the Zwelethemba process is the notion that economic, social and cultural rights count. Or put differently, civil and political rights are of value if they are associated with processes that promote economic, social and cultural values at local levels. Human rights within the logic of the model must be seen to promote not simply individual rights but community well-being. There are several forms of community well-being that the Zwelethemba model promotes, the well-being that comes from the construction of peace as a foundational order as well as the well-being that emerges when self-direction is realized. In addition, the model seeks to put funds that can be used to promote development directly into the hands of Peace Committees. These committees are required to dispense these resources in ways that respond to local needs and concerns, as measured both through the deliberative processes of peace gatherings and through community surveys and gathering that bring people together specifically to identify collective needs and concerns. For every dispute that is resolved within the constraints of the regulatory framework a small amount of money is accredited to a Peace Building account to support developmental initiatives. Committee members are encouraged to develop plans in collaboration with other community members that use these funds (which have to date been provided by donor funding, in particular from the Finnish Government) to lever other resources both financial and in-kind. The conception lying behind this is to tie a dispute resolution or Peace Making process that respects individual human rights to a process that promotes economic, social and cultural well-being. The objective is to relate self-direction to development by establishing the possibility of self-directed development. This focus on Peace Building means that the emphasis is not simply on disputes but includes broader issues such as public health, food, shelter, waste management, education, recreation and the like. Peace is extended beyond a Hobbesian concept on peaceful co-existence through the provision of physical security to more general questions of human security (Wood & Shearing, 2007).

6. RECONCILING THE PAST AND THE FUTURE IN HUMAN RIGHTS

In the previous sections we have tried to demonstrate that it is possible to develop local models of dispute resolution that manage to reconcile

universal human values with local norms as well as to integrate different sets of human rights. In this section our focus shifts, as we discuss the role of "rights" in relation to how conflicts may be solved, in particular as to how a concern with the past and the future might be managed.

The criminal justice system has not been immune to the rise of human rights over time. The human rights community has been instrumental in promoting greater attention to the rules of due process for suspects and offenders. Criminal justice continues, however, to be based on some core assumptions as to how human conflicts should be managed: first, that it is reasonable to characterize a conflict as a crime with a defined offender and victim; secondly, that it is reasonable to respond to the crime through a past-oriented logic of retribution; and, thirdly, that a reasonable way of solving conflicts is to organize criminal proceedings as adversarial legal processes.

It is now well established that victims and offenders are frequently dissatisfied with the ways their problems are handled by the criminal justice system (Wright, 1996; Strang, 2002). Feminist legal analysis have questioned whether the dichotomous and adversarial character of legal rights may not be alien to women's experiences and have elaborated on the possibility of organizing legal processes with a stronger focus on outcome (Binion, 1995). Christie (1977), in particular, has been a spokesman for returning conflicts from the criminal justice system back to the society. In his view the criminal justice system "steals" conflicts that are needed within communities as a mechanism for reconciliation and growth.

A potential problem with the manner in which the criminal justice system constructs conflicts is that it is not always well adjusted to empirical realities, where thin and frayed lines may exist between offending and victimization. Parties to conflicts of some duration are often cast in long-lasting relationship where roles frequently alternate; the offender today might have been yesterdays' victim, and vice versa. Putting the blame where it belongs becomes a more complicated matter than thinking about crime as isolated instances of harmful behaviour. Christie (1977) once argued that Barotse law, "allowing the conflicting parties to bring in the whole chain of old complaints and arguments...", might have been a good instrument for norm-setting and problem-solving on many occasions. What this might indicate is that the process of seeking to reveal the chain of causes through which a conflict has nurtured and intensified, and debating the consequences thereof for the parties involved, might be significant elements of a restorative form of problem-solving. Christie seems to suggest that conceiving of the conflict as a one-incident encounter with clearly defined roles might sometimes constrain the collective attempt to search for fair and reasonable outcomes.

Moore (2004, p. 88) suggests that it might actually be more fruitful to think of conflicts and relationships as "managed", more than resolved, through legal (or restorative) processes. In recommending a more future-oriented way of thinking he claims that "[T]here may be less transformation as a result of the process, and more transformation as a result of the outcome. Change comes from an action plan that is put into practice..." (*Ibid.*, p. 89). Within such a future-oriented approach to justice the primary objective might be defined as to offer disputants a hope for a better and more peaceful tomorrow. The reasoning of these scholars seems to indicate the possibility of a more open-ended experience of justice, beyond the assumption of legal practices (Pavlich, 2002, p. 98).

As argued by Yamin (2005) there are significant limitations when relying too heavily on litigation and court-centric strategies to address human rights violations. She emphasizes the necessity of advocacy strategies that move beyond adversarial, dyadic relationships that state problem solving forums tend to promote to ones that give a greater role to non-state actors. She argues that contemporary innovative human rights advocacy concern itself with:

> Understanding and promoting the enabling conditions in which people can feel themselves to be self-authorized subjects who can then claim and use the tools necessary to enjoy their different rights. (*Ibid.*, p. 1222)

6.1. Avoiding a "Crime" Construction

According to the Zwelethemba model, individuals directly involved in the conflict are understood as participants or "parties" rather than "victims" and "offenders". The victim/offender binary is viewed within the model as serving to separate, exclude and to pre-judge. In practice it is commonplace for a "case" brought to the attention of local peacemakers (called "Peace Committees") to be regarded as no more than a single slice in time that should be located within a history of conflict between the parties. Within this context the "offending" party and the "harmed" party may, and probably do, change places over time. In other words, today's "offender" may have been yesterday's "victim". The model is based on the argument that the language of "victim" and "offender" structures the meaning of what happened in the past in ways that make it difficult for parties involved to understand and articulate their own reality or lived experience.

6.2. Identifying Root Causes

The model does contain a backward-looking mechanism, but not one that is focused on the blaming or shaming of the behaviour of a pre-defined offender. Instead, the disputants and other participants are encouraged to engage in a collective search for underlying "root causes" that have contributed to the dispute. Before a solution is reached, it is regarded as important to reveal the series of events that has contributed to and nurtured the conflict:

> ... It is important to follow the steps. It can be very dangerous to go too quickly for a solution. You must first see what the cause is. For instance, if one of the disputants cries, show regret, that is not enough, you must ask and tell, try to locate the cause. If not, people will do it again. Before the solution, you must find the underlying cause. You must not jump at a solution. That can be very dangerous...[3]

6.3. A Future Orientation

The goal of Peacemaking Gatherings is the establishment of a future-oriented solution to the conflict that will "make for a better tomorrow" that most, and ideally all, parties present agree to. In this regard, the model stresses a deliberative approach that end in consensus building (Shearing & Wood, 2003). The model is designed, to borrow from LaPrairie (1995, p. 80), "...to return the conflict to its rightful owners..." (see also Christie, 1977). During the Peacemaking Gathering, or at its termination, it may indeed be the case that considerable affect (anger, sadness, remorse, etc.) is displayed, but emotional transformation is not the goal of the process. It is regarded as "nice if it happens" but not as essential. The goal is instrumental. The key question guiding the peacemaking process (and the set of steps established for this) is, "how do we make a better tomorrow?" This focus on the future has its roots in the life experience of poor people who are required daily to get on with the business of living. With its instrumental focus on the future, the process may produce the outcome of reintegration as described by Braithwaite (1989) but once again reintegration is a "nice if it happens" consequence but not a goal.

Accordingly the term "reintegration", however, is not an appropriate one to use in characterizing this local capacity model, as it suggest that there existed a prior collectivity (small or large) to which an individual or individuals were bound to, or integrated with. This is certainly not always or even usually the case. The notion of reintegration implies that a certain relationship or "bundle of life" that needs to be "restored". This may indeed be the case, and this restoration process may indeed be an outcome of a Gathering. However, living in peace and making a better future may simply involve an agreement between parties that they will avoid each other in the future and an agreement by their associates that they will work to ensure that this happens.

An example from Zwelethemba serves to illustrate this. One of the conflicts brought to a Zwelethemba Peace Committee was by neighbours of a family who were worried that the ongoing conflict between a daughter-in-law and her husband's mother would escalate into serious violence. A Gathering was convened of the persons regarded as most likely able to contribute to a resolution of the conflict. The invitation to the Gathering was to persons who were seen in a position to be helpful in an instrumental sense – they were not invited to attend as "supporters" of the conflicting parties. The Gathering quickly concluded that the chances of restoring a "happy family", if there had ever been one, were minimal. The Plan of Action agreed to involve moving the son and the daughter-in-law's informal house to another part of the township far away from the mother-in-law.

6.4. Justice as a Future Guarantee of Peace

The uniqueness of the Zwelethemba model, compared to both retributive and some restorative justice arrangements, is that the matters of dispute are not addressed through a backward-looking process that seeks to balance wrongs with burdens but through a forward-looking one that seeks to guarantee that the disputants' moral goods will be respected in the future. Contrary to what one might expect from the discourses of many moral philosophers with a deontological approach, this is experienced by the parties to the dispute, and by members of the community, as both a just and an instrumentally effective outcome. Justice, as a moral outcome, is given meaning within a future-focused framework (Shearing & Johnston, 2005).

6.5. Increasing the Likelihood that Agreements will be Honoured

Reaching agreements is not sufficient. The credibility of the model also depends on the degree to which the agreements are honoured by the parties to the conflict. The likelihood for future peace, however, is related to the way that agreements are reached. The Zwelethemba model underscores that resolutions must be reached by the disputants themselves and never enforced upon them by others. It is considered to be important to check if that is indeed the case. As one PeaceMaker pointed out:

> ... It is important to use time, because of the solution and the peace. Both disputants must feel free, be satisfied. We must know that the agreement is the right one. At the end, we will see it in their faces, that it is correct. That it brings the peace. We often ask the friends and relatives who are present if they think that the solution is correct...[4]

Because the status of the Peace Committees is so closely related to the likelihood of agreements being honoured they are forced to take this issue very seriously. A Peace Gathering organized in Khayelitsha in May 2003, attended by one of us, helps to illustrate this point. The dispute concerned a money-lending issue, for which a solution was not so difficult to reach. The agreement entered into by the parties was that the husband of disputant number two would pay disputant number one Rands 200 a month, until the agreed upon amount had been paid. However, when, for a variety of reasons, no one else was present at the meeting beside the disputants and the PeaceMakers they decided to arrange for a new Peace Gathering. The Peace Committee felt that it was necessary to commit additional members of the disputants' families and community to the agreement, particularly the husband of disputant number two, as he was to be the source of the money to be paid.

A follow up study was recently conducted to evaluate the extent to which the peace agreements entered into had been kept by the disputants for a period of three to six months after the gathering. Twenty-five cases of dispute resolution organized by three PeaceCommittees were randomly selected for study and a total of twenty-six disputants were interviewed. In 16 of 17 cases in which the interviewers were able to get hold of one or both of the disputants (others had moved, were drunk or were otherwise un-accessible, witnessing to the fragility of life in the townships) the peace contracts were acknowledged to have been honoured. No disagreement of opinions was registered in those cases when both parties to the dispute were interviewed. Only in one case was the status of the agreement more ambiguous. Twenty-two of the disputants were overwhelmingly positive of the Peace Gathering process they had experienced, confirmed that they would use the model again if required, and stated many reasons for why they preferred Zwelethemba to other forms of public or private justice. Besides being satisfied with the process and the outcome, disputants frequently reported that they preferred the Peace Committee due to its capacity for solving conflicts "in a rational way", "just sitting down and talk", with "no violence involved". Many also emphasized how the model made it possible to solve conflicts before "things go too far" and without people getting arrested and being put in jail. Four disputants had more mixed feelings towards the process, two of whom were quite negative because they did not get the outcome they wanted from the Gathering.

6.6. Monitoring the Peace Agreements

An important function to increase compliance with the peace contracts is to monitor the implementation of action plans. One or several of the participants at a Gathering, frequently, but not always, members of the Peace Committee, are selected to make sure that those who have committed themselves to the peace contract fulfil their promises. Compared to other community structures involved in solving local conflicts the Peace Committees appear to put more emphasis on this function, as one representative of a civic organization (SANCO) in Khayelitsha noted: "We do see that the peace committee uses much more time to follow up cases, we do not have the capacity for that."[5] The members of the Peace Committees recognize that the capacity to monitor agreements is an important and advantageous feature of their practice:

> ... Most of the disputants follow up the agreement. If some do not, we try to encourage them to keep their promises. For instance, in money-lending cases, we ask: "Could you manage to pay 50 R a month", like that. We try to encourage the disputants to keep their promises. People say to us: "We like the way you follow up". The monitoring, it is important for being trusted. Monitoring, we think of it as marketing...[6]

6.7. Preventing Escalation

In considering the activities of Peace Committees, it is not just the work that they do that is significant, but the counterfactual possibilities avoided. While disputes are for the most part minor, and easily handled, they could easily have escalated into more serious disputes. The dispute resolution activities of Peace Committees are seen, from a police perspective, as a demand reduction mechanism that frees valuable resources for other activities. Further, had disputants taken their dispute to other less regulated popular forums the "resolution" itself might have escalated the disorder (Nina, 2001).

From the standpoint of transition to a democratic society PeaceMaking gatherings operate as a terrain in which democratic and human rights values are being enacted as routine local practices. This contributes to a culture of democratic deliberation.

7. CONCLUSION

As Goodhart (2003) has suggested, one way of thinking about the universality of human rights is as a question of effectiveness in achieving particular values. If so, we need to distinguish between different ways of structuring processes which we organize to attain such values. Uncoupling values from processes opens a conceptual space that allows one to scrutinize the extent to which such values can be effectively realized through different kinds of institutions and mechanisms (Shearing, Wood, & Font, in press). It is quite possible that justice is delivered and human rights protected through forms of practices that are not explicitly established or normally recognized as promoting such values.

In this paper we have presented a model of local conflict management, developed in South Africa that, while not being conceived as a Human Rights NGO, in practice promotes as range of such values. We have underscored the capacity of the model to reconcile core tensions in human rights, as conceptualized by scholars and practitioners. The model negotiates a terrain of nested PeaceMaking and PeaceBuilding forums that mobilize local knowledge and norms within the limits of rules and principles associated with universal rights, that allow for a dual approach to civil/political and developmental human rights, and that combines a concern for the past with a strong emphasis on the prospects of building a more peaceful tomorrow.

As a conclusion we hope to have illustrated that a bottom-up perspective, emphasizing the relevance and potential of local human rights-oriented practices, such as the Zwelethemba model developed by poor and marginalized communities in South Africa, might have something to offer the human rights discourse and the human rights community. The time seems to be ripe to embrace a "nodal approach" to human rights. It is becoming more and more obvious that a state-centred focus is insufficient. The future challenge lies in finding new ways of building alliances among a range of actors, knowledges and capacities in human rights.

NOTES

1. Member of the Khayelitsha Peace Committee, individual interview, May 2003.
2. Member of the Mbekweni Peace Committee, group interview, May 2003.
3. Member of the Nkqubela Peace Committee, interview no. 1, May 2003.
4. Member of the Mbekweni Peace Committee (Lonwabo), group interview May 2003.

5. Member of the civic organization (SANCO) in Khayelitsha, interview no. 14, May 2003.
6. Member of the Khayelitsha Peace Committee, interview no. 11, May 2003.

REFERENCES

Alston, P. (2005). Ships passing in the night: The current state of the human rights and development debate seen through the lens of the millennium development goals. *Human Rights Quarterly, 27,* 755–829.

Alves, J. A. (2000). The declaration of human rights in postmodernity. *Human Rights Quarterly, 22,* 478–500.

Baxi, U. (2002). *The future of human rights.* Delhi: Oxford University Press.

Binion, G. (1995). Human rights: A feminist perspective. *Human Rights Quarterly, 17,* 509–526.

Braithwaite, J. (1989). *Shame and reintegration.* Cambridge: Cambridge University Press.

Chandler, D. (2001). The road to military humanitarianism: How the human rights NGOs shaped a new humanitarian agenda. *Human Rights Quarterly, 23,* 678–700.

Christie, N. (1977). Conflicts as property. *British Journal of Criminology, 17,* 1–15.

Donnelly, J. (2001). The universal declaration of human rights: A liberal defense. *Human rights.* Working Papers, No. 12. http://www.du.edu/humanrights/workingpapers/papers/12-donnelly-02-01.pdf

Douzinas, C. (2000). *The end of human rights.* Oxford: Hart Publishing.

Erman, E. (2005). *Human rights and democracy. Discourse theory and global rights institutions.* Aldershot: Ashgate Publishing.

Felice, W. (2004). Respecting, protecting and fulfilling economic and social rights: A UN security council? *Human rights & human welfare.* Working Papers, No. 12.

Fields, A. B., & Narr, W-D. (1992). Human rights as a holistic concept. *Human Rights Quarterly, 14,* 1–20.

Fitzpatrick, P. (2006). Is humanity enough? The secular theology of human rights. *Human rights & human Welfare.* Working Papers, No. 32.

Forsythe, D. P. (2005). International humanitarianism in the contemporary world: Forms and issues. *Human rights & human welfare.* Working Papers, No. 22.

Freeman, M. (1994). The philosophical foundation of human rights. *Human Rights Quarterly, 16,* 491–514.

Gaay de Fortman, B. (2001). Laborious law. *Human rights.* Working Papers, No. 15. http://www.du.edu/humanrights/workingpapers/papers/15-degaayfortman-09-01.pdf

Galanter, M. (1981). Justice in many rooms: Courts, private ordering and indigenous law. *Journal of Legal Pluralism and Unofficial Law, 19,* 1–48.

Goodhart, M. (2003). Origins and universality in the human rights debates: Cultural essentialism and the challenge of globalization. *Human Rights Quarterly, 25,* 935–964.

Guilhot, N. (2005). *The democracy makers.* New York: Columbia University Press.

Habermas, J. (1988). Law and Modernity. In: S. M. McMurrin (Ed.), *The tanner lectures in human values* (Vol. 8). Salt Lake City: University of Utah Press.

Habermas, J. (1997). *Legitimation Crisis.* Cambridge: Polity Press.

Johnston, L., & Shearing, C. (2003). *Governing security: Explorations in policing and justice.* London: Routledge.

Langlois, A. J. (2002). Human rights: The globalisation and fragmentation of moral discourse. *Review of International Studies, 28,* 479–496.

LaPrairie, C. (1995). Some reflections on new criminal justice policies in Canada: Restorative justice, alternative measures and conditional sentences. *The Australian and New Zealand Journal of Criminology, 32,* 139–152.

Mertus, J. A. (1999). Doing democracy differently: The transformative potential of human rights NGOs in transnational civil society. *Third World Legal Studies (1998–1999),* 205–234.

Moore, D. B. (2004). Managing social conflict – The evolution of a practical theory. *Journal of Sociology and Welfare, 31,* 71–91.

Nina, D. (2001). Popular justice and the 'appropriation' of the state monopoly on the definition of justice and order: The case of anti-crime communities. In: W. Scharf & D. Nina (Eds), *The other law: Non-state ordering in South Africa* (pp. 98–120). Lansdowne: Juta.

O'Manique, J. (1990). Universal and inalienable rights: A search for foundations. *Human Rights Quarterly, 12,* 465–485.

Otto, D. (1996). Nongovernmental organizations in the United Nations system: The emerging role of international civil society. *Human Rights Quarterly, 18,* 107–141.

Pavlich, G. (2002). Deconstructing restoration: The promise of restorative justice. In: G. M. Weitekamp & H.-J. Kerner (Eds), *Restorative justice. Theoretical foundations* (pp. 90–109). Cullompton, UK: Willan Publishing.

Perry, M. J. (1997). Are human rights universal? The relativist challenge and related matters. *Human Rights Quarterly, 19,* 461–509.

Pollis, A. (1996). Cultural relativism revisited: Through a state prism. *Human Rights Quarterly, 18,* 316–344.

Preis, A-B. S. (1996). Human rights as cultural practice: An anthropological critique. *Human Rights Quarterly, 18,* 286–315.

Sano, H.-O. (2000). Development and human rights: The necessary, but partial integration of human rights and development. *Human Rights Quarterly, 22,* 734–752.

Shearing, C., & Johnston, L. (2005). Justice in the risk society. *The Australian and New Zealand Journal of Criminology, 38,* 25–38.

Shearing, C., & Wood, J. (2003). Governing security for common goods. *International Journal of the Sociology of Law, 31,* 205–225.

Shearing, C., Wood, J., & Font, E. (in press). Nodal Governance and Restorative Justice.

Skogly, S. I. (1990). Human rights reporting: The "nordic" experience. *Human Rights Quarterly, 12,* 513–528.

Skogly, S. I. (2002). Is there a right not to be poor? *Human Rights Law Review, 2,* 59–80.

Smith, J., Pagnucco, R., & Lopez, A. (1998). Globalizing human rights: The work of transnational human rights NGOs in the 1990s. *Human Rights Quarterly, 22,* 379–412.

Stammers, N. (1995). A critique of social approaches to human rights. *Human Rights Quarterly, 17,* 488–508.

Strang, H. (2002). *Repair or revenge. Victims and restorative justice.* Oxford: Clarendon Press.

Tilley, J. J. (2000). Cultural relativism. *Human Rights Quarterly, 22,* 501–547.

Twining, W. (2006). Human rights: Southern voices. Francis Deng, Abdullahi An-Na'im, Yash Ghai, and Upendra Baxi. *Review of Constitutional Studies, 11,* 203–279.

Udombana, N. J. (2000). The third world and the right to development: Agenda for the next millennium. *Human Rights Quarterly, 22,* 753–787.

Wellman, C. (2000). Solidarity, the individual and human rights. *Human Rights Quarterly, 22*, 639–657.

Wood, J., & Shearing, C. (2007). *Imagining security*. Cullompton, UK: Willan Publishing.

Wright, M. (1996). *Justice for victims and offenders. A restorative response to crime*. Winchester: Waterside Press.

Yamin, A. E. (2005). The future in the mirror: Incorporating strategies for the defense and promotion of economic, social and cultural rights into the mainstream human rights agenda. *Human Rights Quarterly, 27*, 1200–1244.

JUSTICE AND HUMAN RIGHTS FOR ABORIGINAL PEOPLES IN SASKATCHEWAN: MAPPING THE ROAD AHEAD

James P. Mulvale

1. INTRODUCTION

Aboriginal peoples living in what is now known as the province of Saskatchewan, Canada, have experienced great troubles and systematic injustices in their dealings with the white man since his arrival in their territory over three centuries ago. In this chapter, I will outline the effects of racism, internal colonialism, and cultural genocide as manifested in the interactions of Saskatchewan's Aboriginal peoples with the contemporary criminal justice system. I will also examine proposals for changes in the criminal justice system, and more broadly in the relationship between Aboriginal peoples and political institutions and social formations in Canada. Specifically, I will examine how the reports and recommendations of three landmark public commissions of inquiry into Aboriginal peoples and the criminal justice system have shaped and advocated these proposals for change. The Royal Commission on Aboriginal Peoples worked at the national level and carried out a very comprehensive examination of the social, legal, constitutional, and institutional relationships between

Crime and Human Rights
Sociology of Crime, Law and Deviance, Volume 9, 215–238
Copyright © 2007 by Elsevier Ltd.
ISSN: 1521-6136/doi:10.1016/S1521-6136(07)09009-4

Aboriginal and non-Aboriginal peoples in Canada, delivering its Final
Report in 1996. The Commission of First Nations and Métis Peoples and
Justice Reform in Saskatchewan examined the comprehensive workings of
criminal justice system and related systems in this province, and delivered its
Final Report in June 2004. The Inquiry into the Death of Neil Stonechild,
under the direction of Justice D. H. Wright, investigated a case of police
racism and violence towards Aboriginal people in the city of Saskatoon,
Saskatchewan, and reported to the provincial government in September
2004.

The analysis and recommendations of these three commissions speak to
the need to reform, and perhaps even fundamentally reconstruct, criminal
justice processes as they affect First Nations and Métis peoples. Many of the
changes proposed by these commissions have the potential to correct
historical injustices towards Aboriginal peoples as they have been
manifested in the criminal justice system. The commissions' blueprints also
have the potential to put into practice innovative aspects of human rights
that are consonant with Aboriginal cultures, and that could lower the
incidence and harms of criminal behaviour committed by and against
Aboriginal peoples.

The term "Aboriginal peoples" is used here as inclusive of both First
Nations and Métis people. The term "First Nations" refers to communities
of indigenous people that share a common language, history, and set of
religious beliefs and cultural practices, that function collectively in some
form of cohesive social organization, and that are located within a definable
geographic territory. First Nations in Canada generally have signed Treaties
with the British Crown (now acting through the federal government in
Ottawa). The First Nations of Saskatchewan are Cree, Saulteaux,
Assiniboine and Dene people who adhere to numbered Treaties Four,
Five, Six, Eight and Ten (www.otc.ca). They are organized into over 70
bands or reservations across the province, and also act politically in larger
units called Tribal Councils. Métis people can be defined is this way:

> Aboriginal people of mixed First Nation and European ancestry who identify themselves
> as Métis people, as distinct from First Nations people, Inuit or non-Aboriginal people.
> The Métis have a unique culture that draws on their diverse ancestral origins, such as
> Scottish, French, Ojibway and Cree. (www.fnmr.gov.sk.ca/glossary.htm)

Métis peoples have the opportunity to act politically through the Métis
Nation – Saskatchewan. They are not signatories to Treaties with the
Crown, and do not have a reserved land base. However Métis people in
Saskatchewan do operate or partner in a wide range of organizations that

provide education, social services, economic development, and cultural preservation and enhancement to Métis communities and others.

Aboriginal peoples in Saskatchewan constitute 13.5% of the population of Saskatchewan, which is a province of slightly less than one million people. First Nations people constitute approximately two thirds of this Aboriginal population, and Métis people one third. The demographics of Saskatchewan are shifting dramatically. As a proportion of the total provincial population, Aboriginal peoples have grown from 7.8% in 1986, and will increase (according to projections) to 28% by 2035 and 33% by 2045 (www.fnmr.gov.sk.ca/html/demographics/index.htm).

2. THE HISTORICAL CONTEXT AND THE PRESENT CHALLENGE

The first contacts of Aboriginal peoples with Europeans in what is now western Canada occurred during the era of European exploration and establishment of the fur trade in the late 1600s and into the 1700s (Bourgeault, 1986; Waiser, 2005, pp. 23–28). The commercial agents of French and British imperialism, especially the Hudson's Bay Company in the case of the British, were interested in trading for animal furs for their home market. During this era the dealings of Aboriginal peoples with their French and British guests were characterized by a significant degree of reciprocity and cooperation. Fur traders from France and Britain recognized that the help of First Nations was essential to them if they were to navigate the vast terrain, survive the rigours of living on the land, and actually obtain the animal furs that they sought as a commercially valuable commodity destined for European markets.

The relationship between Aboriginal peoples and Europeans on the Canadian prairie and boreal forest to the north changed markedly in the late nineteenth century. As the fur trade declined, officials of the Canadian government were eager to secure land on the Great Plains for the transcontinental railroad then under construction. This ribbon of steel would bring homesteading farmers from eastern Canada and various parts of Europe, and would enable the young white settler Dominion to extend its political control from Atlantic to Pacific, thereby preventing the loss of the Canadian hinterland to the ambitious and aggressive republic to the south. To effect this plan of extending its sovereignty across what was then referred to as the northwest territories of Canada, the British Crown (acting through

Canadian government officials) signed Treaties with First Nations living in what later (in 1905) became the province of Saskatchewan. In these Treaties, the First Nations surrendered most of their traditional territory (on which the buffalo, the staple of First Nations' survival, had been largely decimated as a result of European incursions). In exchange, the First Nations received guarantees from the Crown of parcels of reserved land, annual payments, schools, agricultural implements, and hunting and trapping rights off reserve. In general terms, the Treaty relationship was to consist of mutual respect and harmony based on the honour of the Crown and the integrity and prosperity of First Nations.

On a less peaceful note, the Canadian government used armed force to put down rebellions by Métis people on the Canadian prairies in 1871 and 1885. The Métis resistance was caused by the threat to their traditional land and way of life, as settlers, farmers and surveyors arrived in increasingly large numbers from central Canada. The Métis were never afforded the opportunity to sign Treaties, and in fact were treated contemptuously by Ottawa and the incoming white settlers as "half-breeds". The Métis were socially devalued and economically marginalized, and only in recent decades has there been some social and legal recognition of their cultural distinctiveness, political aspirations, and unique contributions to Canadian history.

Even for First Nations who were parties to Treaties, however, the real intentions of the Canadian government became clear in the decades of the late nineteenth and twentieth centuries. Treaty provisions to do with land entitlement, economic development, and protection of indigenous languages and cultures were ignored or abrogated by Canadian politicians and government officials. A set of assumptions, beliefs, and explicit policies that can be characterized as internal colonialism and cultural genocide shaped and guided the treatment of Aboriginal peoples by the Canadian government. A particularly malevolent aspect of this approach was the operation of residential schools by Roman Catholic religious orders and Protestant churches on behalf of the federal government. Aboriginal children were taken from their families and sent off to these schools, where they were forbidden to speak their own languages and taught English, and were instructed in Christian religious beliefs. They were expected to assimilate white culture and behaviours. These children were also subjected (as has been revealed in recent years) to systematic emotional, physical, and sexual abuse at hands of their religious teachers and caretakers. The individual damage and community disorganization that resulted from the residential school experience has taken a tremendous toll on First Nations, and the healing process is still in relatively early stages in the early twenty-first century. The payment of financial compensation by churches and the federal government to the victims of residential schools has been a subject of great political and legal contestation for years, even as the number of survivors declines with the passage of time.

The manifestations of decades of entrenched racism towards Aboriginal peoples in Canada, and government laws and policies based on internal colonialism and cultural extinction, are multiple and profound. First Nations and Métis peoples experience poverty, unemployment, low educational attainment, poor health, substandard housing, addiction, and suicide at much higher rates than non-Aboriginal people in Canada. They are also much more likely to become enmeshed in the various aspects of the criminal justice system, including police contacts, court appearances, and incarceration in the correctional system. Aboriginal people are also much more likely to be victimized by crime. Data from 2004 (Statistics Canada, 2006) indicate that "Aboriginal people were three times more likely than non-Aboriginal people to be victims of violent crime, specifically sexual assault, robbery and physical assault". Aboriginal people are also more likely to be jailed than their non-Aboriginal peers. According to the Correctional Service of Canada, who deal with convicted persons sentenced to two years or more of imprisonment, "Aboriginal peoples represent 2.8% of the Canadian population, but account for 18% of the federally incarcerated population" (www.csc-scc.gc.ca/text/prgrm/correctional/abissues/know/7_e.shtml). Of 3,850 federally sentenced offenders from Saskatchewan, just over three quarters are Aboriginal. In the provincial correctional institutions of Saskatchewan (for offenders sentenced to less than two years), Aboriginal adult offenders comprise 80.2% of the inmate population even though they are slightly less than 10% of the adult population as a whole (Statistics Canada, 2006).

The incidence of actual crime, the criminalization of individual behaviours and circumstances, and the widening of the carceral net in regard to Aboriginal people in Saskatchewan and Canada have multiple and complex causes. They include the general historical legacies of internal colonialism and racism (as discussed above), but also the more specific and immediate practices of court officials, police, correctional officers, and other players in the criminal justice system. Understanding and addressing the causes of mistreatment and racism towards Aboriginal peoples in the criminal justice system are not easy tasks. However, we do have at our disposal useful diagnoses of the problems and blueprints for positive change in the criminal justice field that have been advanced by the three government commissions mentioned at the beginning of this chapter. The reports of these commissions provide roadmaps for developing and implementing new models of Aboriginal justice, and to thereby overcome systemic racism, correct historical and current injustices, and contribute to the realization of civil, political, social, economic, cultural, and collective rights for First Nations and Métis peoples in Saskatchewan and Canada. Key themes and recommendations of each of these three commissions are examined in turn below.

3. ROYAL COMMISSION ON ABORIGINAL PEOPLES

The *Royal Commission on Aboriginal Peoples* (RCAP) was commissioned by the Canadian federal government under Conservative Prime Minister Brian Mulroney in 1991, and was charged with a very formidable task.

> The Commission of Inquiry should investigate the evolution of the relationship among aboriginal peoples (Indian, Inuit, and Métis), the Canadian government, and Canadian society as a whole. It should propose specific solutions, rooted in domestic and international experience, to the problems which have plagued those relationships and which confront aboriginal peoples today. (www.ainc-inac.gc.ca/ch/rcap/sg)

Over the subsequent period of slightly over two years, RCAP "visited 96 communities, held 178 days of hearings, heard briefs from 2067 people and accumulated more than 76,000 pages of testimony", and "commissioned more than 350 research project". RCAP (1996a) produced its final report in five volumes in 1996, and made a total of 454 recommendations.

One aspect of the work of RCAP (1996b) that is of particular interest here is its publication entitled *Bridging the Cultural Divide: A Report on Aboriginal People and Criminal Justice in Canada*. The general conclusion contained in this report was blunt and condemning.

> The Canadian criminal justice system has failed the Aboriginal peoples of Canada – First Nations, Inuit, and Métis people, on-reserve and off-reserve, urban and rural – in all territorial and governmental jurisdictions. The principal reason for this crushing failure is the fundamentally different world views of Aboriginal and non-Aboriginal people with respect to such elemental issues as the substantive content of justice and the process of achieving justice. (RCAP, 1996b, p. 309)

RCAP also recognized that crime rates were higher among Aboriginal peoples, leading to their overrepresentation in police contacts, court dockets, and prisons. However the Commission pointed to systemic root causes of higher rates of crime and victimization in Aboriginal communities, and argued that the incidence of crime and the treatment of Aboriginal offenders and victims were part of the legacy of racism, cultural genocide, residential schools, lack of education and employment, and related social problems such as addiction and family violence (RCAP, 1996b, pp. 26–53).

As a starting point for a process of change, the RCAP recommended that

> [F]ederal, provincial and territorial governments recognize the right of Aboriginal nations to establish and administer their own systems of justice pursuant to their inherent right of self-government, including the power to make laws, within the Aboriginal nation's territory. (RCAP, 1996b, p. 224)

This right to establish their own laws and operate justice institutions is based not only on Aboriginal peoples' inherent right to self-determination and self-government. It is also recognized in British jurisprudence going back to the Royal Proclamation of 1763, in Treaties signed between the Crown and First Nations, and in Section 35 (1) on Canada's *Constitution Act* of 1982 which states that "[t]he existing aboriginal and treaty rights of the aboriginal peoples of Canada are hereby recognized and affirmed".

The concepts of legal and judicial pluralism – derived from the idea that societies can function comfortably and adaptively with more than one legal code and more than one set of recognized and legitimate justice institutions – are the subject of contentious debate in many quarters. One definition of legal pluralism is "a situation in which two or more legal systems coexist in the same social field", where legal system can be defined broadly "to include the system of courts and judges supported by the state as well as non-legal forms of normative ordering" (Merry, 1988, p. 870). The concept of legal pluralism underpins RCAP's commitment to the right of Aboriginal peoples to articulate their own laws and to control their own justice institutions.

In the Canadian context, Borrows (2002, p. 23) warns that "[f]ull respect for and acceptance of First Nations law will not be easy to accomplish". He proposes a variation on the theme of legal pluralism for Canada, with Aboriginal law operating independently within Aboriginal communities, and also in tandem with Canadian jurisprudence in broader legal and judicial contexts. He argues that Aboriginal law can and should re-shape the contours of Euro-Canadian law, while at the same time incorporating elements of the latter in its own evolution. Aboriginal legal understandings and practices will have particular benefits beyond court rooms "in less formal settings, both within Indigenous communities and in the interactions of Indigenous peoples with their neighbours" (Borrows, 2002, p. 26). He is optimistic that there are many practical mechanisms for incorporating First Nations law into

Canadian jurisprudence, not the least of which is "legally trained members of
First Nations" who in many instances are "bicultural and/or bilingual and
who have learned law from their Elders as well as from Canadian legal and
academic institutions" and who "can bridge the gulf between First Nations
and European legal systems and help to make the law truly intersocietal"
(Borrows, 2002, pp. 24–25). The task of explicating Aboriginal law, drawing
on both written codes and oral teachings, will require "work and
imagination". But this effort must be part of the reinvigoration and further
evolution of Aboriginal cultures, and has the potential to greatly enhance the
entire fabric of Canadian law and society (Borrows, 2002, p. 27).

While proposing fundamental restructuring of Canadian courts and law,
RCAP (1996b, p. 78) also concerned itself with the implementation of
effective interim reforms to the existing criminal justice system. The
Commission recommended follow-up and implementation of reforms in
10 areas that had been identified as crucial by earlier commissions
investigating the treatment of Aboriginal peoples in the criminal justice
system (RCAP, 1996b, p. 285):

1. cross-cultural training for non-Aboriginal staff working in the criminal
    justice system;
2. more Aboriginal staff in all areas of the justice system;
3. more community-based alternatives in sentencing;
4. more community-based programs in corrections;
5. more specialized assistance to Aboriginal offenders;
6. more Aboriginal community involvement in planning, decision making
    and service delivery;
7. more Aboriginal advisory groups at all levels;
8. more recognition of Aboriginal culture and law in service delivery;
9. additional emphasis on crime prevention programs for Aboriginal
    offenders;
10. self-determination must be taken into account in planning and
    operation of the criminal justice system.

RCAP's emphasis on both broad, bold new concepts such as Aboriginal
self-determination and legal pluralism, and specific, practical steps to
improve the existing system, could be considered a strength rather than a
contradiction. This dual approach also characterized the work of another
Commission that operated in the province of Saskatchewan a decade later,
which I will now examine and discuss.

4. COMMISSION ON FIRST NATIONS AND MÉTIS PEOPLES AND JUSTICE REFORM

For many years police services in Saskatchewan were notorious for their frequent use of "starlight tours" – taking Aboriginal men (and some women), who may have been intoxicated and causing a minor disturbance in the community, and driving them out of town and leaving them on the empty prairie in temperatures that in winter can dip down to minus 30 degrees or below. Two young Aboriginal men who were victims of this practice and who died as a result were Lawrence Wegner and Rodney Naistus. Partly as a response to anger and concern about these two deaths, particularly among Aboriginal people in Saskatchewan, and partly due to general concerns about the treatment of First Nations and Métis people by police and other elements of the criminal justice system, the *Commission on First Nations and Métis Peoples and Justice Reform* was established by the government of Saskatchewan in November 2001. Although a creature of the provincial government, the Commission was to carry out its work in partnership with and deliver its reports to the Federation of Saskatchewan Indian Nations (FSIN) and the Métis Nation – Saskatchewan (MNS), the political bodies that represent Aboriginal peoples in the province, as well as to the federal government. The Commission was given the mandate

> to review the justice system with the intent of devising solutions to overcome systemic discriminatory practices and address attitudes based on racial or cultural prejudice.

Unlike RCAP at the national level, with its emphasis on self-government and legal pluralism, the Commission in Saskatchewan took an inclusive, or what could be called one-society-with-cultural-variations approach in its work on justice reform in the interests of Aboriginal peoples. This was very much reflected in its statement of its vision (in English, Cree, and Dene):

> One Community – working together to create a healthy, just,
> prosperous and safe Saskatchewan
> meyo wahkotowin
> dene araya who teeya al then. (Final Report, 2004, p. 9)

The Commission strongly emphasized relationship building and cultural bridging between Aboriginal and non-Aboriginal peoples, which was reflected in its Mission Statement:

> To create change and make a difference by:
> • Listening to people
> • Building relationships

- Promoting respect and change
- Recognizing successes, and
- Making recommendations for future justice reform.

This approach based on system reform and the healing of relationships was also reflected in a statement about justice that was offered by an Elder at a Community Dialogue that was held by the Commission, that is prominently featured in the Introduction to the Commission's Final Report:

> Justice is something that Creator gave us. It has to do with love. It had to do with benevolence. It has to do with the ability to forgive and to do something in restitution of whatever it is that we do wrong. Comes from within here. We had that. (Final Report, 2004, p. 9)

This kind of sentiment, and the concerns of the Commission with fixing the problems of the existing justice system as it affects Aboriginal people, contrasts markedly with RCAP's general emphasis on cultural distinctiveness and political autonomy and co-equality (under Treaties where they exist). RCAP premised its analysis and recommendations on the right to political self-determination for Aboriginal peoples, and the independence of Aboriginal law and justice from the prevailing Euro-Canadian system. The Justice Reform Commission's more accomodationist and reformist approach was opposed by the Federation of Saskatchewan Indian Nations, which recommended the creation of parallel and independent justice institutions under First Nations' control (FSIN, 2004). In fact the FSIN elected official with responsibility for the Justice portfolio refused to attend the media event surrounding the release of the Final Report of the Commission. FSIN Vice-Chief Lawrence Joseph explained the shortcomings of the Commission's Report (which was optimistically entitled "Legacy of Hope") in this way (www.fsin.com/mediareleases/index.html):

- it focuses on improvements to existing programs or the implementation of new programs rather than the actual reform of the justice system;
- it recommends initiatives that are "aboriginal" in nature that include both Métis and non-aboriginals without acknowledging the distinct status of treaty people;
- and, it does not address the constitutional treaty right of First Nations to the inherent right to self-government.

Notwithstanding these fundamental criticisms, in this same media report Vice-Chief Joseph pointed to the practical value of many of the specific recommendations made by the Commission. It can also be argued that, despite their differing political and ideological premises, the Commission on

First Nations and Métis Peoples and Justice Reform (reporting in 2004) and the Royal Commission on Aboriginal Peoples (reporting in 1996) share broad similarities in regard to conclusions and recommendations for practical reforms. It is a worthwhile exercise to focus on some of these specific prescriptions as they are articulated in the more recent report from Saskatchewan. Adopting and implementing the proposals for practical reforms within the criminal justice system would certainly enhance the immediate protection of civil and political rights of Aboriginal peoples who are enmeshed in this system. Other proposals address the *root causes* of the mistreatment and overrepresentation of First Nations and Metis peoples in the criminal justice system, which include cultural genocide, poverty, unemployment, addiction, mental health and other disabilities, and family dysfunction. Action addressing such root causes includes anti-racism education, economic development and income security measures, and effective treatment and healing programs under Aboriginal control. Such strategies would arguably advance the social and economic rights for Aboriginal persons in Saskatchewan.

The Commission made key recommendations to protect civil and political rights in regard to police accountability and behaviour. As mentioned above, it was racist treatment of Aboriginal individuals by police resulting in death in some cases which was the precipitating issue that led to the establishment of the Commission in the first place. The Commission clearly documented the mistrust, fear and resentment that existed towards the Royal Canadian Mounted Police (which serves rural areas and First Nations reserves) and city police services (particularly in Saskatoon). For instance, in its Final Report the Commission stated that it

> heard many wise words from Elders on the subject of policing and its history. One Elder referred to the Treaty signing by his people in 1876 and the negotiations that took place. Speaking in Cree, he explained that "the Red Coats [RCMP] at that time were to be a servant of the people, not the dominator like we have been accustomed to all these years. The Red Coats were here in our community, our reservations, with the thought and belief from our people that they were there to protect us and to serve us and not to work against us." (Final Report, 2004)

To combat police racism, the Commission made several recommendations that encompassed (Final Report, 2004):

• the development of a comprehensive anti-racism strategy by the Saskatchewan Police Commission (Recommendation 5.1);

- the involvement of First Nations and Métis people in the evaluation and improvement of cultural awareness training for police officers (Recommendation 5.2);
- the hiring of First Nations and Métis people as police officers in numbers that reflect their proportion of the general population (Recommendation 5.3);
- measures to ensure that community policing is effective and accountable, including support to local boards overseeing and working with local police officers (Recommendations 5.4 and 5.5);
- use of increased discretion with youth, and their diversion into extra-judicial processes whenever possible (Recommendation 5.6);
- establishing community-based detoxification facilities for intoxicated adults and youth, to divert such individuals from police custody and the "drunk tank" (Recommendations 5.7 and 5.8);
- use of video recording equipment and Aboriginal liaison workers to ensure appropriate treatment of (especially First Nations and Métis) persons in police custody (Recommendation 5.9);
- the creation of an independent body partly overseen by First Nations and Métis organizations to handle public complaints about police conduct (Recommendation 5.10).

The Department of Justice in Saskatchewan acted on the last recommendation in April 2006, through the implementation of a Public Complaints Commission comprised of civilians to oversee the work of the Saskatchewan Police Complaints Investigator. Saskatchewan Justice also widened access to police complaints process through the designation of the FSIN Special Investigations Unit and rural RCMP detachments as sites at which complaints against police can be lodged (Saskatchewan Justice, 2006).

The Commission devoted an entire chapter of its Final Report (Vol. 1, Chapter 4) to restorative justice as the overarching strategy for "restoring justice in Saskatchewan" (as stated in the chapter title), especially for First Nations and Métis peoples. Aspects of this proposed broad strategy include:

- the recognition, diversion from criminal justice, and appropriate treatment for persons with mental disorders and disabilities (Recommendation 4.1);
- funding from "all levels of governments" for "therapeutic resources with a First Nations and Métis focus" for those needing help with drug addiction and other problems. These programs would involve "Elders, healers, and support for families" (Recommendation 4.2);

- better funding and support for the Aboriginal Court Worker Program to provide advice, support and advocacy for those appearing in court (Recommendation 4.3);
- dealing with "system generated charges" of both youth and adult offenders (e.g. breeching probation conditions) through community teams rather than through the courts (Recommendation 4.4).

Additional practical measures to enhance restorative justice and community-based justice approaches, and thereby enhance the civil and political rights for First Nations Métis people in relation to the institutions of the criminal justice system, are recommended in Volume 1, Chapter 6. The provincial and federal governments (working in partnership with Aboriginal governments) are urged to:

- increase the number of First Nations and Métis jurors, lawyers, judges, and members of the National Parole Board;
- extend a pilot project to conduct court hearings in the Cree language court both "geographically and linguistically";
- extend the knowledge and ensure the availability of translation services for speakers of indigenous languages;
- in remote and isolated communities where it is not possible to hold court hearings, provide "suitable video and audio links";
- establish a "Therapeutic Court, preferably mobile, with the capacity to address issues such as alcohol and other addictions, fetal alcohol spectrum disorders, families in crisis and family violence" that would "facilitate an integrated response to the root causes of criminal behaviour";
- provide "extensive and well resourced use of Alternate Measures (including spousal assaults and excepting homicide)";
- establish and fund Community Justice Committees;
- provide "a toll free telephone line where people can get reliable, up-to-date information on family law matters";
- extend Legal Aid services;
- increase the availability of "cultural and spiritual programming, whether traditional or religious" to First Nations and Métis prisoners;
- expand prison programs for incarcerated Aboriginal women;
- ensure adequate planning and resources for community treatment of young offenders.

It is thus evident that the Commission was very much concerned with practical measures to protect and enhance the civil and political rights of Aboriginal peoples in relation to the police and other aspects of the criminal justice system. The Commission was particularly concerned about youth – both their proper treatment in the system, and broad prevention strategies to prevent their coming into contact with criminal justice in the first place. This concern was illustrated by the second chapter of the Final Report (Vol. 1), and by the Commission's Interim Report entitled *A Dialogue in Progress: Focus on Youth* (released in January 2003) (www.justicere formcomm.sk.ca/reports.gov).

The Commission also addressed a host of issues related to protection and enhancement of social, economic and cultural rights with the aim of getting at the root causes of crime and achieving a broad vision of justice for First Nations and Métis peoples in Saskatchewan. A prominent theme in the Commission's Report is "Creating Healthy, Just, Prosperous and Safe Communities in Saskatchewan" (Chapter 2, Vol. 1). It is stated that "[i]mproving quality of life by dealing with social and economic problems will also strike at the root causes of crime" (Final Report, 2004, p. 2–4). The Commission points to the need to make advances on many fronts in order to overcome social exclusion of Aboriginal peoples, and to develop a comprehensive approach to crime prevention. These areas that must be addressed include the elimination of poverty, education, employment, housing, and support to single and young parents. Services and resources must also be developed and enhanced for First Nations and Métis people struggling with specific problems such as substance abuse, family violence, involvement with gangs, Fetal Alcohol Spectrum Disorder, and other disabilities. While the Commission, with its mandate to address specific problems in the criminal justice system, did not develop detailed plans or make precise recommendations in all of these various areas, it did ground its analysis in this broader and holistic framework related to social and economic rights. It also specifically mentioned the importance of "artistic, cultural and recreational activities [that] encourage youth to stand out and make a community proud" (Final Report, 2004, Vol. 1. p. 3–1).

In an interesting and very detailed submission to the Commission on First Nations and Métis Peoples and Justice Reform, Paul Joffe and Wilton Littlechild (the latter being the head Commissioner) make the case that "international human rights norms relevant to Aboriginal peoples in Saskatchewan should be incorporated into the reforms for improving the administration of justice in the province" (Joffe & Littlechild, 2004). They call for a strategy that addresses

root causes of crime [that] emanate from a wide range of factors that unjustly impact on Aboriginal peoples. The criminal justice system cannot resolve these pressing problems alone. For example, such matters as colonialism, dispossession and racial discrimination, may be considered by some observers as external to the "administration" of justice. Yet they remain central in addressing questions of fairness, honour and justice itself.

Joffe and Littlechild (2004) argue for "respect for both Aboriginal and treaty rights in any framework for the administration of justice", and indeed for a broader "human rights culture that is relevant to First Nations and Métis peoples to be entrenched in the administration of justice". Justice reform must be guided by a principled framework that stipulates that "self-determination of Aboriginal peoples be a central element for all reforms". Additionally, Joffe and Littlechild (2004) insist that "relevant international human rights norms be incorporated in all implementation strategies, with a view to uplifting existing standards".

It is evident in this very thoughtful, well researched, and lengthy legal brief by Joffe and Littlechild (2004) that the head Commissioner (along with his co-author) are strongly committed to the concept of self-determination and collective rights for Aboriginal peoples, and "the sacred nature and historical and contemporary significance of treaties". This focus is some-what different from the overall thrust and tone of the Commission's Final Report, which emphasizes specific reforms in the justice system, "one community", and reconciliation and consensus building between Aboriginal and non-Aboriginal communities. The conceptual framework underlying the brief by Joffe and Littlechild is not dissimilar from conceptual departure points in the work of RCAP. For instance, both posit the inherent right to and constitutional protection of Aboriginal self-government (although Joffe and Littlechild place a much heavier emphasis on the importance of international human rights instruments).

The Commission, in its concluding set of recommendations of its Final Report (2004, Vol. 1, Chapter 10), called upon the

governments of Canada and Saskatchewan, the Federation of Saskatchewan Indians and the Métis Nation – Saskatchewan ... [to] jointly support and establish an Office of the Implementation Commissioner.

This approach was not adopted in the follow-up to the release of the Commission's Final Report in June 2004. Almost a year later, the government of Saskatchewan announced that it would spend $48 million "to attack the root causes of racism in the justice system" including "more affordable housing and better access to education for aboriginal children" (Cook, 2005). It also committed funds to "the appointment of a police complaints commission with the power to investigate complaints against police". However parts of this funding package were set aside for projects not related directly to the recommendations of the Commission on First Nations and Métis Peoples and Justice Reform, such as the replacement of a decrepit wing at the Regina jail, and the inclusion of forensic pathology services in the Coroner's Office.

Commission Chair Littlechild expressed some disappointment that an Implementation Commissioner was not appointed, but said to the media that he was "willing to live with the government plan to implement the findings through meetings with stakeholders". On the other hand, Vice-Chief Lawrence Joseph of the Federation of Saskatchewan Indian Nations "expressed pessimism at the idea of trying to improve the existing justice system rather than making wholesale structural changes". Joseph stated that "creating better living conditions is a worthy but off-the-mark goal because the changes are driven by the government's agenda" and that the government was doing things "for us, not with us" (Cook, 2005). In a FSIN (2005) media release, Joseph expressed his view that

> There is new money for more police to put Indians in jail, more Aboriginal positions within the provincial government structure, and more symbols to placate First Nations. What we need, however, is more capacity and control over justice in our own communities, and we won't get that through this plan.

On the other hand, Joseph (FSIN, 2005) also indicated that "there are a few excellent plans and initiatives contained in the province's response" and that

> First Nations people are encouraged by the province's willingness to recognize that a more holistic or integrated approach is necessary, and by the province's readiness to explore options for First Nations self-administered policing in Saskatchewan.

5. REPORT OF THE STONECHILD INQUIRY

In November 1990 the frozen body of 17-year-old Neil Stonechild was found in a field in an industrial area on the edge of the city of Saskatoon, Saskatchewan. The Aboriginal teen had been in police custody the night he went missing. As a result of family efforts and media coverage, the Saskatchewan government set up the *Commission of Inquiry Into Matters Relating to the Death of Neil Stonechild* headed by Mr. Justice David H. Wright. Judge Wright undertook his work in February 2003, and issued his Final Report (Wright, 2004) 18 months later.

He concluded that Neil Stonechild's death was investigated in a totally inadequate fashion by the Saskatoon Police Service, and that for many years senior police officials "rejected or ignored reports from the Stonechild family members and investigative reporters" (Wright, 2004, p. 212). The Stonechild Inquiry made eight recommendations (Wright, 2004, p. 213), and for the most part they were similar to recommendations made by the Commission on First Nations and Métis Peoples and Justice Reform. The Stonechild Inquiry called for "in-depth training in race relations" for police officers, the recruitment of more Aboriginal police officers, and improved procedures for handling complaints about police misconduct.

The death of young Neil Stonechild was in fact one manifestation of the common police practice over many years in Saskatchewan of targeting Aboriginal people for "starlight tours". The Final Report by Judge Wright is very much focussed on the evidence of this particular case, in keeping with his Inquiry's Terms of Reference. Unlike RCAP and, to a lesser extent, the Commission on First Nations and Métis Peoples and Justice Reform, Judge Wright does not engage in fundamental critical analysis of the colonialist power relations and racist ideology that perpetuate the mistreatment and subordination of First Nations and Métis people in Saskatchewan. In fact, he seems to trace police misconduct back to a somewhat "voluntaristic" explanation of "two solitudes" choosing not to communicate with one another.

> As I reviewed the evidence in this Inquiry, I was reminded, again and again, of the chasm that separates Aboriginal and non-Aboriginal people in this city and province. Our two communities do not know each other and do not seem to want to. (Wright, 2004, p. 208)

In a similar vein, Judge Wright stresses his sympathy for "the past and present members of the Saskatoon Police Service who have worked hard, often in trying circumstances, to protect and serve the people of this community" (Wright, 2004, p. 211). He adopts a "few bad apples in the barrel" explanation of the extant problems between the Aboriginal community and the police.

The most important impact of the Stonechild Inquiry, in regard to eliminating racism and advancing political influence and human rights of Aboriginal peoples in Saskatchewan, probably derives not from the Final Report and Recommendations but from the media coverage of the hearings. This tragic, dramatic and evocative case saturated the provincial media for several months. There was particularly poignant testimony from Neil Stonechild's mother, Stella Bignell (Wright, 2004, pp. 24–27), and from Neil's friend Jason Roy (Wright, 2004, pp. 33–49) who was with Neil on the night that he was apprehended by police and subsequently died. Judge Wright strongly emphasized the love, dedication, and determined hard work of Ms. Bignell for her deceased son. The Judge also strongly emphasized the credibility of Mr. Roy, and commended him "for his tenacity in pursuing this matter over many years" (Wright, 2004, p. 49). This very public praise from a respected judge of Euro-Canadian background for a young Aboriginal man, who historically in Saskatchewan would be seen as marginalized and non-credible due to his Aboriginal identity and his status (at that time) as a young offender with a substance abuse problem, was widely reported in the media. Judge Wright was, intentionally or not, challenging decades of entrenched police beliefs and practices that deemed Aboriginal people as not worthy of belief, of no importance as human beings, and in fact dispensable.

In its coverage of the Inquiry, the media also gave sustained and close attention to the tragic circumstances of the death of Neil Stonechild, and to the denial of responsibility by the police and their complicity in covering up their involvement. This media coverage can reasonably be assumed to have had a significant impact on the public consciousness in Saskatchewan and beyond. Political justification and theoretical articulation are necessary elements in defining, protecting and enhancing human rights. But popular understanding and the mobilization of public opinion are also necessary ingredients if we are to act collectively to end racism and foster equality, dignity, and human rights for Aboriginal people. The Stonechild Inquiry played a very valuable role, through the media, in such popular education and mobilization of popular opinion. In this sense, the Inquiry served as a concrete and dramatic exemplar of the broader and more complicated work of the Commission on First Nations and Métis Peoples and Justice Reform (that was working at the same time) and of the Royal Commission on Aboriginal Peoples (whose work took place a decade earlier).

6. INDIGENOUS HUMAN RIGHTS AT THE INTERNATIONAL LEVEL

The United Nations Declaration on the Rights of Indigenous Peoples (www.unhchr.ch/huridocda/huridoca.nsf/(Symbol)/E.CN.4.SUB.2.RES. 1994.45.En?OpenDocument) is an important initiative that has catapulted the definition and realization of human rights for Aboriginal peoples into national and international forums of political debate. The Declaration provides the basis for Aboriginal peoples to influence and shape the criminal justice institutions that affect them, and potentially to take control of their own justice institutions in the context of self-determination and self-government within a broader international human rights framework. The draft Declaration was adopted by the Human Rights Council in June 2006 and is currently under review by the General Assembly. This document mirrors arguments advanced in the Final Report of the Royal Commission on Aboriginal Peoples in Canada in 1996 on the question of Aboriginal self-determination and self-government. Article 3 of the Declaration states that

> indigenous peoples have the right of self-determination, and that by virtue of that right they freely determine their political status and freely pursue their economic, social, and cultural development.

Article 21 states that "[i]ndigenous peoples have the right to maintain and develop their political, economic and social systems". Specifically in regard to law, Article 4 of the Declaration endorses a position of legal pluralism:

> Indigenous peoples have the right to maintain and strengthen their distinct political, economic, social and cultural characteristics, *as well as their legal systems,* while retaining their rights to participate fully, if they so choose, in the political, economic, social and cultural life of the State. (italics added)

In regard to the rendering of justice in practical terms, Article 33 asserts that

> Indigenous peoples have the right to promote, develop and maintain their institutional structures and their distinctive juridical customs, traditions, procedures and practices, in accordance with internationally recognized human rights standards.

Article 23 speaks of Indigenous control of the structuring and delivery of programs, including (presumably) those that would assist individuals in conflict with the law and experiencing related problems in their lives:

> [I]ndigenous peoples have the right to determine and develop all health, housing and other economic and social programmes affecting them and, as far as possible, to administer such programmes through their own institutions.

Of course, a difficulty with the Declaration is that a number of countries have refused to sign it, including Canada. Canada's previous support for a United Nations Declaration on the Rights of Indigenous Peoples, which first wavered under the Liberal government, was pulled back under the subsequent conservative government over concerns it would run counter to the constitution, defense laws and existing land deals. In late 2006 the Canadian Minister of Indian Affairs recently faced an angry group of Aboriginal protestors in front of the Parliament buildings (Bailey, 2006). The protestors saw a direct link between the new Conservative federal government's failure to implement a funding agreement to address the needs of Aboriginal peoples, and the government's failure to accept the Declaration of the Rights of Indigenous Peoples. The funding agreement that the newly elected Conservative government refused to support was the Kelowna Accord, which had been agreed to by federal and provincial first ministers and Aboriginal leaders in the dying days of the previous Liberal federal government in November 2005. The Accord would have invested over $5 billion over five years to improve education, health, housing, community infrastructure, and economic opportunities for Aboriginal peoples.

The Assembly of First Nations (www.afn.ca) expressed "outrage" at the successful efforts of the Canadian government (in collaboration with the African Union, the United States, Australia, and New Zealand) to delay adoption by the United Nations of the Declaration of the Rights of Indigenous Peoples. KAIROS (http://www.kairoscanada.org) is an ecumenical organization of Christian churches in Canada advocating for social justice. It endorses the position of Amnesty International that there is an "urgent need for the Declaration":

> The Declaration has been under development for more than 20 years, making it one of the intensely debated and carefully scrutinized human rights instruments in UN history. Uniquely, the primary beneficiaries of the Declaration, Indigenous peoples themselves, have been an integral part of its development. Over these two decades, it has become apparent that a small handful of states are intractably opposed to the Declaration for reasons of domestic politics. However it is also clear that the majority of states and Indigenous peoples' organizations that participated in the elaboration of the text have been able to find common ground on the legitimate needs of states and Indigenous peoples. The General Assembly itself has made it clear that no time should be wasted in bringing forward the Declaration for adoption.

Support from Canada for the UN Declaration of the Rights of Indigenous Peoples would be an important tool to protect and foster the rights and interests of Aboriginal peoples worldwide. The Declaration in and of itself would not be sufficient to redefine and reshape criminal justice systems as they affect Indigenous persons. But in places like Saskatchewan, the Declaration would aid in efforts being made by various parties to transform the criminal justice system. The Declaration has the potential to add moral legitimacy, political clout, and practical leverage to the efforts of Aboriginal people and organizations, as they challenge current practices in policing, courts, and corrections that manifest systemic oppression against them. The Declaration could also boost efforts to transform state-centred punitive practices into community-owned and community-controlled restorative ones, thereby helping to prevent, minimize, and make amends for interpersonal harm as it affects both Aboriginal and non-Aboriginal people.

7. CONCLUSIONS

It is apparent from the above discussion that First Nations, Métis and other Aboriginal people in Canada have mapped ways forward to improve and potentially transform the criminal justice system. This system has historically served to marginalize and oppress Indigenous people in Saskatchewan as of part of a broader process of internal colonialism and cultural extinguishment.

The three Commission Reports discussed in this chapter can be seen as roadmaps for change. They point to ways in which improvements can be made to the protection of basic civil and political rights of Aboriginal persons who are caught up in the criminal justice system. Such improvements would include the right to freedom from police violence and mistreatment, the right to a fair and culturally appropriate judicial hearing, and availability of healing and alternative measures in corrections. The Commission Reports also point to how root causes of crime can be addressed through attention to social and economic rights, such as decent and affordable housing, economic security, relevant and high quality education, and cultural development and expression.

These roadmaps for change, finally, call for and are underpinned by "third generation" collective rights of Aboriginal peoples – including the rights to self-determination and self-government for Aboriginal peoples, in conjunction with existing and pending Treaties, and within the broader framework of the Universal Declaration of Human Rights and associated UN Covenants and Conventions. Making simultaneous progress on all of these levels is necessary, if we are to devise long-term, systemic solutions to the problem of human rights abuse of Aboriginal peoples in the criminal justice system. In other words, system change is necessarily part of a broader struggle for social justice.

In Saskatchewan, there has been a consciousness of the link between the private troubles of Aboriginal individuals enmeshed in criminal justice system, and the public issues of rights, justice, and self-determination for First Nations and Métis people. One way in which this has been evident at the provincial level has been the early and strong commitment of players in the criminal justice field in Saskatchewan – both Aboriginal and non-Aboriginal, those based in the community and those working in government – to restorative justice and cultural specificity in the delivery of programs to offenders, victims, family members, and communities affected by crime. Saskatchewan is recognized as something of an ideological trailblazer in regard to restorative justice and Aboriginal approaches in the criminal justice field. However even in this province it is difficult to change entrenched, traditional thinking and practices. Based on first hand research carried out in Saskatchewan, Handel (2003) concludes that

> resources provided by governments, and within communities, are often inadequate to support community-based restorative justice initiatives in some First Nations communities.

Similarly, Tomporowski (2004) concludes that

> restorative agencies [in Saskatchewan] are vulnerable to practices such as the fragmented way in which funding is provided from multiple departments and government's focus on measurable outcomes.

The latter researcher (Tomporowski, 2004) also refers to the link between criminal justice reform and a broader imperative of community building, pointing to the "importance of expanding restorative approaches to address non-criminal matters and community issues".

There is, needless to say, much that remains to be done by Aboriginal leaders and communities and their non-Aboriginal allies in implementing a broad human rights approach in criminal justice that will lead to practical benefits for First Nations and Métis peoples in Saskatchewan. This work can build on the recognition and affirmation of "existing aboriginal and treaty rights of the aboriginal peoples of Canada" in Section 35 (1) of the Constitution Act (1982), as well as on the increasing attention being paid to Aboriginal rights at the international level, *in casu* of the International Labour Organization (ILO, 1989). This work can also draw liberally on the comprehensive analysis and thoughtful recommendations of the Royal Commission on Aboriginal Peoples from a decade ago, as well as on the analysis and recommendations of recent Commissions at the provincial level in Saskatchewan.

Sometimes there is great cynicism that government appointed commissions are exercises in futility, that they are just a way to stall action and dodge political responsibility. And to be sure, recommendations from such commissions are not often implemented as promptly, completely, or transparently as those who sit on or work for such commissions would wish. On the other hand, the consultative processes and written outcomes of bodies such as the Royal Commission on Aboriginal Peoples and the Commission on First Nations and Métis Peoples and Justice Reform can produce lasting effects. They can provide enduring knowledge bases, help to shift social and political discourses in fundamental ways, and provide inspiration and practical guidance to those working to change systems and advance human rights and social justice.

REFERENCES

Books, Reports and Articles

Assembly of First Nations. (2006). *Assembly of first nations expresses disappointment and concern regarding the vote to delay consideration of the UN declaration on the rights of indigenous peoples*. Media release, 28 November. Accessed at: http://www.afn.ca/article.asp?id=3189

Bailey, S. (2006). *Indian Affairs minister shouted down and frozen out by angry native crowd* (Accessed on-line.). Toronto: Canadian Press NewsWire.

Borrows, J. (2002). *Recovering Canada: The resurgence of indigenous law*. Toronto: University of Toronto Press.

Bourgeault, R. (1986). *Class, race and gender: Political economy and the Canadian fur trade, 1670s to 1820s*. Unpublished M.A. thesis. University of Regina, Regina, SK.

Commission on First Nations and Métis Peoples and Justice Reform. (2004). *Final Report* (Volume 1 – *Legacy of hope: An agenda for change*; Volume 11 - *Submissions to the commission*.) Regina, Saskatchewan: Commission on First Nations and Métis Peoples and Justice Reform. Accessed at: http://www.justicereformcomm.sk.ca

Cook, T. (2005). *Sask. government releases plan for aboriginals alienated by justice system* (Accessed on-line at: http://proquest.umi.com/pqdweb?index=0&did=840905061&SrchMode=1&sid=1&Fmt=3&VInst=PROD&VType=PQD&RQT=309&VName=PQD&TS=1184104836&clientId=12307). Toronto: Canadian Press NewsWire.

Federation of Saskatchewan Indian Nations. (2004). *Recommendations for justice reform fall short of expectations, FSIN*, 22 June. Accessed at: http://www.fsin.com/mediareleases/index.html

Federation of Saskatchewan Indian Nations. (2005). *Saskatchewan's response to JRC restrictive, FSIN*, 12 May. Accessed at: http://www.fsin.com/mediareleases/index.html

Handel, M.B. (2003). *Pushing the boundaries: Restorative justice practice in a First Nations community*. Unpublished M.A. thesis. University of Regina, Regina, SK.

Joffe, P., & Littlechild, W. (2004). *Administration of justice and how to improve it: Applicability and use of international human rights norms* (http://www.justicereformcomm.sk.ca/volume2/15section12.pdf). Regina: Commission on First Nations and Métis Peoples and Justice Reform.

KAIROS. (2006). *The UN declaration on the rights of indigenous peoples: Righting historic wrongs, embracing a future of justice and hope*. Ottawa: Amnesty International (Canada).

Merry, S. E. (1988). Legal pluralism. *Law and Society Review, 22*, 869–896.

Royal Commission on Aboriginal Peoples. (1996a). *Report of the royal commission on aboriginal peoples* (On-line at: http://www.ainc-inac.gc.ca/ch/rcap/index_e.html). Ottawa: RCAP.

Royal Commission on Aboriginal Peoples. (1996b). *Bridging the cultural divide: A report on aboriginal people and criminal justice in Canada*. Ottawa: Minister of Supply and Services Canada.

Saskatchewan Justice. (2006). *Annual report of the Saskatchewan police complaints investigator,* *2005–2006* (Accessed at: http://www.saskjustice.gov.sk.ca). Regina: Government of Saskatchewan.

Statistics Canada. (2006). *Aboriginal people as victims and offenders.* ("The Daily" posted on 6 June). Ottawa: Statistics Canada. http://www.statcan.ca/Daily/English/060606/d060606b.htm

Tomporowski, B. (2004). *Exploring restorative justice in Saskatchewan.* Unpublished M.A. thesis. University of Regina, Regina, SK.

Waiser, B. (2005). *Saskatchewan: A new history.* Calgary: Fifth House.

Wright, J. D. H. (2004). *Commission of inquiry into matters related to the death of Neil* *Stonechild* (Accessed at: http://www.stonechildinquiry.ca/finalreport/Stonechild.pdf). Regina: Government of Saskatchewan.

Official Websites

Dolha, L. (2004). *Justice report falls short of FSIN hopes.* Accessed at http://www.firstnationsdrum.com/Summer%202004/TrtySask.htm

First Nations and Métis Relations of the Government of Saskatchewan, www.fnmr.gov.sk.ca

International Labour Organization, Convention C169 on the Indigenous and Tribal Peoples (1989). http://www.ilo.org/ilolex/english/convdisp1.htm

Office of the Treaty Commissioner of Saskatchewan, www.otc.ca

United Nations Declaration on the Rights of Indigenous Peoples, www.unhchr.ch/huridocda/huridoca.nsf/(Symbol)/E.CN.4.SUB.2.RES.1994.45.En?OpenDocument

CRIMINOLOGY, HUMAN RIGHTS AND INDIGENOUS PEOPLES

Chris Cunneen

1. INTRODUCTION

Criminology, human rights and Indigenous peoples: how do we understand the connections between these three terms? For too long the voices arguing to connect criminology with human rights were isolated and marginalized. At best, the possible links were seen as peripheral to the main concerns of criminology. At worst, bringing a human rights understanding to definitions of crime and criminal justice was seen as undermining criminology's search for scientific status. And as for Indigenous people? They were seen as part of the "crime problem", a segment of the problem population whose criminality needed explanation. Human rights apparently had nothing to do with their offending behaviour. The problem for criminology was why did so many Aboriginal people in places like Canada or Australia commit so much crime?

However, over the last decade or so the intellectual terrain has shifted significantly. Discourses on human rights have emerged in social science disciplines, and now clearly provide one frame for how we analyse and interpret the world. In addition the development of concepts like "state crime" (which until recently had been largely ignored in criminology) has breathed fresh life into understanding the relationship between the

Crime and Human Rights
Sociology of Crime, Law and Deviance, Volume 9, 239–261
Copyright © 2007 by Elsevier Ltd.
All rights of reproduction in any form reserved
ISSN: 1521-6136/doi:10.1016/S1521-6136(07)09010-0

development of modern political states and the violent and at times genocidal dispossession of Indigenous peoples. Perhaps more importantly for Indigenous people, human rights have emerged as a fundamental and global political discourse and have provided a platform for the articulation of specific Indigenous demands. This articulation has been achieved largely through supranational bodies like the United Nations, and now finds expression through organs like the UN Permanent Forum on Indigenous Issues.

As a result of these developments we can see at least three strands to how we might bring criminology to a more intellectually robust understanding of Indigenous people and human rights. The first point is that Indigenous people have been victims of profound historical injustices and abuses of human rights which can be at least partially understood as state crime. The second point is that contemporary justice systems are often seen in the context of the abuse of Indigenous people's human rights. The third strand is an analysis of how claims to specific Indigenous rights impact on current criminal justice processes, and how those claims might broaden our understanding of reform and change.

2. HISTORICAL INJUSTICES AND HUMAN RIGHTS ABUSES OF INDIGENOUS PEOPLES

We know the widespread role of state institutions, often sanctioned by law, as the perpetrators of some of the greatest crimes against humanity. One estimate is that modern political states have been responsible for the murder of over 169 million people between 1900 and 1987, excluding deaths in wars, judicial executions and the killing of armed opponents and criminals (Green & Ward, 2004, p. 1). The modern political state has been integral to the commission of genocide and other human rights abuses. Genocide and modernity have gone hand in hand (Bauman, 1989), and the specific modernity of genocide is that the vastness and totality of "final solutions" could only be pursued by the modern state with access to resources, administrative capacities and law-making functions (Gellately & Kiernan, 2003, p. 4). This is at the heart of our contemporary understanding of state crime. That genocide, the "crime of all crimes", should have been absent from criminology for so long deserves full explanation in itself (Morrison, 2004). A part of the problem has been the positivist approaches in law and criminology that define "crime" as a breach of state criminal law, and count crimes from the data driven by state agencies. Within such state-centric discourses it is difficult to conceptualize the incidence and nature of state crime (Morrison, 2005).

The colonial context adds a further dimension to how we understand the connections between the development of the modern political state and the globalized nature of gross violations of human rights. As Marx noted, the dawn of capitalist production was made possible through the exploitation of the peoples and resources in Africa, Asia and the Americas. It was the "extirpation, enslavement and entombment in mines of the aboriginal population [in the Americas], the beginning of the conquest and looting of the East Indies, and the turning of Africa into a warren for the hunting of black-skins" that laid the foundations for capitalist development (Marx quoted in Morrison, 2005, pp. 300–301).

The modern political state is built on the human rights abuses of colonized and enslaved peoples. Indeed racism, slavery and its consequent effects in Africa and America could be the subject of much criminological research. However, the focus of this chapter is on Indigenous people and it is primarily to Australia, New Zealand and North America that the discussion is drawn, although I will use the example of the Mayan people in Guatemala as an example of contemporary state genocide against an Indigenous people. The claims concerning historical injustices and human rights abuses against Indigenous peoples are multilayered. At the highest level is the claim that particular colonial practices against Indigenous people constituted genocide. Below genocide are claims of mass murder, racism, ethnocide (or cultural genocide), slavery, forced labour, forced removals and relocations, the denial of property rights, and the denial of civil and political rights. The claims of genocide against Indigenous people in the settler-colonies of North America, New Zealand and Australia have been controversial (Van Krieken, 2004). However there seems little doubt that genocide is the appropriate description for specific colonial laws and practices at particular times and places (Churchill, 1997; Moses, 2000). More broadly, the concept of ethnocide or cultural genocide captures the aggressive attempt to "civilize" Indigenous peoples through a range of state-endorsed laws, policies and practices.

2.1. Genocide

The United Nations Convention on the Prevention and Punishment of the Crime of Genocide (1948) defines genocide as any of the following acts committed with the intention to destroy, in whole or in part, a national, ethnical, racial or religious group by:

a) killing members of the group;
b) causing serious bodily or mental harm to members of the group;
c) deliberately inflicting on the group conditions of life calculated to bring about its physical destruction in whole or in part;
d) imposing measures intended to prevent births within the group;
e) forcibly transferring children of the group to another group.

The crime of genocide has been levelled against colonial regimes in their treatment of Indigenous peoples in Australia and the Americas. In relation to genocide and Native Americans, Ward Churchill has noted the following:

> During the four centuries spanning the time between 1492 ... and 1892 when the U.S. Census Bureau concluded that there were fewer than a quarter million Indigenous people surviving within the country's claimed boundaries, a hemispheric population estimated to have been as great as 125 million was reduced by something over 90 percent. The people had died in their millions of being hacked apart with axes and swords, burned alive and trampled under horses ... intentionally starved and frozen to death during a multitude of forced marches and internments, and in an unknown number of instances, deliberately infected with epidemic diseases. (Churchill, 1997, p. 1)

Intention is a key element of genocide, and much of the recent analysis draws distinctions between the intentional killings of Indigenous people by colonial forces as distinct from the deaths of Indigenous peoples arising from introduced diseases (Stannard, 1993, p. xii). Massacres of Indigenous people by colonial state forces occurred across North America and Australia during the colonial period. On both continents, Indigenous men, women and children were murdered. As Stannard has noted in relation to the US,

> the European habit of indiscriminately killing women and children when engaged in hostilities with the natives of the Americas was more than an atrocity. It was flatly and intentionally genocidal. For no population can survive if its women and children are destroyed. (Stannard, 1993, pp. 118–119)

There are well documented massacres of Aboriginal people in Australia in the nineteenth century. In Western Australia and Queensland authorities spoke of police "teaching the blacks a lesson" and "dealing out a fearful punishment" (Cunneen, 2001a, p. 50). It is clear that colonial processes meant that the rule of law as a constraint on arbitrary power and as a guarantee of equality before the law was suspended in relation to Aboriginal people. What ensued can only be described as mass murders.

There were relatively recent massacres in Australia in the early part of the twentieth century. The last recorded massacre occurred in 1928 in Coniston, Northern Territory when some 60 to 70 Walpiri people were killed over several weeks by a police party. Murray, the officer in charge openly admitted to a policy of shoot to kill. According to a missionary who spoke to survivors of the killings, "the natives tell me that they simply shot them down like dogs and that they got the little children and hit them on the back of the neck and killed them". Murray admitted killing 31 people. Other estimates by missionaries put the figure at between 70 and 100 Aboriginal people killed. An inquiry, headed by a police inspector, was established into the killings. Aboriginal people were refused legal representation. The inquiry cleared those who were involved (Cunneen, 2001a, p. 55).

2.2. The Civilising Mission and the Forced Removal of Children

The civilising mission involved changing natives from savages to civilized Christians. It was a task that occupied the European empires over several centuries, and continued into the twentieth century in settler states like Australia and North America. Yet the civilising process was also often brutal. Native Americans were placed on church missions where the deaths tolls were horrific. While many of these deaths were caused by European-introduced diseases, the conditions on these missions also directly contributed to the large number of deaths. Living spaces for captive Indians "averaged about seven feet by two feet per person ... common rooms contained a single open pit for a toilet" (Stannard, 1993, p. 138). Severe malnutrition resulted from the inadequate diets and long hours of forced labour. Grotesque forms of punishment were used against the rebellious.

One way of ensuring the civilising process was through the removal of Indigenous children. The Canadian residential school policy was based on assimilation – of changing Indigenous peoples from savage to civilized by educating the young away from the influences of their parents and tribes. As Milloy (1999, p. xv) has noted in the Canadian context, the process was "violent in its intention to 'kill the Indian' in the child for the sake of Christian civilization. In that way, the system was, even as a concept, abusive".

In Canada the residential school system stretched for more than a century from the 1870s to the 1980s. There was a nationwide network of schools operated by the Anglican, Catholic, Presbyterian and United Churches. Thousands of Indian, Inuit and Metis children were to pass through the schools. The system was a church-state partnership with the Department of Indian Affairs providing the funding, setting the standards and exercising legal control over the children who were wards (Milloy, 1999).

In Australia Aboriginal children had been forcibly removed from their families by colonizers since the beginning of European occupation of Australia. However by the late nineteenth and early twentieth centuries there developed a systematic and state-sponsored policy of removal which was far more extensive than any previous interventions (see NISATSIC, 1997, pp. 25-149). In many states of Australia, Aboriginal children were placed in church-run institutions, while in some states like New South Wales the institutions were operated by the state.

The Australian removal policies rested on specific assumptions about race, "blood" and racial hygiene. Aboriginal people were divided according to the amount of European "blood" they might possess. Law became fundamental to the categorization and separation of individuals within racialized boundaries. According to the social Darwinist ideas, so-called "full blood" Aboriginal people were bound to die out because of their inferiority. However, the concern for the state was the apparently rapidly growing population of "mixed blood" children. It was these children that became the target of intervention. By permanently removing them from their families and communities it was believed that this group of children would, over generations, eventually be biologically absorbed into the non-Indigenous population. Their Aboriginality would be "bred" out. Eugenicist arguments required a proactive state to manage, cleanse and maintain the "white" population. Law provided the foundation through which an administrative edifice would define Indigenous people as "full blood", "half caste", "quarter caste" and so on.

Both the Canadian and the Australia authorities saw the removal process as part of a civilising mission and spiritual duty to uplift the "natives". Yet in both countries, the system was never properly resourced or supervised, and shocking neglect and physical abuse were common. In Australia a federal inquiry in 1997 found that basic safeguards which protected non-Indigenous families were cast aside when it came to Indigenous children. The main components of the forced removal of Indigenous children which were unlawful were deprivation of liberty, deprivation of parental rights, abuses of power, and breach of guardianship duties. In relation to international human rights the main obligations imposed on Australia and breached by a policy of forced removals were the prohibitions on racial discrimination and genocide. The policy continued to be practiced after Australia had voluntarily subscribed to treaties outlawing both racial discrimination and genocide (NISATSIC, 1997). In 1996 the Canadian Royal Commission on Aboriginal Peoples (RCAP, 1996) released its final report. As a result the Canadian Government has acknowledged past injustice and apologized to Indigenous peoples, particularly in relation to the effects of the residential school system.

2.3. Racism

Racism was a precondition for the colonial genocides and the systematic abuse of human rights of Indigenous peoples in Australia and the Americas. As Stannard (1993, p. 247) notes, Spanish and Anglo-Americans saw the natives of the Americas as racially inferior beings. Racial discrimination provided an overarching basis to governmental law and policy towards Indigenous people throughout much of the eighteenth, nineteenth and twentieth centuries. The suspension of the rule of law and the use of terror and violence by colonial authorities against Indigenous people was also contextualized and legitimated within racialized constructions of Indigenous people as inferior, lesser human beings. There is no doubt that these racialized constructions changed during the eighteenth, nineteenth and twentieth centuries: in Australia this move was from notions of barbarism to views about a race "doomed" to extinction. Indeed competing views about race were often prevalent at the same time. However, what is important is that racialized constructions of Indigenous people inevitably facilitated discriminatory intervention. Institutionalized and legalized discrimination reached a peak during the "protection" period of the twentieth century.

After the 1940s ideas about cultural assimilation came to the fore. However, the ultimate goal was still the same: the disappearance of Indigenous people as a distinct group of people. In Australia, cultural assimilation was seen as leading to a form of "equality" with European Australians. However, this equality was to be one defined on the assumption of the superiority of white Anglo-Australian cultural, economic and political institutions. It was to be the equality of "sameness": where everyone could participate on a social terrain defined by the colonizer. The goal of equality still authorized racial discrimination. To reach the level of equality the colonial subject required tutelage. They had to be taught and trained to be equal. As a result, in the post 1945 period there was intensive supervision and surveillance through a range of state agencies including child welfare and criminal justice agencies.

There were a range of specific harms which occurred as a result of racial discrimination and the policies and practices of the "protection" and assimilation periods of the twentieth century. These include such matters as stolen wages, missing trust monies, and under-award payments for Indigenous workers. There were negligent and, at times corrupt and dishonest practices which lead to the withholding of moneys from Aboriginal wages that had been paid into savings accounts, and trust funds. In addition to these practices there were also under-award payments to Aboriginal workers. The denial of civil and political rights included numerous legislative controls and restrictions on movement, residence, education, health care, employment, voting, worker's compensation and welfare/social security entitlements. In Australia the right to vote in either state or federal elections varied between States. It was not until 1962 that Commonwealth amendments to electoral laws removed any remaining prohibitions on voting at the federal level. States began to dismantle their discriminatory laws during the same period. Restrictions on Indigenous voting rights in Queensland were not removed until 1965. Discriminatory restrictions on eligibility for social security benefits for Aboriginal people were not completely lifted until 1966. State legislation which restricted the citizenship rights of Indigenous people living on reserves in Queensland remained in place until the 1980s (Chesterman & Galligan, 1997).

2.4. Reparations

Many of the harms against Aboriginal peoples in Australia and North America relied on law for their legitimacy. Many were essentially aimed at destroying Indigenous cultures. They were cultural harms in the broadest sense: colonial laws, policies and practices which, at various times, sought to assimilate, "civilize", and Christianize Aboriginal peoples through the establishment of reservations, the denial of basic citizenship rights, the forced removal of children and forced education in residential schools, the banning of language, cultural and spiritual practices, and the imposition of an alien criminal justice system (RCAP, 1996; NISATSIC, 1997; Tsosie, 2004).

Many of the harms caused by colonial polices are the subject of litigation, including the removal of children, missing wages and stolen trust fund money. How we address these historical injustices raises important questions for criminology, in particular how do we understand the purpose of prosecutions for crimes against humanity? Do we hold individuals accountable for state crime? And what is the purpose of punishment or reparations in these cases? Is it retribution: to punish the evil actions of those who committed crimes against humanity? Is it consequentialist: to achieve specific and general deterrence so that these systematic human rights abuses do not re-occur? Is it expressive: to reaffirm our commitment to human rights as an international standard?

The historical abuse of Indigenous people's human rights requires a comprehensive response to the past. The survivors and descendants of the victims have a case for reparations and compensation. Criminology as a discipline can make an important contribution to understanding how and why we might develop a more systematic approach to reparations for historical injustices through its interests in punishment.

3. CONTEMPORARY RELATIONS BETWEEN INDIGENOUS PEOPLES AND STATE CRIMINAL JUSTICE SYSTEMS

Indigenous people today total some are 370 million people across 70 nations. As distinct peoples they have retained social, cultural, economic and political characteristics which distinguish them from the dominant societies in which they live. Indigenous peoples are also among the most disadvantaged and vulnerable groups of people in the world (Permanent Forum on Indigenous Issues, 2006). It is inaccurate to generalize about the specific nature of Indigenous cultures given their variety. Also the experiences of colonization varied depending on when it occurred, where and by whom. The discussion in this chapter focuses on Indigenous peoples experiences in the settler colonies of Canada, the USA, New Zealand and Australia, and some of the commonalities found in Indigenous peoples' relations with dominant criminal justice systems in those countries.

3.1. Imprisonment

A starting point in understanding contact between Indigenous peoples and criminal justice systems is the massive over-representation of Indigenous people. Data shows that Māori are over-represented at every stage of the New Zealand criminal justice system. In 1998 they were 3.3 times more likely to be apprehended for a criminal offence than non-Māori. They were more likely to be prosecuted, more likely to be convicted, and more likely to be sentenced to imprisonment. The result was that Mäori made up 14 per cent of the general population and 51 per cent of the prison population. Evidence suggests the gaps are widening, not narrowing (Doone, 2000, p. 8). In Canada Aboriginal people comprise 3 per cent of the general population, but Aboriginal offenders make up 17 per cent of inmates in the federal penitentiary system. The situation is even worse in some provincial institutions, particularly in Manitoba, Saskatchewan and Alberta, where Aboriginal people make up more than 60 per cent of the inmate population in some penitentiaries. In Saskatchewan, for example, Aboriginal people are incarcerated at a rate 35 times higher than the mainstream population (Cunneen, 2001b, p. 108). In the United States, on any given day an estimated one in 25 American Indians 18 years old and older is under the jurisdiction of the nation's criminal justice system. This is 2.4 times the rate for whites and 9.3 times the per capita rate for Asians but about half the rate for blacks. The number of American Indians per capita confined in state and federal prisons is about 38 per cent above the national average. The rate of confinement in local jails is estimated to be nearly four times the national average (Greenfeld & Smith, 1999). In Australia, in 2005, Indigenous imprisonment rates were 2,021.2 per 100,000 compared to 162.5 for non Indigenous people, and some 22 per cent of the total prisoner population were Indigenous people (ABS, 2005, p. 3).

There have been major inquiries into the relationship of Indigenous people with the criminal justice system, particularly in Australia (the Royal Commission into Aboriginal Deaths in Custody) and Canada (the Manitoba Aboriginal Justice Inquiry, and the Royal Commission into Aboriginal Peoples). There is a wealth of information which these inquiries and subsequent research has provided on the problematic processes of criminalization and Indigenous people. For the purposes of the current discussion I have concentrated on the human rights issues which have arisen in the context of Indigenous peoples in Australia.

3.2. Freedom from Torture and Cruel, Inhuman and Degrading Treatment

Freedom from torture and cruel, inhuman and degrading treatment is a fundamental human right and protection from state abuse. There have been long-running concerns over police violence against Indigenous people in Australia. Amnesty International has accused Australia of a "wavering commitment to human rights" and noted that:

Aboriginal Australians have been ill-treated and abused by state officials, and suffer systemic discrimination. Incidents of ill-treatment by police have gone unpunished. The government has also taken decisions that appear to undermine its stated commitment to human rights. (Amnesty International, 1997, p. 3)

Problems associated with police violence against Indigenous people were a key part of the National Inquiry into Racist Violence undertaken by the Australian Human Rights and Equal Opportunity Commission (HREOC) in 1991. The Inquiry found that racist violence is an endemic problem for Aboriginal and Torres Strait Islander people in Australia and that "Aboriginal – police relations have reached a critical point due to the widespread involvement of police in acts of racist violence, intimidation and harassment" (HREOC, 1991, p. 387).

3.3. Special Considerations for Children and Young People

There are special human rights obligations which are applicable to children and young people. These include:

- detention as a last resort, the utilization of alternatives to detention and the availability of a variety of sentencing dispositions;
- treatment with humanity and respect, treatment suitable for age, and treatment to promote a child's sense of dignity; and
- the promotion of the child's reintegration into society.

The evidence shows clearly that Indigenous young people are less likely to receive diversionary options like youth conferencing compared to non-Indigenous youth, are more likely to be proceeded against by way of arrest, are more likely to be refused bail and remanded in custody, and are more likely to be sentenced to a period of detention (Cunneen & White, 2007, pp. 141–170). In other words, the specific human rights protections which have been developed for children and young people are less likely to be applied when the young person is Indigenous.

3.4. Freedom from Racial Discrimination

A major area of concern with the operation of criminal justice systems has been the impact of policing and the use of public order or "street" offences legislation against Indigenous people. The argument has been that the high levels of discretion available to police in utilising this type of legislation, allows for racially discriminatory decisions to be made. As a result, Indigenous people are much more likely to be criminalized for minor offences, and required to "move-on" in public places. For example, it has been found that in New South Wales' townships with large Aboriginal populations, police used their move-one powers at a rate 30 times higher than across the State generally (Chan & Cunneen, 2000).

3.5. The Use of Arrest as a Last Resort

A critical issue examined by the Royal Commission into Aboriginal Deaths in Custody was the high level of criminalization of Indigenous people. Research has continually called into question the issue of over-policing in Indigenous communities, particularly in relation to public order offences. The evidence also shows that police are more likely to use arrest when dealing with Indigenous people rather than alternative processes. In several jurisdictions detentions for public drunkenness are a major reason for contact with the police.

3.6. The Right to a Fair Trial

A fair trial demands that the accused understands the charges and can answer the case against them. Many Indigenous people in remote communities do not speak English and there is a lack of interpreters. Legal representation for Indigenous accused in remote communities may also be limited. The right to a fair trial is a requirement of the International Covenant on Civil and Political Rights. However, the problem of interpreters and legal representation has been identified for decades as significantly reducing the ability of Indigenous people to utilize the courts in a fair and equitable manner.

3.7. The Use of Detention and Imprisonment as a Sanction of Last Resort

As indicated above, Indigenous people are significantly over-represented in prison. The evidence shows that Indigenous people are more likely to receive a sentence of imprisonment than non-Indigenous people. There are a number for reasons for this. It is more likely that Indigenous people have prior criminal records and this affects sentencing decisions. It is also less likely that Indigenous people sentenced in rural and remote areas will have access to a full range of non-custodial sentencing options.

3.8. Deaths in Custody: The Failure to Exercise Appropriate Duty of Care

Indigenous deaths in custody continue to occur in controversial circumstances. Investigations of those deaths show that negligence and lack of care are still endemic despite the accepted legal view that authorities have a duty of care for those in their custody. However, basic failings mean that deaths occur in preventable circumstances:

* hanging points remain common place in custodial environments;
* medical assessments and other vital information are not communicated or do not impact on decision-making;
* there is a lack of training in how to respond to vulnerable persons such as the mentally ill; and
* there is a failure of custodial authorities to follow instructions or procedure (Cunneen, 2006).

The challenge for a human rights perspective in criminology is to understand how contemporary criminal justice systems work in a way that criminalizes Indigenous peoples and entrenches them within that system. At a deeper level this requires an understanding of how specific human rights which in theory guide the operation of criminal justice systems, appear to be disregarded or suspended when it comes to Indigenous people. At least part of this understanding will involve an analysis of institutional racism in the justice system.

4. A CONTEMPORARY INDIGENOUS GENOCIDE

Lest we think that the genocide of Indigenous people is a matter of historical interest only, it is worth considering the more recent events in Guatemala – a relatively small Central American country of 12 million people, of whom about 40 per cent are Indigenous. From the 1960s through to a peace accord in 1996, the country suffered what has been recognized as one of the worst internal armed conflicts in the region. The Guatemalan Commission for Historical Clarification was formed after the peace accord and reported in 1999. It found that massacres occurred in some 626 villages, while 200,000 people were documented to have been killed or disappeared during the period of conflict. Some 83 per cent of those killed were Indigenous Mayans. State forces, in particular the Guatemalan army, police and paramilitary groups, were responsible for 93 per cent of the human rights violations. The Commission also noted the role of the US Central Intelligence Agency in the events which had occurred in Guatemala (Sanford, 2003, p. 14), for which President Clinton was later to express regret, saying the US involvement and support of the military-sponsored human rights abuses was wrong.

According to the Commission for Historical Clarification (1999), the army was responsible for genocide against the Maya, particularly in the years between 1981 and 1983 when more than half the massacres occurred. The National Security Doctrine was based on identifying and targeting Mayans and all political opposition for elimination. The Commission noted that

> The Army's perception of Mayan communities as natural allies of the guerrillas contributed to increasing and aggravating the human rights violations perpetrated against them, demonstrating an aggressive racist component of extreme cruelty that led to the extermination en masse, of defenceless Mayan communities purportedly linked to the guerrillas – including children, women and the elderly – through methods whose cruelty has outraged the moral conscience of the civilised world. (Commission for Historical Clarification, 1999, para 85)

The number of deaths in Guatemala exceeded the deaths tolls of conflicts in El Salvador, Nicaragua, Argentina and Chile combined. In addition there were forced displacements of up to one and a half million Indigenous people during the 1980s. The Commission found that Mayans suffered arbitrary execution, forced disappearance, and the torture and rape of men, women and children, "the effect of which was to terrorize the population and destroy the foundations of social cohesion, particularly when people were forced to witness or execute these acts themselves" (Commission for Historical Clarification, 1999, para 114). The "scorched earth" operations involved burning entire villages and collectively worked fields and harvests to the ground. In the Ixil region the Commission found that "between 70% and 90% of villages were razed" (Commission for Historical Clarification, 1999, para 116).

The Commission, whose report was titled "Guatemala: Memory of Silence", also found racism to be an "underlying cause" of the armed conflict (1999, para 12). Indeed, Seils (2002) argues that one of the reasons the Guatemalan conflict received so little attention internationally was that at least from the 1980s it was essentially a war of racial persecution against Mayan peoples. In one of its strongest conclusions the Commission found, that in the four regions most affected by the violence, the Guatemalan state through its agents had committed acts of genocide against groups of Mayan people (1999, para 122).

Of the 626 massacres documented by the Commission for Historical Clarification, only two cases relating to mass killings during the conflict have been successfully prosecuted in the Guatemalan courts. As Human Rights Watch has noted, Guatemalans seeking accountability for these abuses face considerable obstacles.

> The prosecutors and investigators who handle these cases receive grossly inadequate training and resources. The courts routinely fail to resolve judicial appeals and motions in an expeditious manner. The army and other state institutions fail to cooperate fully with investigations into abuses committed by current or former members. The police do not provide adequate protection to judges, prosecutors, and witnesses involved in politically sensitive cases. (Human Rights Watch, 2006)

Political violence and the victimization of Indigenous people continue to be a significant problem. According to Human Rights Watch, there is a widespread consensus that those responsible for the violence and intimidation are affiliated with private, secretive, and illegally armed networks who "appear to have links to both state agents and organized crime-which give them access to considerable political and economic resources" (Human Rights Watch, 2006).

What do we make of the genocide in Guatemala in terms of criminology? In the first instance it is a contemporary example of state crime of the worst kind against Indigenous people. Secondly a critical criminology built on a human rights perspective, has specific analytical tools for understanding how that crime developed and was operationalized in state law and policy, and in practice with allegiances between military, police and paramilitary groups. Thirdly, a critical criminology can contribute to our understanding of the processes of redress and remedy. How and why do we punish those responsible for crime? And what can we put in place to alleviate the harm caused to victims?

5. INDIGENOUS RIGHTS IN A GLOBAL CONTEXT: THE IMPLICATIONS FOR CRIMINOLOGY

Indigenous aspirations for human rights occur on a global stage. Over the last decades the struggle for Indigenous rights has become a matter of global politics in which nation states can no longer claim Indigenous rights are merely issues of domestic policy. The importance which Indigenous peoples have placed on the development of international human rights standards is not surprising when it is understood that modern states have been at the forefront of denying basic rights to Indigenous peoples.

The growth of Indigenous peoples' claims at the international level is reflected in the Declaration on the Rights of Indigenous Peoples, adopted by the General Assembly of the United Nations in March 2007 (United Nations, General Assembly, 2007). The Declaration was developed by the United Nations Working Group on Indigenous Populations (WGIP) during the 1980s and 1990s and brought a new level of internationalism to the question of Indigenous rights. The WGIP was a body that was representative of Indigenous peoples from around the world, and the draft declaration it developed is widely seen as a document reflecting the aspirations of Indigenous peoples, rather than the interests of states. Indigenous people also now have a permanent presence at the United Nations. The Permanent Forum on Indigenous Issues was established as an advisory body to the Economic and Social Council in July 2000, with a mandate to discuss Indigenous issues related to economic and social development, culture, the environment, education, health and human rights.

The Declaration on the Rights of Indigenous Peoples contains a preamble and 46 articles covering matters of self-determination, nationality, security, culture, religion, language, education, media, employment, land and resources. The preamble rejects racism and affirms that Indigenous people should be free from discrimination. It recognizes that Indigenous peoples have been deprived of their human rights through colonization and the taking of their land. It recognizes the urgent need to respect the rights of Indigenous peoples, particularly their rights to self-determination, and to their land and resources. It recognizes that respect for Indigenous knowledge, cultures and traditional practices contributes to sustainable and equitable development and proper management of the environment.

It is not possible in the context of this chapter to deal with all the human rights issues covered in the Declaration. However, a number of the rights outlined in the Declaration have specific relevance to criminology. The Declaration states that Indigenous peoples have the right to self-determination and the right to keep their distinct characteristics. It is these two rights which I explore further below: the right to self-determination and the right to freedom from genocide and ethnocide.

5.1. Freedom from Genocide and Ethnocide

Given the history of the attempted destruction of Indigenous peoples, and the historically entrenched discrimination and dispossession, it is not surprising that a fundamental right claimed by Indigenous peoples is the right to exist as distinct "peoples" with their own language, culture and institutions.

Several articles of the Declaration are concerned with the rights to life and existence. Indigenous peoples are to be free from genocide and their children must not be removed from their communities. They have the right to their culture and identity. They have the right to stay on their land and must be specially protected in time of war. Of particular relevance is the right to existence as a collective right of Indigenous peoples to maintain and develop their distinct identities and characteristics. It has been recognized that a major theme of the Declaration is the "protection of the unique character and attributes of Indigenous peoples, including culture, religion and social institutions" (Coulter, 1995, p. 127). Articles 7 and 8 of the draft Declaration deal with genocide, forced assimilation and destruction of culture (ethnocide).

Prohibitions against genocide fit firmly within a criminological frame – genocide is the crime of violence *par excellence*, so it is not difficult to see the relevance to criminology. However, ethnocide and cultural assimilation are also relevant rights for proper criminological understandings. Article 8 (d) of the Declaration prohibits "any form of forced assimilation or integration by other cultures or ways of life imposed on them by legislative, administrative or other measures". The provisions which prohibit forced assimilation and integration have implications for how we think about the development of institutions which may seek either directly or indirectly to impose the standards and cultural and social mores of the dominant group on Indigenous communities. We might think about this in relation to the criminal justice system at a number of levels: does the criminalization of certain activities discriminate against Indigenous people? Do legal processes recognize cultural differences, for example by providing for a role for Indigenous Elders in sentencing? Do legal processes recognize language differences, for example by providing interpreters? Do penal regimes adequately cater for cultural differences of Indigenous people?

5.2. Self-Determination

Indigenous peoples base their claims to self-determination on the fact that they were the first peoples in their territories. Self-determination means the right of Indigenous peoples to choose their political status and to make decisions about their own development. Article 4 of the Declaration notes that in exercising self determination, Indigenous peoples "have the right to autonomy or self-government in matters relating to their internal and local affairs", and in Article 5 that Indigenous peoples have "the right to maintain and strengthen their distinct political, legal, economic, social and cultural institutions". Article 34 asserts that:

> Indigenous peoples have the right to promote, develop and maintain their institutional structures and their distinctive customs, spirituality, traditions, procedures, practices and, in cases where they exist, juridical systems or customs, in accordance with international human rights standards.

It is not surprising that Indigenous peoples might wish to re-assert their claims to develop Indigenous law and processes for dealing with dispute resolution. The criminal justice systems of colonial states developed as state activities fundamentally captured within the wider historical trends of colonization and nation building-and nation-building occurred at the expense of dispossessed and excluded peoples, including Indigenous peoples. While western liberal democratic states may see their criminal justice systems as essentially neutral, fair and universal in their application, it is clear that for many Indigenous peoples state criminal justice systems are seen as oppressive. The process of re-asserting Indigenous rights may require significant institutional change on the part of state criminal justice agencies, especially when a central component of the Indigenous critique of policing and the criminal justice system has been that Indigenous rights have been ignored, in particular the right to self-determination.

Self-determination can take a variety of forms. As the Australian Indigenous leader Michael Dodson has noted,

> [E]very issue concerning the historical and present status, entitlements, treatment and aspirations of Aboriginal and Torres Strait Islander peoples is implicated in the concept of self-determination. The reason for this is that self-determination is a process. The right to self-determination is the right to make decisions. (Dodson, 1993, p. 41)

Henriksen (1998, p. 32) has discussed four existing ways of arranging Indigenous autonomy and self-government. These are not meant to be exhaustive of all possibilities nor are they meant to suggest that the existing solutions are necessarily adequate, but rather they provide an illustrative way of thinking about the issue. The four arrangements include:

- Indigenous autonomy through contemporary Indigenous political institutions (for example, Saami Parliaments in the Nordic countries);

- Indigenous autonomy based on the concept of an Indigenous territorial base (for example, the Comarca arrangement in Panama, the Torres Strait Regional Authority in Australia, or Indian jurisdictions in the United States);
- Regional autonomy within the state (for example, the Nunavut territory in Canada or Indigenous autonomous regions in the Philippines);
- Indigenous overseas autonomy (for example, Greenland Home Rule).

The right of self-determination is also often linked to Indigenous claims of sovereignty. Sovereignty can have multiple meanings in the context of Indigenous political claims. It can refer to the historical claim that Indigenous people have never relinquished sovereignty – particularly pertinent in Australia where there were no written treaties recognized by the Crown. Or it can be used to refer by Indigenous people to the residual and unextinguished rights to self-government and autonomy which were recognized to varying degrees through treaties in New Zealand and North America. More generally, the political claim of a right to self-determination implies the right and ability to exercise some level of sovereign power – even if within the boundaries of existing nation states.

In practice Indigenous peoples' experience of sovereignty under colonial regimes varies widely depending on the particular historical circumstances. In the USA, Indigenous peoples have had sovereignty recognized within the confines of the overarching authority and jurisdiction of the federal government. Federal Indian law is founded on the doctrine of inherent sovereignty. "The essential claim of tribal Indians that distinguishes them from other groups is their claim of sovereignty – the inherent right to promulgate and be governed by their own laws"(Scott Gould, 1996, p. 815). Sovereignty in international law is usually seen as inextricably tied to territory:

> Sovereignty demands a territory over which the governmental authority of the sovereign extends. Control over territory is the most essential element of sovereignty. (...) Territory thus represents both the encompassing limits of a state's jurisdiction over its resident population and the barriers to outside jurisdiction. (Royster, 1995, pp. 1–2)

However, sovereignty is also a dynamic concept with transformed meanings in different political and historical contexts. It is neither static nor absolute. Despite the apparent claims of the nation state to a concept of sovereignty which privileges a particular political relationship and concept of power, sovereignty is in a state of flux. From an Indigenous perspective, it can be conceptualized in terms of jurisdictional multiplicity and divisibility rather than monopoly and unity.

While sovereign power remains central to the nation state, trends towards globalization have also seen the state deal with competing modes of governance. Although "the liberal-democratic nation-state retains a central role in redistributing elements of sovereign power and national jurisdiction" (Stenson, 1999, p. 67), there has also been a "redistribution" of sovereign powers. In the criminal justice area, we can see sovereign power moving out of the state to international bodies for courts and policing (United Nations and regional-based courts, regulatory bodies, investigatory bodies and so forth). Sovereign power can also bee seen as moving downwards to more regional and local spheres of government and governance such as multi-agency crime control partnerships (Stenson, 1999, p. 68).

The challenge that Indigenous claims to sovereignty and self-determination pose for criminology are both theoretical and practical. The theoretical challenge is to understand that basic categories and definitions of crime are fundamentally circumscribed by historical and political contexts. The very legitimacy of the institutions used to control crime is not universally accepted. The praxis issue this raises is how do we develop legal institutions which are capable of dealing with multiple jurisdictions and differential citizenship claims (Cunneen, 2005). In other words, how do criminal justice system institutions develop in a manner that can deal fairly with competing citizenship demands and maintain legitimacy for different social groups?

6. CONCLUSION

The intersection between human rights, criminology and Indigenous peoples opens up new and important terrain for understanding how criminal justice systems operate and their impact on specific groups. As I have identified in this chapter a human rights perspective on Indigenous issues and criminology falls broadly across three areas: the historical relationship between Indigenous people and colonial states, the contemporary operation of criminal justice systems in nations with significant Indigenous minorities, and the contemporary human rights claims of Indigenous peoples in the international arena and the effect this is likely to have on domestic systems of justice.

A criminology informed by human rights can bring new scholarship to the historical relationship between Indigenous people and colonial states. Part of this will necessarily involve a re-interpretation of the historical development of criminal justice systems in the context of the colonial imperative of controlling Indigenous people. However the task is not only one of "history". A key contemporary demand by Indigenous peoples is the claim for reparations for past human rights abuses. Criminology can also offer insights and analysis into how processes for reparations might develop – particular given criminology's traditional interests in punishment and victims, and its developing interests in restorative justice.

As indicated in this chapter, Indigenous people are significantly over-represented in the criminal justice systems of former colonial states. A criminology informed by human rights can offer a significant analysis of the nature and impact of that over-representation. It can also offer guidance as to how criminal justice systems might develop in a way that is respective of key internationally accepted human rights standards (like the Convention on the Rights of the Child, and the Covenant on Civil and Political Rights).

Finally, Indigenous people are increasingly using international human rights mechanisms to develop their own specific claims. In particular, the Declaration on the Rights of Indigenous Peoples represents a key document in understanding the current political aspirations of Indigenous people. The aspirations of Indigenous people in regard to law and justice open up some exciting and challenging possibilities for criminologists. Those aspirations require us to re-think how criminal justice institutions operate, and how they might be developed in a way that allows for cultural multiplicity.

The bulk of criminological research in relation to Indigenous people has been narrowly confined to "Indigenous crime" and traditionally sees state criminal justice responses as the more or less technical application of laws, policies and procedures to control crime. Most government-employed "administrative" criminologists steer as far away as possible from the issue of human rights. Bringing a human rights perspective to criminology and Indigenous people is an important task. It opens up a new level of research, analysis and theory building, and can directly contribute to identifying and remedying human rights abuses.

REFERENCES

Amnesty International. (1997). Australia: A champion of human rights? *Focus, 27*(1), 3–6.

Australian Bureau of Statistics (ABS). (2005). *Prisoners in Australia.* Catalogue No. 4517.0, Canberra: ABS.

Bauman, Z. (1989). *Modernity and the holocaust.* Cambridge: Polity Press.

Chan, C., & Cunneen, C. (2000). *Evaluation of the implementation of the New South Wales police service aboriginal strategic plan.* Sydney: Institute of Criminology.

Chesterman, J., & Galligan, B. (1997). *Citizens without rights.* Melbourne: Cambridge University Press.

Churchill, W. (1997). *A little matter of genocide: Holocaust and denial in the Americas, 1492 to the present.* San Francisco: City Lights Books.

Commission for Historical Clarification. (1999). *Guatemala: Memory of silence.* Report of the Commission for Historical Clarification, http://www.shr.aaas.org/guatemala/ceh/report/english/toc.html, Accessed 15/03/07.

Coulter, R. (1995). The draft UN declaration on the rights of indigenous peoples: What is it? What does it mean? *Netherlands Quarterly of Human Rights, 13,* 123–138.

Cunneen, C. (2001a). *Conflict, politics and crime. Aboriginal communities and the police.* St. Leonards: Allen and Unwin.

Cunneen, C. (2001b). *The impact of crime prevention on aboriginal communities.* Sydney: New South Wales Crime Prevention Division and Aboriginal Justice Advisory Council.

Cunneen, C. (2005). Consensus and sovereignty: Rethinking policing in the light of indigenous self-determination. In: B. A. Hocking (Ed.), *Unfinished constitutional business. Rethinking indigenous self-determination* (pp. 47–60). Canberra: Aboriginal Studies Press.

Cunneen, C. (2006). Aboriginal deaths in custody: A continuing systematic abuse. *Social Justice, 33*(4), 37–51.

Cunneen, C., & White, R. (2007). *Juvenile justice. Youth and crime in Australia* (3rd ed.). Melbourne: Oxford University Press.

Dodson, M. (1993). *Aboriginal and Torres Strait Islander social justice commissioner first annual report.* Sydney: HREOC.

Doone, P. (2000). *Report on combating and preventing maori crime.* Wellington: Crime Prevention Unit, Department of Prime Minister and Cabinet.

Gellately, R., & Kiernan, B. (Eds). (2003). *The spectre of genocide. Mass murder in historical perspective.* Cambridge: Cambridge University Press.

Green, P., & Ward, T. (2004). *State crime. Governments, violence and corruption.* London: Pluto Press.

Greenfeld, L., & Smith, S. (1999). *American Indians and crime.* Washington, DC: Bureau of Justice Statistics.

Henriksen, J. (1998). *Implementation of the right of self-determination of indigenous peoples within the framework of human society.* Paper presented to the UNESCO conference on the implementation of the right to self-determination as a contribution to conflict prevention, 21–27 November, Barcelona, Spain.

Human Rights and Equal Opportunity Commission (HREOC). (1991). *Racist violence. Report of the national inquiry into racist violence.* Sydney: Human Rights and Equal Opportunity Commission.

Human Rights Watch. (2006). *Human rights overview. Guatemala,* http://www.hrw.org/english/docs/2006/01/18/guatem12208.htm, Accessed 30/11/06.

Milloy, J. (1999). *A national crime. The Canadian government and the residential school system 1879 to 1986.* Winnipeg: The University of Manitoba Press.

Morrison, W. (2004). Criminology, genocide and modernity: Remarks on the companion that criminology ignored. In: C. Sumner (Ed.), *The Blackwell companion to criminology* (pp. 68–88). Oxford: Blackwell Publishing.

Morrison, W. (2005). Rethinking narratives of penal change in global context. In: J. Pratt, D. Brown, M. Brown, S. Hallsworth & W. Morrison (Eds), *The new punitiveness. Trends, theories, perspectives* (pp. 290–307). Cullompton: Willan Publishing.

Moses, D. (2000). An antipodean genocide? The origins of the genocidal moment in the colonisation of Australia. *Journal of Genocide Research, 2,* 89–106.

National Inquiry into the Separation of Aboriginal and Torres Strait Islander Children from Their Families (NISATSIC). (1997). *Bringing them home*. Report of the National Inquiry into the Separation of Aboriginal and Torres Strait Islander Children from Their Families. Sydney: Human Rights and Equal Opportunity Commission.

Permanent Forum on Indigenous Issues. (2006). *About UNPFII history*, http://www.un.org/esa/socdev/unpfii/en/history.html, Accessed 15/03/07.

Royal Commission on Aboriginal Peoples (RCAP). (1996). *Report of the royal commission on aboriginal peoples*. Ottawa: Canada Communication Group.

Royster, J. V. (1995). The legacy of allotment. *Arizona State Law Review, 27*(1), 1–78.

Sanford, V. (2003). *Buried secrets: Truth and human rights in Guatemala*. New York: Palgrave Macmillan.

Scott Gould, L. (1996). The consent paradigm: Tribal sovereignty at the millennium. *Columbia Law Review, 96*, 809–903.

Seils, P. (2002). Reconciliation in Guatemala: The role of intelligent justice. *Race and Class, 44*, 33–59.

Stannard, D. (1993). *American holocaust*. New York: Oxford University Press.

Stenson, K. (1999). Crime control, governmentality and sovereignty. In: R. Smandych (Ed.), *Governable places: Readings on governmentality and crime control* (pp. 45–74). Aldershot: Ashgate.

Tsosie, R. (2004). *Acknowledging the past to heal the future: The role of reparations for native nations*. Paper presented at Reparations: An Interdisciplinary Examination of Some Philosophical Issues Conference, 6–8 February, Queens University, Kingston Ontario, Canada.

United Nations, General Assembly. (2007). *Declaration on the rights of indigenous peoples*, A/Res/61/178 of 6 March 2007, www.un.org/esa/socdev/unpfii

Van Krieken, R. (2004). Rethinking cultural genocide: Aboriginal child removal and settler-colonial state formation. *Oceania, 75*, 125–151.

ABOUT THE AUTHORS

Hans-Jörg Albrecht is Director at the Max Planck Institute for Foreign and International Criminal Law in Freiburg/Germany (MPI), and teaches criminal law, criminal justice and criminology at the University of Freiburg. He has been a guest professor at various universities in China and at the University of Teheran, and holds a doctorate *honoris causa* from the University of Pécs. His research interests cover various legal, criminological and policy topics ranging from sentencing theory, juvenile crime, drug policies, environmental crime and organized crime, evaluation research and systems of criminal sanctions.

Kai Ambos is a professor of criminal law, criminal procedure, comparative and international criminal law at the Georg-August-University of Göttingen and the Head of the Department for Foreign and International Criminal Law. He is a former (senior) research fellow at the Max-Planck-Institute for Foreign and International Criminal Law in Freiburg, where he was in charge of the sections on International Criminal Law and Spanish-speaking Latin America. He is also a judge at the State Court of Göttingen.

Dieter Burssens is a doctoral researcher at the Leuven Institute of Criminology at the Katholieke Universiteit Leuven. He is a social worker and a criminologist by training, and is interested in juvenile criminology, restorative justice for juveniles and crime prevention. He is a member of the European Governance of Public Safety Research Network.

Marc Coester has studied pedagogical sciences at the Eberhard-Karls-University of Tübingen, and is currently a research associate at the Institute of Criminology of the same university. His main focus is on issues of criminology, social psychology, hate crimes and victimology.

Chris Cunneen is the NewSouth Global Chair in Criminology at the Law Faculty of the University of New South Wales in Sydney, after having served as the Director of the Institute of Criminology at the University of Sydney. He is the chairperson of the Juvenile Justice Advisory Council, which advises the Minister on juvenile justice matters, and a member of the Attorney-Generals Taskforce on Child Sexual Assault in Aboriginal

Communities. His research interests lie in the area of juvenile justice, policing, restorative justice and indigenous issues.

Jan Froestad is an associate professor at the Department of Administration and Organisation Theory of the University of Oslo. He has been closely involved in the Community Peace Programme at the University of the Western Cape in Cape Town.

Jack R. Greene is professor of criminal justice and Dean of the College of Criminal Justice at Northeastern University in Boston (Massachusetts). He was the Director of the Center for Public Policy at Temple University for 10 years, and served as the Senior Consultant to the Chief of the Los Angeles Police Department for projects on rebuilding patrol services, increasing strategic management, and building partnerships with community organizations. His current research deals with terrorism from a criminological perspective, police service delivery, organization change, and community interactions.

Nils Meyer-Abich is a lawyer and social anthropologist and a research fellow at the Department for Foreign and International Criminal Law at the Georg-August-University of Göttingen. He currently performs his legal preparatory service at the judiciary of Hamburg.

James P. Mulvale is an Associate Professor and currently serves as Head in the Department of Justice Studies, University of Regina, Canada. He teaches in the areas of social justice theory, and work and economic security. His research interests include basic (or guaranteed adequate) income, Indigenous peoples' perspectives on justice, and the practical and contemporary implications of Treaties with First Nations. His professional background includes community development work in the fields of developmental disability and community mental health.

Stephan Parmentier is professor of sociology of law, crime and human rights at the Faculty of Law of the Catholic University of Leuven, and the Head of the Department of Criminal Law and Criminology. Stephan Parmentier has been a visiting professor at the International Institute for Sociology of Law in Oñati (Spain), and a visiting fellow at the universities of Stellenbosch, New South Wales (Sydney) and Oxford. His research interests and publications relate to political crimes, transitional justice and human rights, and the administration of criminal justice. He has served as the vice-chairman of the Flemish Section of Amnesty International.

Dieter Rössner is professor at the Faculty of Law and Director of the Institute of Criminology at the Philipps-University Marburg. He held previous appointments in criminology at the universities of Tübingen, Göttingen and Halle, and also served as a judge and a prosecutor. His main research is in the field of empirical criminology and crime prevention, with a particular interest in victim-offender mediation and the prevention of delinquency.

Clifford Shearing holds a South African Research Chair in African Security and Justice at the University of Cape Town where he is also the professor of Criminology and the Director of the Institute of Criminology. He also holds appointments at the University of Toronto and the Australian National University in Canberra, and is currently a visiting professor of Security Governance at the University of Oxford. His main research interests are in the fields of policing, security, and conflict resolution.

Ann Skelton is an advocate with the children's litigation project at the Centre for Child Law, University of Pretoria. Her doctoral thesis, completed in 2005, focused on restorative justice and child justice. She previously worked at Lawyers for Human Rights, and directed a UN technical assistance project on juvenile justice. Her research interests lie in the fields of restorative justice, youth crime and children's rights.

Lode Walgrave is an emeritus professor of criminology at the Leuven Institute of Criminology at the Katholieke Universiteit Leuven. He has served as a visiting professor at the University of Montréal and the Australian National University in Canberra, and as the founding co-director of the International Network for Restorative Justice for Juveniles. His main research covers the areas of juvenile delinquency and restorative justice.

Elmar G. M. Weitekamp teaches criminology at the Institute of Criminology at the Eberhard-Karls-University of Tübingen, and is a special guest professor in victimology and restorative justice at the K.U. Leuven. He serves as the co-director of the Post-graduate Course in Victimology, Victim Assistance and Criminal Justice of the World Society of Victimology, and has been a visiting professor at the University of Melbourne. His research interests and publications relate to victimology, restorative justice, and juvenile gangs.

AUTHOR INDEX

SUBJECT INDEX

Printed in the United States
103884LV00001B/15/A